THE MAN WHO SUPERCHARGED BOND

The extraordinary story of Charles Amherst Villiers

PAUL KENNY

FOREWORD BY LORD MONTAGU OF BEAULIEU

Haynes Publishing

First published in September 2009

A catalogue record for this book is available from the British Library

ISBN 978 1 84425 468 2

Library of Congress catalog card no 2009923205

Published by Haynes Publishing,
Sparkford, Yeovil, Somerset BA22 7JJ, UK
Tel: 01963 442030 Fax: 01963 440001
Int.tel: +44 1963 442030 Int.fax: +44 1963 440001
E-mail: sales@haynes.co.uk
Website: www.haynes.co.uk

Haynes North America Inc.,
861 Lawrence Drive, Newbury Park, California 91320, USA

Designed and typeset by James Robertson
Printed and bound in the UK

CONTENTS

FOREWORD

by Lord Montagu of Beaulieu

This book finally fills a gap which I urged Amherst Villiers himself to fill more than 20 years ago!

I had long considered him a British motor racing hero. His name adorned the supercharger of the Blower Bentley which had done battle with Mercedes at Le Mans. His development work on a pair of little Bugattis had given his great friend Raymond Mays the capability to dominate the hill-climb and sprint scene of the mid-1920s. Thanks to Amherst, the car which began life as a Vauxhall TT, and became first the *Vauxhall Villiers* and then the *Villiers Supercharge*, enjoyed a longer spell on the front line of British motor sport than any other car.

When Amherst came to live at Palace House, my home at Beaulieu, for several spells during the 1970s, I came to appreciate the full breadth of the man. I learned how seriously he took his painting; his favourite medium may have been portraiture, but much of his time at Beaulieu was actually devoted to the depiction of a 13th century Italian miracle. He told me of his aero engine work before the War, of his design for a 6-engine, trans-Atlantic passenger plane during it, and of his contributions to rocket and missile development over the course of more than 20 years in the United States.

Amherst told his stories with such skill, such humour and such charm, that I felt that he should record his life for posterity. I introduced him to a journalist of my acquaintance to support him in the task of writing an autobiography. Unfortunately, nothing came of this, and in hindsight I think that Amherst was the sort of man who was so inspired by whatever project currently held his attention that he could not devote any time to look back and review his long and fascinating life.

That is why, when Paul Kenny first came to see me in the autumn of 2006, and told me of his plans to write Amherst's biography, I was only too happy to support him.

Paul has diligently researched each of the many strands of Amherst's life and woven them into a fascinating narrative. He has also caught the aspects of Amherst's complex personality which prevented him, in spite of his breadth of talent, from achieving true, lasting greatness.

Paul should be congratulated on a book which gives an authoritative, overdue account of an extraordinary man.

Palace House, Beaulieu
2009

ACKNOWLEDGEMENTS

I owe so much to the huge cast who have made this book possible. My lovely, long-suffering wife Jane originally suggested to me that I should write an article on Amherst Villiers during a short career break, and when she realised that the piece, which appeared in *Motor Sport*, had merely whetted my appetite for writing rather than satiated it, she somehow stuck by me and encouraged me through the much longer career break in which I did the bulk of the research for this book. My wonderful children, Ben, Fleur and Alice, have been equally patient. My love and thanks go to them all.

Paul Fearnley may, in some motor racing enthusiasts' eyes, be known as the man who changed the cover of *Motor Sport* from its traditional British Racing Green to red, but for me he will always be the man who first took a punt on me and encouraged me to have a go at writing. I am equally grateful to his successor as *Motor Sport* editor, Damien Smith, for publishing my piece on Amherst.

Amherst's daughter Janie assisted me with that article and provided the illustrations for it, for which I thank her. Her brother Charles kindly showed me an image of the portrait Amherst painted of him as a boy, and provided a wonderful description of a project on which he worked with his father.

Lord Montagu of Beaulieu deserves special mention. Not only did he invite me into his wonderful home to share with me his memories of Amherst and lend me his correspondence with him, but he kindly agreed during our very first meeting to write the foreword to this book, and proposed that I approach Haynes as publishers. I am enormously grateful to him.

From the moment John Haynes, founder and chairman of Haynes Publishing, replied enthusiastically by return to my initial approach and synopsis, I felt in good hands. In particular, Haynes' editorial director Mark Hughes and his team, including Flora Myer, Jane Hutchings and Peter Nicholson, have been very supportive.

I have many people at Brooklands Museum Trust to thank. The invitation of director Allan Winn and Penny McKechnie for me to give a lecture at the museum on Amherst was the final prompt that encouraged me to commit to the book, and John Pulford and Mike Davison were just two of many who gave me assistance in the wonderful research library.

Special mention must also go to the late Bertie Guest. A cousin of Amherst, Bertie spent the last years of his life working on a twin-volume history of the Guest clan. He invited me to his home and shared with me the relevant parts of his research. Sadly, upon receiving my copy of *The Guest House* and sending him my congratulations, I learned from his daughter Veronica that he had passed away. It is a source of regret to me that Bertie did not live to read even a draft of my first chapter, but, as Veronica says, he lives on through his own book.

Desmond Fitz-Gerald, the 29th Knight of Glin and owner of the beautiful Glin Castle on the banks of the River Shannon in Ireland's County Limerick, is Amherst's nephew. A committed and utterly objective historian in his own right, Desmond has been enormously helpful, sharing with me his father's diary, family photograph albums and an extensive archive of family correspondence. My deepest thanks go not only to Desmond and his wife Olga for their hospitality and support, but also to Ken Bergin, the special collections librarian at the University of Limerick, where the Glin Archive is housed, and his assistants Jean Turner and Siobhan Morrissey.

Similarly, Trevor Dunmore, clubhouse librarian at the Royal Automobile Club, and his assistant Karen Jacobs, have been generous in their time and support. That lovely library overlooking Pall Mall, with its beautiful oak-lined bookshelves and open fires at each end, is probably my favourite place in London.

I have more books on my own shelves by Doug Nye than any other single author. He is a giant in the field of motor racing history and is, of course, *the* oracle on British Racing Motors (BRM). That he has taken time out from his busy schedule to talk to me about Amherst, introduce me to others who could help, and even read my chapter on BRM and suggested ways of improving it, demonstrates what an extraordinarily kind and enthusiastic man he is. I cannot thank him enough.

Rolls-Royce historian Tom Clarke played a similarly vital role in my chapter on Amherst's supercharging of Jack Kruse's Phantom.

Others who kindly gave of their time and knowledge include Kathy Ager of LAT Photographic Digital Archive; Vibeke Andersson; Mark Askew of Jeep Promotions; Malcolm Barber of Bonhams & Butterfields; John Bentley; Alan Bodfish of the W.O. Bentley Memorial Foundation; Greg Bradford; Melanie Britt of the Air Accidents Investigation Branch; John Burningham; Philip Bye, senior archivist at the East Sussex Record Office; Dexter Brown; Margaret Cadwaladr; Beatrice Canning Brown; Piers and Eleanor Carlson; Jacqueline Cox of Cambridge University Archives, and the staff of the Manuscript Reading Room at Cambridge University Library; James Cox, archivist at Gonville & Caius College, Cambridge; Nick Coyle; Jon Day of the National Motor Museum's picture library at Beaulieu; Dr Deepa Deo; Michael Downes; John Dyson; Sarah Fairburn and Carly King of the Ian Fleming Archive; Bill Ficken; Stephen Forge; Lucy Fleming; Bert and Brenda Flower; Jonny Flower of the Rolex Watch Company; Ian Flux; Brad Frank; Jeff Gale; Jon Gilbert of the Adrian Harrington bookshop; Jonathon Glancy of *The Guardian*; Andrew Gold; Dan and Evi Gurney; David and Sue Hanley; Tom Hanley; Clare Hay; Vince Higgins; Steve Holter; Bernard Horrocks of the National Portrait Gallery; Dr Tom Houston; Bob Hurst; Peter Irvin QC; David Jackson of The A. J. Jackson Aviation Collection; Peter Janson-Smith, Bette Hill; Caroline Johnson of the National Motor Museum's reference library at Beaulieu; Claire Kenny; Digby Lamb; Gordon Leith of the Royal Air

Force Museum; Ursula Leslie; Rear Admiral Guy Liardet; Jan Kruse; Paula McColl; Jenni McMurrie of EON Productions; Alan Mann; Stanley Mann; Joanna Millar; David Morys of the Bugatti Trust Photo Archive; John Nicholson; Alec Osborn; Ralph Pegram; Bruce Pounds; Nick Pourgourides; Jon Pressnell; Bruce Ricketts; Gordon Riley; Jonathan Rishton; the Revd Ian Robson; Emma Sargent; Michael Sargent; David Sewell; the late Amanda Severne; Selina Skipwith, Keeper of Art at The Fleming Collection; Julian Spencer of the Rolls-Royce Enthusiasts' Club; Antonia Spowers; Hugo Spowers; Quentin Spurring; Ken Thomas, chief historian with Hamilton Sundstrand's Space Hardware Heritage Team; Catherine Trippett; Maxine Trost, archivist at the Lawrence Livermore National Laboratory; David Venables; Wing Commander Eric Viles; Frans Vrijaldenhoven; Robert Wade; Mick Walsh; Susan David Williger; and Eoin Young.

My thanks go to all of the above, and my apologies to those who helped me and whom I have not acknowledged. Any omissions or errors in the following pages are mine and mine alone.

Paul Kenny
Teddington, Middlesex
2009

Author's note: Contemporary values have been translated to current values using Table 1 of the Office of National Statistics paper, *Consumer Price Inflation Since 1750*, and its table *CPI-CT December 2003 onwards*. The conversion rate between the US dollar and pound sterling varied enormously during the writing of this book, but I have settled on $1.35/£1.

INTRODUCTION

This book is the result of a visit I paid to London's National Portrait Gallery five years ago. I was absorbed by the images of the British heroes adorning the walls of what was then known as the Twentieth Century Room – aviators John Brown and Amy Johnson, explorer Ernest Shackleton, writers Aldous Huxley and Dylan Thomas, and composer William Walton, to name but a few.

Then I spotted a picture, painted in 1961, of racing driver Graham Hill, sporting a trim moustache and a pair of pale blue Dunlop overalls and dark blue rally jacket. He looked for all the world as though he was staring out at the World Championship he would pip Jim Clark to the following year. The painting below was of James Bond's creator Ian Fleming, in his trademark short-sleeved blue shirt and bow tie, and sporting that unique nose he reprofiled against the head of Henry Douglas-Home, brother of the future prime minister, in an Eton football match.

The same man painted both portraits. He also helped to design the engine that drove Hill to that 1962 championship, supercharged the Blower Bentley driven by Bond in *Casino Royale*, *Live and Let Die* and *Moonraker*, and provided Fleming with the first illustrations for *Chitty-Chitty-Bang-Bang*. He held dual British and US citizenship and was just at home on either side of the Atlantic. He was equally adept at making racing cars, planes and rockets go faster, and he was a regular Anglican churchgoer who painted a pope and studied the teachings of a yogi saint.

His name was Charles Amherst Villiers, pronounced Vill-ers. If you plan to read this book out loud to your children or grandchildren (and why not?), do please bear in mind that he was most insistent that he had a two-syllable surname. While his second wife Nita called him Charles, and his colleagues during a two-decade sojourn in North America called him Charlie, or even – much to his chagrin – Chuck, in his home country he was generally known as Amherst, so that is how I shall refer to him.

His two-syllable family name is also a clue as to why, in among all the cars, aircraft, rockets, paintings and court cases, one thing you will find missing from his story is mention of the three-syllable Villiers engines. When the Sunbeam bicycle company opened new premises in Villiers Street, Wolverhampton, in 1898 to manufacture pedals, it called the operation the Villiers Cycle Component Company. By the First World War it had become the Villiers Engineering Company and had begun manufacturing its splendid engines. It may be that the company was named after the road, or perhaps it was named after the local MP who had died in 1898. But since the road was named after the MP, the company's name stems either directly or indirectly from Charles Pelham Villiers, the UK's longest-ever serving Member of Parliament. He was Amherst's great-uncle, and this distant familial link is the only one that existed between the engine manufacturer and Amherst.

Given that Amherst lived to the ripe old age of 91, and has been dead now for over 17 years, it seems astonishing that a story as extraordinary as his has not been told before. He himself was given more than one opportunity to tell it in his own words. In 1963, when a limited edition of *On Her Majesty's Secret Service* was released with his portrait of Fleming as a frontispiece, the publishers of the James Bond canon, Jonathan Cape, asked Amherst to write an autobiography, focused on speed and space. But Douglas Aircraft had invited Amherst out to California to work on a Mars project, his spare time was spent restoring a Blower Bentley, and the moment passed.

Then, in the late 1980s, when Lord Montagu of Beaulieu tried to help settle out-of-court a dispute between Amherst and Rolls-Royce, he proposed that Amherst should focus instead on an autobiography, and introduced him to a freelance journalist to support him in the task. Amherst, who had a high level of trust in his fellow man, and an equally strong belief in the English legal system to put right breaches in that trust, chose to have his day in court.

So the honour – and that is exactly what it has been – of telling Amherst's story has fallen to me. I hope that I have managed to convey something of him as a man, as well as his myriad achievements, between these covers.

Chapter 1

FIEL PERO DESDICHADO

Amherst was born on Sunday, 9 December 1900, at his family's home in Hyde Park Square, a few hundred yards from the northern perimeter of one of London's finest parks. The 63-year reign of Queen Victoria was drawing to a close, and her son, the future King Edward VII, would succeed her within seven weeks. The old Queen had survived numerous attempts on her life and her days were ending peacefully, but the 25th President of the United States, William McKinley, would be less fortunate, succumbing to an assassin's bullet nine months after Amherst's birth, to be succeeded by his vice-president, Theodore Roosevelt.

In the fields in which Amherst would come to excel, development was patchy to say the least. Karl Benz's patent for his motor car may have been 15 years old, but in Britain motorists who had rejoiced at the 1896 Locomotives on Highways Act (later known as the Emancipation Act), which rid them of the need to have a man walk ahead of them waving a red flag, still had to contend with a national speed limit of 14mph.

Little wonder that man's early steps in his quest for speed were taken on the roads of France. Each armed with an electric car, the Count Gaston de Chasseloup-Laubat and Camille Jenatzy had spent the early months of 1899 pushing the world land speed record from under 40mph (approx 64kmh) to in excess of 65mph (approx 105kmh). This last effort, by Jenatzy, had been the first to raise the

Fiel pero desdichado ('Faithful, though unfortunate'), the motto of the House of Marlborough.

bar above 100kmh, and had been the subject of much comment from medical experts who feared for his health at such speed.

The aeroplane had, quite literally, not got off the ground. Amherst had celebrated his third birthday by the time of Orville Wright's inaugural powered flight at Kitty Hawk.

As for the rocket, the Chinese had used it as a weapon for centuries, and *The Star-Spangled Banner*, with its reference to 'the rockets' red glare', reminds us that the Royal Navy had used rocket-launched shrapnel bombs against Fort McHenry as long ago as 1812. However, at the time of Amherst's birth, space exploration lay more than half a century away. That Amherst would become an accomplished automotive, aeronautic and astronautic engineer, and a fine portrait painter, too, says much for the way he was educated, and also for the determined, free-thinking spirit he inherited from his parents.

His father, Ernest Amherst Villiers, was born in the Essex village of Tolleshunt Knights in November 1863. The common middle name shared by father and son was a tradition of the time, for it was the maiden name of Ernest's mother, Florence Amherst, who was sister of the first Lord Amherst of Hackney. Ernest's father, Charles, had been chaplain to the bishops of Carlisle and Durham in the late 1850s, and was subsequently rector of Croft, near Darlington in Yorkshire. Charles was the nephew of the fourth Earl of Clarendon, but for Amherst to subsequently claim direct descent from the House of Clarendon depended on nothing less than a royal licence, personally granted by Queen Victoria.

In the frank terms of *Burke's Peerage & Baronetage*, Charles had been born 'either illegitimately or through a secret marriage'.[1] Today, members of the extended family are upset by the reference to illegitimacy, and are certain that Charles's parents, Thomas Villiers and Charlotte Hart, were indeed married. However, Thomas's family felt he had married beneath him, and were horrified at the thought that a son of the union would become the fifth earl if his uncle did not have a son himself. Indeed, for much of his life, Charles did not know that throughout his childhood he had been heir to the peerage.

When he was just 2 years old his father died and his uncles banished his unfortunate mother and raised him as Charles Lawrence. But he had friends in high places: as a young man he had taught divinity to the future King Edward VII, and this seems to have been the reason for the Queen's personal intervention. Her decree, 'given at our Court at Saint James's the Eighth Day of July 1876', laid down 'that he and his issue may take the surname of Villiers only and bear the Arms of Villiers with due and proper distinctions'.[2] So it was that when Amherst's father Ernest joined Uppingham School in the East Midlands of England (where a future client of Amherst's, Sir Malcolm Campbell, was also taught), he was a Lawrence, but by the time he left for Peterhouse College, Cambridge, he was a Villiers.

Ernest followed his father into the Church. In 1893 he was ordained as a deacon at Wakefield, Yorkshire, and then went to nearby Halifax as chaplain. He was also a keen fisherman who once caught more than 30 salmon in a single day on a Swedish river. He moved to London in 1896 to become chaplain of St George's, Hanover Square, and it was here that he met his future wife, the Hon. Elaine Augusta Guest.

Elaine came from a privileged background. Her father was Ivor Bertie Guest, the first Baron Wimborne. His immense fortune had been generated in the ironworks of Dowglais, Glamorganshire, by his father, John Josiah Guest, and consolidated first by the sale of the family firm to Arthur Keen's Patent Nut and Bolt Company in 1900, and then, two years later, by the acquisition by the company of one of the world's leading manufacturers of screws and fasteners, Nettlefolds Ltd. Thus was born Guest, Keen & Nettlefolds. Initially admired for its vast breadth of focus – from mining, via iron- and steel-making, to the nuts, bolts and screws that made it a household name – a century on, GKN remains one of the UK's most important engineering groups, employing more than 40,000 people in over 30 countries, with revenues in excess of £4.6 billion (US$6.2 billion).

Ivor Bertie Guest was the embodiment of how the entire basis of influence in the British establishment had shifted. The Industrial Revolution and the importation of cheap US grain had substantially weakened the significance of land as the foundation for wealth. Commerce and industry mattered more now, and if Old Wealth was to survive, it had to marry New. Thus it was that John Guest had married Lady Charlotte Bertie (pronounced Bar-tie, and another maiden name which would be passed down through the generations). She was the daughter of the ninth Earl of Lindsay, and it was Charlotte who arranged for the purchase of a modest house near the village of Canford in Dorset in 1846, and who commissioned the prize-winning architect of the Houses of Parliament, Sir Charles Barry, to transform it into a country seat worthy of the Guest dynasty – Canford House. Similarly, in 1868, Ivor married Lady Cornelia Churchill, eldest daughter of the seventh Duke of Marlborough. Two years later, he purchased the Duke of Hamilton's home on Arlington Street, just off Piccadilly, and a decade on, when he became Baron Wimborne, he and Cornelia renamed their London base Wimborne House.

Cornelia was a highly influential woman, with several abiding interests. She was a staunch supporter of the 'low' Protestant faith, and had a strong antipathy to both the Anglican High Church and Catholicism. She was also keen for girls to enjoy the same educational opportunities as boys, and the two interests dovetailed when she joined an organisation known as Allied Schools, which managed such famous educational establishments as Stowe and Wrekin College. Cornelia would later arrange for Canford House to be sold to Allied Schools, and Canford remains a highly respected school to this day.

Most of all, Cornelia had an overwhelming passion for politics. Four of her sons, Ivor Churchill (note, Cornelia's maiden name), Henry, Freddy, and the much younger Oscar, all became MPs, and she took a particular interest in the parliamentary career of her nephew, Winston Churchill. She watched his maiden speech from the House of Commons' Ladies' Gallery, and when the Conservative Colonial Secretary Joseph Chamberlain proposed the charging of import duties, Wimborne House swiftly became the headquarters of the Liberal opposition 'Free Traders'. Cornelia wrote to Churchill, telling him 'there is no future for Free Traders in the Conservative Party. Why tarry?' Within a year, he had famously crossed the floor of the House to sit on the Liberal benches, to be followed in due course by both Ivor and Freddy.

Churchill enjoyed a close social and political bond with his Guest cousins. It was at Canford House that he learned the bricklaying skills that helped to sustain him during his 'wilderness years', and he recuperated there after contracting a serious illness shortly after winning his first position in office. Freddy proofread his first book, *The Story of the Malakand Field Force* (and failed to spot numerous misprints), while Cornelia set aside a room for him in Wimborne House when he wrote the rather more serious, twin-volume biography of his father Randolph.

When, in 1915, in the wake of his disastrous strategy for the Dardanelles, Churchill lost his position as First Lord of the Admiralty, and he and his wife Clementine were therefore obliged to leave their home in Admiralty House, Ivor gave them respite at Wimborne House. In the winter of the following year, David Lloyd George became Prime Minister, and Freddy, as his Chief Whip, arranged for Churchill to speak first at the secret session of the House of Commons which marked the start of the new premiership. Within three months of Churchill's rousing 75-minute speech, he was back in a position of influence as Minister of Munitions, and renting Freddy's home in Roehampton, near Richmond Park.

Churchill always remained fond of the extended Guest clan. One might have thought that in July 1951, while he was pressing the Labour Prime Minister Clement Attlee into an autumn general election which would restore him once more to Downing Street, he would have been too busy to deal with a letter from an English rocket engineer living in New Jersey. But Amherst's letter recalled days past at Canford House, and the great man was only too pleased to agree to be godfather to Amherst's son. The boy was named Charles Churchill Villiers (commemorating, Amherst explained to Churchill, the union of the two men's families), and received a copy of Churchill's *My Early Life* as a present.

To return to Amherst's mother Elaine, she was born at Canford House in 1871 and, as we have seen, she had an exemplary background, the produce of Old and New Wealth. As such, she was expected to marry for money. Indeed, her three sisters became the brides of two viscounts and a baron. To Elaine this was no more romantic than the mergers which had created Guest Keen & Nettlefolds. She insisted on marrying for love. That she married a man of the cloth, who was the younger son of a younger son, and whose family had been tainted by the whiff of scandal, was all the more remarkable.

Ernest and Elaine were married at his former place of work, St George's, Hanover Square, on 30 April 1898. Their wedding certificate bears out the huge contrast in their backgrounds. Ernest's father is described as 'Charles Villiers (Deceased), Clerk in Holy Orders'; Elaine's is recorded as 'Ivor Bertie Guest, The Lord Wimborne, Peer of the Realm'.[3]

Fifty years later, Elaine would write to her younger daughter Veronica, 'No one has suffered more from injustice (parental) in her youth than myself and I had very much less than my sisters in every way.'[4] However, family historian, the late Bertie Guest, doubted that Elaine's dowry was any smaller than those of her sisters, and it seems more likely that if Elaine really did receive less than her sisters, it was because Ernest could not bring to the marriage the kind of wealth accruing to a viscount or a baron. Certainly, scrutiny of a pair of documents from the turn of the 19th century makes it clear that for Ernest and Elaine 'injustice' was a relative term. In their Marriage Settlement, drawn up the day before the wedding, Baron Wimborne bestowed on the couple £75,000, to be invested largely in the shares of overseas railway companies and English brewers. The modern-day equivalent is approximately £7 million (US$9.5 million).

The record of the young Villiers family in the 1901 Census is also revealing. They still lived in Hyde Park Square and under 'profession or occupation' Ernest was described as 'living on own means'.[5] In addition to his wife, their two children (Barbara had been born the year before Amherst) and his sister-in-law Gwendola, the Villiers household comprised a further eight people – a nurse, housemaid, under nurse, footman, butler, cook, kitchen maid and sick nurse.

By most people's standards the Villiers were considerably well off, and Amherst had been born into comparative luxury. This is why he was able to work on many of his racing car projects of the 1920s without payment, and also why he was, in the words of his second wife Nita, something of a baby when it came to money, very generous with it, but not good at keeping any!

The newly-weds saw out the final years of the 19th century in the Norfolk parishes of Haveringland and Brandiston, by dispensation of the Archbishop of Canterbury, no less. But with Barbara rising one and Amherst on the way, it was time for a change of direction. Ernest used the provisions of the Clerical Disabilities Relief Act to resign from the Church so that he could prepare for a career in politics, and the family moved briefly to Hyde Park Square, where Amherst was born.

Plans for the launch of Ernest's parliamentary career came to focus on Brighton, on the Sussex coast. The Villiers moved to a beautiful Regency terrace in Adelaide Crescent, overlooking the sea, and Ernest was adopted as one of two prospective Liberal candidates for the Brighton constituency, which was one of relatively few to have survived the Parliamentary reforms of the mid-1880s with two sitting Members of Parliament.

Ernest's task was enormous. Brighton had been a Conservative stronghold for decades, and the Liberals had not even bothered to field a pair of candidates there since 1885. He set about working closely and assiduously with Liberal followers in the town to garner a groundswell of support. As early as July 1903, almost two years before his chance finally came, he rallied supporters on the subject which would lead Churchill to cross the floor of the House, and would finally bring down Balfour's Conservative Government – protectionism. A local newspaper recorded: 'Concluding, Mr Villiers spoke of the aggravated destitution existing in this country at the present time, and said that he felt so deeply the iniquity of the suggestion to tax the food of the people that he should fight against it as long as he had breath.'[6]

Since 1889 the senior Conservative MP in Brighton had been Gerald Loder. In the early months of 1905 he was appointed Junior Minister to the Treasury and was therefore obliged to stand for re-election to Parliament. A by-election was called for 5 April, and Ernest, 'the Free Trade Candidate', stood for the Liberals as Loder's only opponent.

Nothing was left to chance. Every vote was fought for, and Ernest arranged for the Liberals' greatest orator, David Lloyd George, to speak on his behalf the week before the vote. Even so, the general consensus in the media was that Loder would win by a substantial majority, which makes the outcome of the Brighton by-election of 5 April 1905 all the more extraordinary. Loder lost fewer than 500 of the 7,858 votes he had won at the previous general election, yet Ernest, whose Liberal party had not even been represented then, won 8,209 votes, over 300 more than any previous Brighton MP. Balfour's Government was given a severe jolt, and Loder himself was finished as a politician.

When news of the result reached the House of Commons, the scenes were so chaotic that even the following day's *New York Times* recorded them. Under the headline 'Hard Blow for Balfour', it reported:

There was a rush of opposition members from the lobbies shouting with joy over the Liberal victory. 'Villiers is in!' was the cry . . . Mr Lloyd-George (Advanced Liberal) said he had intended to question the Premier on the fate that had befallen a member of the Administration at Brighton. On receiving notice that the question would be raised the Premier had deliberately left the House. The Premier's discourtesy to the House was becoming absolutely offensive . . . Winston Churchill said it looked like the beginning of the end, that it was retribution for the Government's shams and shuffles, and for the manner in which the Premier had treated Parliament.[7]

Four months later, on 8 August, Ernest made his maiden speech in the House of Commons. It is marked in Hansard, the formal record of UK Parliamentary debates, with an asterisk indicating 'revision by the

Member', which is permitted when an MP wants to ensure a speech has been recorded accurately. Since Ernest went to this trouble, and since he so conspicuously ignored the tradition of making an uncontroversial maiden speech, it is worth quoting some extracts here.

Essentially, he stood up in the House and demanded that Balfour call a general election. He told the Prime Minister 'he had outstayed his welcome and his portmanteau was on the doorstep,' and that 'he was doing much to lower the standard of honesty, efficiency and mutual confidence between the governors and the governed.' Ernest said Balfour's 'cooked policy had led to inefficiency on the one side and exasperation on the other, probably unparalleled in the history of Parliament' and that 'personalities were induced, insults pocketed, colleagues betrayed and reputations lost.'[8]

Ernest's extraordinary maiden speech to Parliament might have lacked the brutal frankness of Oliver Cromwell's demand to the Long Parliament, repeated by Leo Amery to Neville Chamberlain in the dark days of 1940, 'in the name of God, go!' but its meaning was just as clear, and within a year Ernest had been granted his wish. The 1906 general election resulted in a landslide victory for the Liberals, and Ernest consolidated his position as Member of Parliament for Brighton, adding a further 850 votes to his record count of the previous year.

With a strong mind for the issues of the day, a gift for oratory and influential relatives, Ernest may have hoped for rapid advancement in the new Parliament. However, when the new Government failed to press on with free trade reforms, and then renewed, without Parliamentary debate, the Brussels Sugar Convention, which had contributed to the great protectionism/free trade arguments of the previous administration, he found that he was ploughing a lone furrow.

On one occasion, he rose in the Commons to ask a representative of the Foreign Secretary, 'What line of defence would the Hon. Gentleman recommend to the members of his party who are endeavouring in the country to vindicate free trade now that the Government have relinquished the principles of free trade?' The Speaker of the House interjected and told Ernest, 'The Government cannot be expected to supply arguments for its own followers.' It is easy to imagine how members on the Opposition benches enjoyed this.[9]

A month later Ernest asked his own Prime Minister, Herbert Asquith, 'Is it the intention of His Majesty's Government to make in future with foreign powers binding agreements affecting the industry and commerce of this country without any reference to Parliament?'[10] Ernest's single minded devotion to the issue that had won him record votes in two elections can only be admired, but it was hardly a policy designed to endear him to his party, or single him out for promotion to office.

It all came to a head on 3 June 1908. In the longest speech of his Parliamentary career, Ernest began by reminding some of his own colleagues, now holding important offices in government, of the cutting criticisms of the original Sugar Convention they had made from the Opposition benches. Then he castigated his own government, not only for renewing the convention, but for doing so without referring the matter back to Parliament.

Hansard's record of the speech concludes,

He had not brought up this subject today without a sense of the gravest possible responsibility. He would perhaps be accused of disloyalty to the Party, but he put free trade before any Party . . . And it was also because of devotion to the Party as well as to free trade that he took up this position. If there was a mistake, better, by far, to put their own house in order than leave it to be wrecked by others at the General Election.[11]

It was, in a sense, Ernest's valedictory speech. At the January 1910 general election, the Liberals suffered heavy losses, though Asquith clung to power in a hung Parliament. After another indecisive result in December, he required a coalition with the Irish Nationalists to give the Liberals a working majority. But Ernest was long gone, having declined to stand for re-election in January. Two months earlier, he had written to *The Times* of 'these days when self interest is appealed to more than ever by politicians'.[12]

Intriguingly, in the letter to her daughter Veronica in which Elaine had complained of having less than her sisters, she continued, 'your father's career was killed for the sake of my brothers.'[13] It may well be that Ernest's embarrassment of his own government led to opposition from Cornelia and her sons, but whatever the reasons for Ernest's departure from the Commons, and whatever strains his dogged single mindedness had caused within his wife's family, the most impolitic political career of the Asquith era was over, and Ernest was left to resume his 'living on own means'.

He and Elaine purchased land near Chichester in Sussex and built a new home for their growing family, Hambrook House. Veronica was born in 1909, and the youngest of their four children, George, arrived three years later. A decade later, the family moved to Speen Court, in the village of Speen, which has now been consumed within the Berkshire market town of Newbury. It was from there that Ernest planned a return to Parliament. He contested the general election of November 1922 as Liberal candidate for the Clapham division of Wandsworth in south-west London. Just as in Brighton 17 years earlier, the seat was a Conservative stronghold, but this time there was no repeat of the heroics of 1905. Ernest took less than 20 per cent of the vote, and came third.

Ernest died 10 months later, on 26 September 1923. The causes of death on his death certificate were given as '(1) Degeneration of the Cortex Cerebri, (2) Coma.'[14] This implies a form of dementia. Alzheimer's disease tends to have a gradual onset and a relatively slow course, so for Ernest to have descended from contesting a general election to coma and death within ten months suggests a more galloping form of the disease. He was buried the following weekend in the picturesque churchyard of St Mary's, Speen. He was just 59.

It seems that Ernest's brief career as Liberal MP for Brighton was largely lost on his elder son, for Amherst spent his formative years in the town developing an early enthusiasm for cars and planes. Indeed, rather than sugar tariffs and free trade, perhaps a question Ernest put to the Secretary of State for the Home Department in May 1908 may have appealed more to the boy: 'How many accidents,' asked Ernest, 'due directly or indirectly to automobiles, occurred in the Metropolitan area during the month of April last; and how many occurred during the same month last year?' The answers, incidentally, were 283 and 250 respectively.[15]

In that same year, 1908, Kenneth Grahame's *Wind in the Willows* was published, but history does not relate if Amherst read about Mr Toad, perhaps the first 'petrol head' in English literature. Rather, his obsession with the internal combustion engine was fuelled initially by the family chauffeur, who let the boy try out not only the family car, a 34/45 Renault, but also his own four-cylinder FN motorcycle. By the age of 14 Amherst was filing up a pair of bronze gears to replace the timing wheels on another motorcycle.

He was equally entranced by the early aviators using the lawns of nearby Hove as a makeshift runway, and he learned that a wet finger in the air could establish the direction of the prevailing wind and determine if there would be any flying that day. He was already pursuing his own chosen path, a trait very definitely inherited from his strong-willed parents, as witnessed by his father's apolitical approach to politics and his mother's bucking of the expectations of her family and her class to marry for love.

Proud though he was of his father's time as an MP, Amherst had a low regard for politics, referring in later life to Westminster as 'Wetminster'. In 1977, when he discovered that the mechanic working on a Ferrari of his had gone into liquidation and was drawing unemployment benefit, he wrote to his sister Veronica that the House of Commons should be dissolved and that airline entrepreneur Freddie Laker should be put in charge of the country!

Amherst was proud, too, of his wider family, and to judge from the way his life would unfold, it is uncanny how true he would be to their mottos. From the House of Clarendon comes *Fidel coticula crux* ('The cross, the test of faith'), and though Amherst would pursue a broad range of paths in paying deference to what he called 'the Creator', he was always first and foremost a Christian. The Guests swore by *Ferro non gladio* ('By iron, not by the sword'), a motto that would apply increasingly to Amherst the longer he lived.

Perhaps the most apt family maxim of all came from his maternal grandmother, Cornelia Churchill. The motto of the House of Marlborough is *Fiel pero desdichado* ('Faithful, though unfortunate'), and in later life Amherst grew increasingly fatalistic, blaming the outcome of many endeavours on the 'rug-pullers'.

All this lay far in the future. Amherst was not yet 11 years old when he took the step which would keep him in Brighton, within walking distance of Adelaide Crescent, when his family moved to Chichester. In the autumn term of 1911 he became a pupil at Windlesham House School and, having been led by the example of his parents to pursue his own mind, England's oldest preparatory school now began to play its part in forming the young Amherst.

Chapter 2

SCHOOL

Charles Robert Malden was born in 1797. He joined the Royal Navy aged just 11 and, while still a teenager, observed the ineffective rocket bombardment of Fort McHenry during the Battle of Baltimore in 1812. He also served at the still more humiliating reverse at New Orleans which confirmed America's independence. He became an expert navigator and, as surveyor on the voyage of HMS *Blonde* to Hawaii in 1825, spotted and explored the tiny uninhabited island in the Pacific Ocean that still bears his name.

Malden is generally credited as being the founder of Windlesham House School. In fact, a cleric named Henry Worsley had originally set it up in Blackheath in south-east London, and then moved it to Newport on the Isle of Wight when he became vicar there in 1832. A year later Malden, who had been training naval cadets on the island, joined Worsley. In 1837 the vicar left abruptly and Malden acquired the lease on the school. His wife Fanny was unimpressed by the smelly drains and enormous rats on the site and insisted on moving. It was she who settled upon Brighton as the new home for the school, and it is this point that has become commonly associated with the founding of Windlesham House. It was also the beginning of a remarkable teaching dynasty.

Initially, Windlesham was simply the establishment in which Charles and Fanny taught their own seven sons, but they also sent a unique message to the town of Brighton: they would look after other parents' children as they did their own. As the Malden boys matured into men, and more sons, daughters, nephews and nieces joined the school, so it grew. Generation after generation of Malden men experienced a highly individual career path, first as pupil, then as assistant, and finally as principal and parent. Unfortunately they shared another common trait – they tended to die young. Thus it was that in 1896 Charles Scott Malden, grandson of the former Navy Lieutenant, died in his early 30s, leaving his widow Grace with the school and £25. She was known as 'Mrs Charles' and would be principal of Windlesham House School for the next 30 years. A profoundly religious woman, what she lacked in a formal education she made up for in moral fibre and courage. She was also very keen on Robert Baden-Powell's embryonic scouting movement.

At the time of Amherst's arrival, the school occupied a two-acre site on Norfolk Terrace in Brighton, less than ten minutes' walk from Adelaide Crescent. He settled in quickly and was placed fourth in class in his first year. He was a particularly keen Scout, performing well at first aid, knot tying, distance judging, cooking and signalling, both Morse and semaphore. He was also a fine singer; he gave a solo performance of the Scottish folk song 'Annie Laurie' at the school's Christmas concert in 1913, and was still considered to be 'reliable in the chorus' even when his voice began to break.

The year 1913 was significant for Windlesham House, as the school moved a couple of miles west to a 37-acre site at Portslade, on the edge of the Sussex Downs. An indication of Windlesham's growing reputation was the list of headmasters of other leading schools who attended the opening ceremony at Portslade, including Harrow's Dr Ford. Amherst missed the event but sent a good luck telegram saying he wished he were there.

It was in the early months at Portslade that Amherst turned out for the school cricket team to compete against Ernest in the Fathers' Match, and won fourth prize in the Cleland Cup for 'boy best at work and play'. The following year, he made further strides, becoming first sub-monitor and then monitor. His scouting career also blossomed, and he was made patrol leader of Hawks Patrol.

It is clear that he had continued to study the aeroplanes flying at

Hove, for in the summer of 1914, volume LXXV of the *School Magazine* records under Scout News: 'Special mention ought to be made of a biplane, designed and made by Patrol Leader Villiers. It is to be finished in the holidays, after which we hope he may present it to the museum.' There was no further mention of Amherst's biplane in subsequent volumes, as the majority of the pages were taken up with the fortunes of old boys fighting in France. Indeed, by this time, half of the Portslade site had been given over to the Royal Engineers for training.

Windlesham House influenced Amherst in other ways, too. Under Mrs Charles, the school had a strong Christian ethic, and in December 1913 Amherst was confirmed by the Bishop of Lewes. His early skills as an artist were honed by another member of the Malden clan, Euphemia Malden, RA, and Amherst enjoyed drawing aeroplanes. His capabilities as a designer were already developing.

By the time Amherst left Windlesham in May 1915, he was in the second form in Classics and the B set for Maths. He may not have reached the ultimate heights of academic endeavour, but he had enjoyed himself enormously, and taken his formative steps as a designer and an artist.

He retained such fond memories of the school that, in 1962, he sent his own son Charles to be educated there, under yet another Mr Malden, whom Amherst considered had a rather attractive wife. This was Charles C. Malden, great-great-grandson of the old naval man turned teacher, and his wife Elizabeth. Under their guidance, Windlesham would blossom into one of the most celebrated preparatory schools in England, but Charles's stay at the school was a short one. Within months of his enrolment, Amherst was headhunted to join Douglas Aircraft in California to work on a Martian space project, and the family returned to the US. Almost half a century after leaving Windlesham House, the draughtmanship and design skills which Amherst first began to acquire as a pupil were still serving him well.

His four years at Windlesham House were the ideal apprenticeship for Amherst to make the most of his next school, Oundle. Situated in the old market town of Oundle, near Peterborough, it was originally founded in 1556 by Sir William Laxton, Lord Mayor of London and Master of the Worshipful Company of Grocers. The school is forever associated with one of the most important educationalists of the late 19th and early 20th centuries, Frederick William Sanderson.

Sanderson was born at Brancepeth in County Durham in 1857. On appointment as an assistant master at Dulwich College in 1885, he introduced a particularly innovative and practical approach to the teaching of chemistry, physics and engineering. His techniques, which enabled boys to experiment with working engines in well-equipped workshops, became highly sought after, and when, in 1892, Oundle's governors at the Grocers' Company wanted to turn round their ailing school with the introduction of a more modern syllabus, it was to Sanderson they turned.

His task was far from easy. Oundle School had fewer than 100 pupils, and with his thick Durham accent, lack of public school education and inexperience of boarding schools, many of his colleagues resented his arrival. However, he soon stamped his authority on the place. Within a year, he opened a preparatory department, the Berystead, where his wife Jane ran the boarding house, and he introduced science and engineering by replicating the laboratories and workshops of Dulwich. Modern humanity subjects such as history and geography were also established, and even the youngest boys were encouraged to undertake original research.

By 1909 Sanderson had rid himself of all but three of the teaching staff he had inherited, and each of Oundle's houses was full, with a total compliment of more than 320 pupils. Pupils were drawn by Sanderson's desire to unlock the potential in each of them. He prided himself in understanding what motivated a boy, and using that understanding to develop a focused curriculum for him.

It was into this febrile environment that Amherst arrived in the autumn of 1915 and he set about exploiting it to the full. He developed a passion for the theatre, playing Lorenzo in *The Merchant of Venice*, Samuel, the Pirate King's lieutenant in *The Pirates of Penzance*, and the rather less well-known part of the River Wye in Sheridan's *The Rivals*.

He was an enthusiastic debater, and in 1916 argued for the motion that 'Cellars are the best place of refuge in a Zeppelin attack.' He was also a handy sportsman, and was a member of his junior house cricket XI and senior house rugby XV. But it was in those famous Oundle workshops that Amherst was at his happiest. In 1917 he readily gave up his summer holidays to remain at school and help make munitions for the war effort, and he was particularly proud when Sanderson gave him responsibility for an old Curtiss Ox V8 aero engine which the Air Ministry had given to the school. He took it from the science block, set it up in a specially constructed test shed on the cricket field, and got it working.

Amherst also established some long-term friendships while at Oundle, the most important of which was with a boy 17 months his senior, T. R. Mays. He was born in August 1899, in his family home at Eastgate House in the Lincolnshire town of Bourne, less than 30 miles from Oundle. His father, Thomas, ran a wool and tannery business from the imposing premises, and was an early motoring enthusiast, owning and racing a succession of Vauxhalls and Napiers. The boy particularly enjoyed hanging around the mechanics who came to tune his father's cars, and angling for ways of joining them on road tests. In his autobiography, *Split Seconds*, Amherst's young friend recalled, 'these speed bursts were to me the supreme thrill, bringing the realisation that to race was the greatest ambition of my life.'[1] He is better known as Raymond Mays, the founder of two of British motor racing's most famous names, ERA and BRM, and Amherst did more than most to help him achieve that ambition. Indeed, as Mays also records in *Split Seconds*, 'the influence of Villiers in particular on my racing career was very marked.'[2]

Mays originally joined the Berystead in 1912, where he formed a deep affection for Jane Sanderson, and graduated to Oundle's School House a year before Amherst's arrival. They were fellow members of the School House rugby XV, and of the group of boys who gave up their summer of 1917 to support the war effort.

The slight difference in age between Amherst and Mays would be key to their relative experience of the First World War. Mays left Oundle in December 1917 to enter Guards Officer Training at Bushy Hall in Hertfordshire. The following May he joined the Grenadier Guards and in October he was shipped out to France. The Armistice came a month later while he was stationed at Mauberge, and he saw in the New Year in Cologne, as part of the Army of Occupation.

Conversely, the younger Amherst left Oundle in July 1918, after Sanderson had arranged for him to gain some valuable experience at Farnborough working for the Royal Aircraft Establishment as a special apprentice. The Armistice would prevent him from satisfying his ambition to fly in action with the nascent RAF.

Sanderson, whose eldest son was killed in the war, came to hold strong views about the role of education in Britain's post-war reconstruction. In June 1922 he had just given a lecture on 'The duty and service of science in the new era' in the old Botanical Theatre at University College, London, when he collapsed and died. His great friend, the author H. G. Wells, who had sent his own boys to Oundle, had chaired the event, and would later write an acclaimed biography of the great educationalist.

In 1983, when Amherst visited his sister Veronica at her home on Vancouver Island, off Canada's Pacific coast, he gave a wide-ranging interview to a local newspaper, *The News Advertiser*. The octogenarian Amherst was still espousing Sanderson's approach to education, some 65 years after he had left Oundle. He argued that natural human inquisitiveness played a vital part in teaching. 'We should say, "What do you wish to learn about?" and, following that, "All right, now tell us about it."' The article continues,

Without that burning desire to immerse oneself in a subject, there is no driving force behind the action. And if a passing grade is the goal, the student need not care beyond meeting that standard. By emphasising examinations, are we producing young people who don't care enough to seek the inner heart of their studies – young people whose aspiration, beyond the usual adolescent dreams, is merely to survive?[3]

Long after Amherst and Mays left Oundle, the school continued making a contribution to the British motor racing and sports car industries. Some ten years behind the pair came Alfred Owen, whose company Rubery Owen acquired BRM and supported it through its most successful years. A decade later Peter Morgan, who would go on to manage the eponymous sports car firm for more than 50 years, could be found in the school's workshops 'making little brass aeroplanes and things like that'.[4] His son, the firm's current corporate strategy director, Charles Morgan, is himself an Old Oundelian.

The output from the modern-day Oundle workshops would have continued to interest Amherst. Just months before he died the *Boot Hill Special*, a battery-operated car designed and built by pupils of the school, set an average speed of 66.42mph (106.89kmh) to break the British land speed record for electrically-powered vehicles, while Oundle boys drove the buggies they had developed in their workshops through the streets of London during the 2006 Lord Mayor's Parade.

Chapter 3

QUICKSILVER

In the spring of 1918, the Royal Air Force was born out of the amalgamation of the Royal Flying Corps and the Royal Naval Air Service. To avoid a clash of initials with what quickly became known as the RAF, the Royal Aircraft Factory was renamed in the summer, so that when Amherst went to Farnborough as a special apprentice it was to the Royal Aircraft Establishment.

A new superintendent, W. Sydney Smith, had been appointed to define a number of specific areas of aeronautical research, and Amherst was able to spend time with K4 Department (Experimental Flight) and E Department (Engines), where he worked on a continuous programme of testing each aero engine, Allied and enemy alike, that came through Farnborough. He personally dismantled the first Liberty engine to arrive in England, and compiled the guide for it.

Amherst enjoyed his brief spell at Farnborough, but a young man of his background and intelligence was expected to go to university. Besides, his old Oundle friend Raymond Mays had made plans to enter Christ's College, and if Amherst also went up to Cambridge, they would be able to renew their partnership. Thus it was that on 22 April 1919 Amherst entered Gonville & Caius College, Cambridge. He was a handsome young man of 18, 6ft 1in tall, with blue eyes and dark hair.

The college, which is generally known as Caius (and pronounced 'Keys'), was originally founded in 1348 by a Norfolk priest named Edmund Gonville, to educate trainee clerics. It became Gonville & Caius in 1557, after Dr John Keys, a renowned physicist who had worked in Italy and 'Latinised' his family name to Caius, had extended it and encouraged it to adopt a Renaissance outlook, even in its physical layout.

Caius commissioned three classical stone gates to reflect the journey that students would take during their time at university. Entry to the college was gained through the Gate of Humility, opposite St Michael's Church on Trinity Street. On the far side of Tree Court lay the arch through which students would pass going about their daily business, the Gate of Virtue. Beyond this lay Caius Court, flanked on one side by the 14th-century chapel, and on the other by the Gate of Honour, which was the triumphal arch under which, by tradition, students passed only once – upon graduation.

At the time of Amherst's admission, talented young men were pouring into Cambridge, either demobbed from war duty or, like Amherst, too young to have seen action. Among the men making their way through the Gate of Humility for the first time (Caius would not admit women undergraduates until 1979) was a fellow Old Oundelian, Joseph Needham, who would go on to become a noted biologist and, eventually, Master of the College.

Another new entrant to Caius was responsible for the sudden marked improvement the college made at athletics. In February 1920, it beat Jesus College in the final of the Inter-Collegiate Athletic Championships, largely because a law undergraduate won the 100 yards, 440 yards, hurdles, long jump and high jump. His name was Harold Abrahams, and his win in the 100 metres Olympic final in Paris four years later would be remembered in *Chariots of Fire*.

Amherst found himself surrounded by brilliant minds. In later life he recalled attending lectures given by Lord Rutherford, the father of nuclear physics, while another influence was the mathematician and philosopher John Venn, who had been President of the College since 1903, and also played a significant part in bringing together the college archives and writing its history. Today, John Venn is more widely remembered as the inventor of the diagram that bears his name.

From the outset, Amherst focused less on his studies and more on extra-curricular activities. There was, for example, the motorcycle he and Mays shared. An early Villiers development was to fit the vehicle with a large leather bag known as a portmanteau, to use as an unorthodox form of side car. Another student prank involved dropping special pellets into the exhaust system, so that he and Mays could leave a smoke screen as they charged round the narrow streets of Cambridge.

The most fascinating of all Amherst's extra-curricular projects at Cambridge must surely be the *Storm Petrel*, an extraordinary hydroplane which soaked and fascinated fellow-users of the River Cam during the summer of 1920. Amherst designed it from scratch, and somehow sourced an old aero engine, propeller, fuselage and floats from which he, Mays and other Cambridge friends gradually assembled a weird-looking craft. Initial tests suggested she worked well enough, but one friend, an undergraduate at Christ's College named Arthur Cotton, tried a little too hard when he sought to impress a lady friend by taking her out for a 'flight' on the river. He opened the throttle too wide and the *Storm Petrel* nosed upside-down and sank. Cotton and his friend were rescued, but legend has it that her jewellery remains in the river to this day.

Amherst's timing in going up to Cambridge was fortuitous. The old Cambridge University Automobile Club (CUAC) had originally been founded in 1902, and among its early members were future luminaries of British motor sport who would have an impact on his career. Mechanical engineering guru Harry Ricardo, whose alcohol-based fuel Amherst would use in Mays's Brescia Bugattis, and whose 3-litre engine for the TT Vauxhall would be supercharged by Amherst, had been secretary of the club 13 years earlier. The future world land speed record holder and founder of KLG Spark Plugs, Kenelm Lee Guinness, who would make part of his Robinhood Engineering Works available to Amherst for the building of Malcolm Campbell's first *Bluebird* record-breaking car, had become a member in 1909. But in the autumn of 1910 the CUAC had folded because of a lack of undergraduate members. Now, in Amherst's first term, he found the following notice posted at garages around Cambridge:

Cambridge University Motor Cycling Club

A club was in existence for several years previous to the war under the above title known more recently as the 'C U Automobile Club', the purpose of which was to collect together keen Motor Cyclists or Car Owners, and to organise sporting events such as Hill Climbs, Reliability Trials and Race Meetings. A comfortable club room was also provided for the use of members.

The events were either held amongst members themselves or else took the nature of inter-Varsity events – several hill climbs etc being arranged in competition with the Oxford University M.C.C.

It has been proposed to revive the Club, provided that sufficient support can be obtained. Would any Motor Cyclists or Car Owners who are sufficiently interested to guarantee their support to the scheme kindly communicate – or better still call in person upon

W. A. FELL SMITH (MAGDALENE COLLEGE)
30 Alpha Road
Cambridge[1]

In the town's Blue Boar Hotel later that term, Mr Fell-Smith chaired a meeting at which it was decided that the CUAC be revived. The pre-war club colours of pink and green on a pale blue background were readopted, and a silver swallow chosen as the club badge. The annual subscription was set at 12s 6d.

There is nothing in the records of the CUAC remaining from this time to suggest that either Amherst or Mays became members immediately, or competed in any of its 1920 events. All that changed when Mays saw a Speed Model Hillman in a Cambridge showroom and persuaded his father to buy it for him. Amherst joined his friend for an initial run on the Huntingdon road, and was intrigued to find that while the Hillman could manage 56mph (90kmh) in top (third) gear, it was capable of 60mph (97kmh) in second.

Mays may have referred to the car in his autobiography as 'then the outstanding 1½ litre sports car', but the gearing on it does seem to have been a little odd.[2] In the first issue of the weekly magazine *The Light Car and Cyclecar* in 1921, the fate of another Speed Model Hillman, stalled and stranded on a hill-climb section of the London–Exeter Trial, was commented upon. The driver had been baulked approaching the hill, prompting the magazine to report: 'The low gear ratio of this machine is unusually high for a touring car, so that unless a hill can be tackled at speed, a successful ascent is rather doubtful.'[3]

As Mays put it, 'Amherst, who had recently gained much knowledge in the experimental department of Aero Engines, at Farnborough, suggested we should experiment with the Hillman and produce more power from somewhere.'[4] Thus, at the tender age of 20, Amherst began his career as a developer of racing and sports cars which would eventually break records at Brooklands and Daytona.

* * * * *

Before describing the nascent steps in Amherst's career, it is necessary first to set out the landscape of British motor sport in the early 1920s.

The earliest British motor sport event of any description took place on Petersham Hill, Richmond-upon-Thames, in June 1899, when approximately 40 entrants competed to set the best time of the day on a 325yd (297m) course with a maximum gradient of 1 in 9. Fastest driver of a genuine motor car that day was one Charles Stewart Rolls, some five years before he met Henry Royce.

The climb had been organised by the Automobile Club of Great Britain and Ireland (ACGBI), the forerunner of the Royal Automobile Club (RAC), as part of a larger event designed to demonstrate to the British public how far the automobile had developed. In the early years of the 20th century, speed hill-climbing had developed swiftly into a competitive sport. This was in spite of the fact that hill-climbs were generally run on public roads, and a national speed limit of 20mph (32kmh) would be in place until 1926. There was, therefore, a particularly important compromise to achieve when organising a hill-climb on the British mainland in the early 1920s. The local police were needed to keep in check crowds who rarely paid much attention to personal safety, yet the constabulary had to be prevailed upon to ignore the speed of the cars the spectators were watching. This uneasy state of affairs would be brought to an end in 1925, in circumstances described in Chapter 4. The other criteria in deciding upon a hill-climb venue were easier to fulfil, which is why there was such a plethora of these events by the early 1920s. A course of rarely more than 1 mile in length, on a hill of testing gradient, with a few bends worthy of the name, were all it took.

Different formulae and classes grew up around the hill-climb scene, but the chief prizes were for the outright quickest ascent of the day, and that set by a car with an engine of no more than 1,500cc capacity. The quickest performance was generally known as 'Fastest Time of the Day', or FTD, but in his seminal book on British speed hill-climbing, *Uphill Racers*, Chris Mason notes that 'time is constant and neither fast nor slow. You can have a fastest speed but not a fastest time.'[5] He preferred 'Best Time of the Day', or BTD, but since Amherst would have been more familiar with FTD, that is the style followed here.

The greatest of all British hill-climb venues, today as it was in the early 1920s, is Shelsley Walsh, situated in rolling countryside in the Teme Valley, some 10 miles west of Worcester. Its origins lay in a steep bridle path connecting two parts of a farm owned in the early days of the 20th century by a member of the Midland Automobile Club (MAC), Montagu Taylor. He agreed to host an event for the club, the path was widened and resurfaced, and the steep, high bank above it was cleared of undergrowth to provide a natural grandstand. The MAC held the first Shelsley Walsh hill-climb in August 1905, which, ignoring interludes for the two world wars, makes the course the world's oldest motor sport venue to have enjoyed continuous use.

Originally 992yd (907m) in length, in 1907 the finish line was pushed a little further up the hill to make the course precisely 1,000yd (914m) long, and a cutting was dug between the first two bends to lessen the gradient at that point. Otherwise, in 1921 the course was much the same as it was in 1905, as indeed it still is today.

Away from the start, the track took a 120-degree left-hand sweep, named Kennel Bend after the nearby home to the local hunt pack, and then a second, open left-hander, The Crossing. A short straight led on to a more pronounced left–right sweep known as the Esses, followed by a straight climb to the finish line. The rise in height from start to finish was 328ft (100m), an average gradient of approximately 1 in 10, although the steepest part of the course was a little under 1 in 6.

The FTD at that 1905 meeting was 77.6 seconds, set by Ernest Instone in a 35hp Daimler. Shelsley Walsh reopened for business after the war in 1920, but at that meeting no one got near the pre-war record, and Joseph Higginson's 55.2 seconds, established in June 1913 in a Vauxhall 30/98, still stood as Mays and Amherst made their way to Shelsley Walsh with the Hillman in September 1921.

The task of setting FTD also existed on the flat, in the form of speed trials. Here, the basic job of the organisers was to find a stretch of straight road of 1 mile or so in length, where the local police were amenable to the effective objective of the meeting being to break the law by as much as possible. Seaside promenades such as Southsea and Blackpool were popular speed-trial venues, and were wide enough to permit two cars to compete at a time, while the dead straight Gloucester Drive on Earl Beauchamp's estate at Madresfield, near Malvern, was also well-loved, and had the additional bonus, being on private land, of having no speed limit to worry about.

As speeds climbed, so the braking area required at the end of the measured distance grew, and some speed-trial organisers found it easier to move off the promenades and on to the beaches themselves. Thus grew up another branch of British motor sport – sand racing.

The sport of sand racing could take the form of straight sprints down a measured distance, or races around a rudimentary track comprising two straights linked by a pair of hairpin bends. These were likely to rut up badly over the course of a race, and incoming tides were another hazard, but, especially once authorities' attitudes to events on public roads hardened in 1925, sand racing grew in popularity. Moreover, beach venues such as Pendine on the South Wales coast, Lancashire's Southport, and Saltburn in Yorkshire were so expansive that they would also play host to world land speed record attempts – the former two successfully.

But in 1921, the home of British motor sport was Brooklands, near Weybridge in Surrey. The circuit was the brainchild of a local landowner, Hugh Locke King. Born in 1848, Locke King was an early advocate of the motor car, and found that an otherwise enjoyable trip to Italy to watch the 1905 Coppa Florio, held on a 100-mile circuit at Brescia, had been spoiled by the fact that no British cars had participated in the race. When he learned that the reasons for this were the low speed limits on British roads and the absence of a suitable alternative venue for cars to race or be tested at speed, he determined to provide such a venue. He made available two of his agricultural holdings, nestling alongside the London & South Western Railway line, Hollick Farm and Wintersells Farm, and called in as designer a colonel in the Royal Engineers who had previously been chairman of the ACGBI, Henry Holden.

Holden's design was for a track 2.77 miles (4.46km) in length, with banked curves to cope with the 120mph (193kmh) speeds envisaged. The circuit would be raced on in an anti-clockwise direction, so that the northern banking, known as the Home or Members' Banking, would form the first bend, with a maximum height of almost 29ft (8.8m). The straight running down to the southern banking was dead level and, since it hugged the railway line, became known as the Railway Straight.

It ran into the Byfleet Banking, which had a wider radius and therefore a lower maximum height, set at just under 22ft (6.7m).

The eastern straight rose away from the end of the Byfleet Banking at a gentle gradient of 1 in 30, and required a slight right-hand dog-leg, because Locke King had sold a portion of land to the east of the site to the British subsidiary of the Itala car manufacturer. The finishing straight ran on from this dog-leg, which thus became known as the Fork, to join the Members' Banking two-thirds of the way round, and rose at its top end at a gradient of 1 in 12.

The circuit was laid out in a 6in (15cm) layer of concrete straight on to the sandy subsoil, and at the point where the Members' Banking crossed the diverted River Wey, the track was carried on a bridge made of steel-reinforced concrete, resting on concrete piers, some of which were sunk into the river bed.

Working at a pace which would surely have the developers of the 2012 London Olympic sites scratching their heads in wonder, 2,000 workers completed the entire project in ten months. It is perhaps this haste, together with the settling of the subsoil and of those piers in the river bed, which led in time to the bumpy nature of Brooklands, and to the notorious hump on the Members' Banking which spawned a thousand images of cars being launched into the air.

The first race meeting was held at Brooklands in July 1907. During a scratch race the following year, the circuit's rudimentary electronic timing recorded Felice Nazzaro in a 15.2-litre Fiat as having completed a lap of the circuit at 121.64mph (195.76kmh), and though there was widespread disbelief at this (stop watches recorded a speed of less than 108mph, or 174kmh), the Brooklands Automobile Racing Club officially recorded it as the outright lap record, and this still stood when Mays and Amherst first took the Hillman to Brooklands in May 1921.

By that time the landscape of the track demonstrated that its primary function during the First World War had been aircraft production and testing. Most notably Vickers had taken over the Itala plant and constructed a factory which backed on to the Fork, and displayed the famous 'Vickers Ltd Brooklands' sign-writing and the company's 'Flying V' logo.

By the 1920s Brooklands was home to a racing club and a flying club, and was as fashionable a sporting venue as Henley, Wimbledon or Ascot. Bill Boddy, the doyen of motor racing writers, and author of the definitive book on Brooklands, remembers it thus:

> *There was a tremendous concourse of people there. I always said it brought everyone together, from rogues to the aristocracy. They were all centred on the paddock because they all liked motor cars and motorcycles, you see? I always thought the topography of the place was wonderful. It was a gentleman's estate with so many aspects to it that the motor racing was incidental really. It was a rather nice country estate in Surrey.[6]*

Amherst's skills in enhancing the performance of a car were first demonstrated not at Brooklands, but on a mundane 750yd (686m) stretch of road running through the estate of the Rothschild banking family in Buckinghamshire, on 5 March 1921. The occasion was the Inter-Varsity hill-climb on Aston Hill, near Aylesbury. The road surface was in reasonable condition, and the hill, with an average gradient of 1 in 14, was not the steepest on the calendar, but the weather was wet and the event would be a test both of Mays's skills as a performance driver, and Amherst's as a development engineer.

Amherst's work was clear to see: the Hillman now sported a pair of slim bucket seats and a new body with streamlined tail, clad in a polished aluminium skin. The wings were fitted with additional stays, secured in place by wing nuts, which enabled their speedy removal so that the car could be switched quickly from 'touring' to 'racing' trim during a meeting. In recognition of the works Hillman car, named *Mercury*, an intricate 'QS' monogram had been applied to the new bodywork, identifying the car as *Quicksilver*. Under the bonnet of *Quicksilver* were further hallmarks of Amherst's work: the gearing had been fixed, the inlet and exhaust ports polished to improve the flow, and the pistons' skirts had had holes drilled in them to make them lighter.

The first marker was laid down by M. H. Rollason, a fellow Cambridge undergraduate also armed with a Speed Model Hillman. He set a time of 50.8 seconds, but Mays went the whole way up the hill in first gear, generating more than 4,000rpm, and set FTD in the light car class in 45.9 seconds. This also enabled Cambridge to defeat Oxford in the team event. In their first competitive test, Raymond Mays and Amherst Villiers had delivered the goods.

The 1921 Brooklands season began with a meeting on Easter Monday. The first race that day was won by Count Louis Zbrowski in a highly modified Mercedes fitted with a 23-litre Maybach engine. The car was the original *Chitty-Bang-Bang* [sic], and more than 40 years later Amherst would come to have a connection with its fictional counterpart.

Though *Quicksilver* was entered for the meeting, Mays and Amherst did not attend as they were busy, further developing the car in preparation for a particularly hectic May. Bertie Kensington-Moir, at that time working for Zenith Carburettors, had taken an interest in their endeavours and given them a number of carburettors to try. Mays had also paid a visit to the Hillman works in Coventry. Much work was being done on *Mercury* to lighten her – works driver George Bedford had even taken to driving in skimpy plimsolls – and Mays came away with 'a few "bits and pieces" from his old engine'.[7]

Amherst and Mays stripped down the engine and fitted the new parts. In spite of much of this work being confined to the evenings, because of the need for the two young men to be seen in at least some lectures, the results were impressive. In tests conducted on the Cambridge–Eaton Scoon Road, they found that from the initial maximum speed of 56mph, *Quicksilver* could now deliver more than 80mph (129kmh), and they approached May in good spirits.

May Day saw the Oxbridge fraternity of car and motorcycle enthusiasts gather together under cloudless skies on Harling Common, near the Norfolk town of Thetford, for the Inter-Varsity Speed Trials. The crowd was particularly large because members of the Norfolk Light Car Club had requested, and been granted, the opportunity to attend the event. They found that the students could organise an event every bit as well as they could drive.

The straight, largely level, 1km (1,094yd) stretch of road, bordered on one side by a wood and the other by a large expanse of undulating countryside, was well-surfaced so that high speeds were anticipated, particularly since flying starts were permitted. An electrical timing system, triggered by the cars and motorbikes breaking threads at the start and finish lines, was highly accurate and allowed times to be announced swiftly.

Mays trounced the opposition, recording precisely the same time on both his runs in *Quicksilver*: 36.6 seconds, equivalent to 61.11mph (98.34kmh). No one else could get near 57mph, and the next quickest Speed Model Hillman driver – Rollason again – could not breach 40 seconds.

Given the flying start, straight course and fine road surface, it can be concluded that the performance of *Quicksilver* that day tells us more about Amherst's development work than Mays's driving, and it is clear that Amherst had given his friend the archetypal 'unfair advantage' over university opposition. It was time to see now how they could fare against the country's finest drivers and cars and, having obtained permission from the authorities in Cambridge, they made their way to Brooklands to participate in the following weekend's Essex Motor Club meeting.

They fared very well. In the Essex Short Handicap, Mays found he had to give second best to a late entrant, Lionel Martin in an early Aston Martin (Aston after the hill-climb, Martin after himself), although *The Light Car* records that Martin 'was hotly pursued by Mays's Hillman (which was going extremely well)'.[8]

In the Essex Light Car Handicap, Mays went up against 12 other drivers over three laps of Brooklands, some 8.5 miles (13.7km). His low profile in the motor racing world was about to end, but it clearly helped him in the handicap, since Bedford in the works Hillman had to give him a 1 minute 21 seconds start. In fact, Bedford headed straight for the paddock when he was finally flagged away from the start, 'giving up the unequal struggle at the outset', wrote *The Light Car*, 'in absolute disgust'.[9]

Perhaps he had more idea than most as to what *Quicksilver* was really capable of. Mays was a quarter of a mile clear at the end of the first lap, and even as the handicap unfolded it was clear that no one would catch him. He wound up winner by some 200yd, in an average speed of 68.5mph (110.2kmh). It was the first of many Brooklands triumphs for Mays.

It is telling that, at the following weekend's Whit Monday meeting at Brooklands, Mays had only a 48-second start over the 'scratch' car, the AC of aviation hero Harry Hawker, for the Short Handicap. *The Light Car* was again complimentary, recording that he handled *Quicksilver* 'in a masterly fashion, getting off the mark very smartly'.[10] However, clutch slip forced him to retire at the end of the first lap, and he was unplaced in either of the other races he entered that day.

Now Mays and Amherst turned their attention to hill-climbs. At these, the competition was much stiffer than at the university events. On occasion, Mays, still not 22 years old and in his first season of competition driving, found some of the courses particularly challenging, and there were no Brooklands handicaps to help him. Results were therefore mixed. A telling image exists of Mays sliding wildly at the exit of the third bend, a right-angled right-hander, at Yorkshire's Holme Moss hill-climb in early June. *The Light Car* published a photograph of Bedford making a much neater exit from the same bend that day, and the respective times of the drivers indicates how much Mays still had to learn as a driver. Bedford set FTD in 94.6 seconds; Mays managed only 140 seconds.

There were days, too, when Amherst's inexperience betrayed itself. Later that month, the South Harting hill-climb was held near Petersfield, Sussex, over a course with an average gradient of 1 in 12, but 1 in 6.7 at its steepest. *The Light Car* reported that Mays 'was not so fast as expected, and his gears apparently did not suit the hill'.[11] Amherst would apply this particular lesson to good effect in the years ahead.

Results improved as the season wore on. At July's Auto-Cycle Union speed-trial meeting, held over a 1km (1,094yd) course on the Duke of Portland's estate at Welbeck Park, Nottinghamshire, Mays took FTD in 43.4 seconds, and a month later, at the Garrowby hill-climb in East Yorkshire, he won the 1,500cc prize.

Mays and Amherst were under no illusions when they made their way to Shelsley Walsh for the first time as competitors. The date was 10 September 1921. Mays records in *Split Seconds*, 'The little Hillman seemed to me to be no more than an impudent parvenu alongside these famous racing machines, and although I reached the summit safely the hill seemed disconcertingly steep and bumpy and the Hillman so slow.'[12] For the record, Mays recorded 82.8 seconds, achieving 4th in class. FTD fell to Chris Bird in his 4.9-litre Indianapolis Sunbeam. He took 3 seconds off Joe Higginson's 1913 record, and left the course record at 52.2 seconds.

All in all, it had been a highly satisfactory first season of motor sport for Raymond Mays and Amherst Villiers, and it had left them with a huge appetite for more. In fact, as the *Quicksilver* campaign of 1921 progressed, all pretence at study ceased. Mays had a further distraction. His father was ill, and he was wanted back in Bourne to help run the family business. For Amherst, the final straw seems to have come when he raised a question about the alloy he had seen used at Farnborough on cylinder heads. The professor advised him the alloy in question would melt and could not therefore be used in an aero engine. It appears this was the moment Amherst felt his immediate future lay outside academia. So, after six terms, he left Cambridge without a degree, and never got to pass through Caius's Gate of Honour.

It is not recorded how Ernest and Elaine received their son's news, but it appears they formed the view that since he loved messing about with engines, he at least ought to do it with a reputable company. It was Ernest's brother Noel who came up with the solution. In December 1905 he had married Dorothy Watson, whose brother William had the good fortune – literally – to have been the great nephew of William George Armstrong, the founder of the Armstrong Whitworth manufacturing group, which had come to dominate the British ship-building and armaments industries. When the old man died in December 1900, some three weeks after Amherst's birth, William Watson inherited his estates.

Watson was never personally involved in the management of the Armstrong Whitworth company. However, he held sufficient influence there that he was able to acquiesce to his brother-in-law Noel's request for help in getting young Amherst into gainful employment, *and* keeping him involved with engines.

Amherst joined the hydraulic machinery division of the group, which was, in fact, the oldest part of Armstrong Whitworth. Sir William Armstrong had still been a practising solicitor in Newcastle upon Tyne when he designed his first hydraulic cranes, and his company had gone on to provide the hydraulic machinery that powered the famous Swing Bridge over the River Tyne, and the original mechanism which raised the spans of London's Tower Bridge.

After a spell working for the development arm of the group in Coventry, Amherst was sent to Oslo in Norway to join the firm A. S. Murea Verkstad, where he studied hydro-electric turbines. We know from a photograph of him working underneath a Bugatti in the paddock at the Madresfield speed-trial of June 1922 that he was not in Norway full time, and in interviews given more than 50 years later to a number of British car magazines, he gives the impression he neither enjoyed the work nor the people he worked for. That winter, he resigned.

Some 40 years later, while living in California, he explained to a fellow ex-patriot British engineer, Bruce Pounds, what triggered the resignation. He had been sent to Italy to establish how quickly an old gun factory, unused since the end of the First World War, could be converted to the manufacture of turbine engines. Not unreasonably, he explained upon his return, that conversion was not feasible; the factory would need to be stripped out and retooled in its entirety. This does not seem to have been the answer for which Armstrong

Whitworth was hoping – maybe, Amherst concluded, there might have been a government grant available for rapid conversion – and a parting of the ways became inevitable.

Amherst had clearly inherited a double-dose of the strong free will previously displayed by Ernest and Elaine. After revelling in Oundle's enterprising culture, he had found the more formal educational environment at Cambridge oppressive, and learned at Armstrong Whitworth that he was no better suited to employment. He longed to apply his skills in a more pragmatic way, yet in a more stimulating atmosphere, and he retained fond memories of the way the partnership with Raymond Mays had developed at Cambridge, from the success with *Quicksilver* to the sheer creativity of the *Storm Petrel*.

It was time for Amherst to pay his old friend a visit.

Chapter 4

CORDON ROUGE AND CORDON BLEU

For long periods during the rest of the 1920s, the Mays family home at Eastgate House in Bourne, Lincolnshire, would be Amherst's base. Behind its imposing, twin-drum façade, its outbuildings not only housed the family business, but provided the workshops in which Amherst and Raymond Mays would develop a succession of notable racing cars. In due course, Bourne would also become home to two of British motor racing's most famous names, ERA and BRM.

Eastgate House, originally built in the 1790s, may have been first a family home and, second, the base to the Mays family's wool and tannery business, but its third function, as a home to numerous British motor racing endeavours, began in 1922. That year Raymond Mays had nominally been an employee of his father's company, but he had also discovered a real talent for wheeler-dealing in support of his motor racing ambitions. He had managed to part-exchange *Quicksilver* for a brand new Brescia Bugatti, and to persuade the financier involved in the deal to accept the £300 difference (over £12,000, or more than US$16,000, in today's money) in 'payments by instalments over an indefinite period, without security'.[1] He had also encouraged the agents of Englebert tyres, Lodge spark plugs and Speedwell oil to provide him with their products free of charge.

Thus armed, Mays had campaigned the Bugatti with considerable success, winning on the beaches at Porthcawl, Saltburn and Skegness, and taking FTDs or class wins at the Aston Clinton, Caerphilly, Chatcombe Park, Kop Hill, Saltersford and South Harting hill-climbs. The speed trials at Bicester, Oxford and Madresfield had also fallen to him. Indeed, it was Mays's Bugatti that Amherst had been photographed working beneath in the paddock at Madresfield.

However, Mays had endured a frustrating Shelsley Walsh, taking almost 25 seconds longer to climb the famous hill than FTD driver, Vauxhall's Matthew Park, when an insect jammed itself in the main jet of his carburettor and cut off the fuel supply.

Now he knew that if he was to achieve his ambition of breaking the record at Shelsley and fend off the increasing competition through a second season with the Bugatti, he would have to generate greater performance from it. Who better to turn to than his old friend? Amherst, in turn, needed little persuasion to apply his ingenuity and engineering skills to the Brescia, even if it meant he would be working for free. At least he would feel fulfilled.

In its original form, the Brescia had been one of the first cars to be manufactured in Ettore Bugatti's own workshop in Molsheim, less than a dozen miles (some 19km) west of Strasbourg, in north-eastern France. Bugatti had been born into a remarkable family in Milan in September 1881. Grandfather Giovanni was an architect and sculptor, and father Carlo a noted art nouveau furniture and jewellery designer, while younger brother Rembrandt would enjoy success as a sculptor of animals. Bugatti's first automotive design won an award at the Milan International Exhibition of 1901, and he spent the first decade of the new century designing cars for other companies to manufacture. A wealthy Spanish banker, Agustin de Vizcaya, owned an estate outside Molsheim and supported Ettore through the early years of developing his own firm and establishing a successful racing pedigree.

The lightweight Type 13, the basis of the Brescia, was one of the first designs to bear Bugatti's own name, and was originally powered by an eight-valve, 1.3-litre engine. Its post-war competition debut was made at Le Mans in August 1920, in the *Coupe Internationale des Voiturettes*. Now fitted with a 16-valve, 4-cylinder engine, it was driven to victory by Ernest Friderich. Thirteen months later, the Italian Grand Prix was held on a triangular circuit of almost 11 miles (18km) in length, close to the Lombardy town of Brescia. The Grand Prix itself was for 3-litre cars, but there was also a *voiturette* class for cars of not more than 1,500cc capacity. For this race, Bugatti bored out his 16-valve engine to 1,453cc, and entered four works cars. They duly romped home 1–2–3–4, and the legend of the Brescia Bugatti was born.

Given that Bugatti would go on to produce some of the most glorious automotive designs of all time, such as the Type 35 and the Royale, it seems hard to credit now how basic the Brescia seemed in appearance. A high, near-horizontal bonnet line was one of a pair of distinctive features to the front, the other being an early version of the classic horseshoe-shaped Bugatti radiator. The exposed, 11-gallon fuel tank, set across the chassis behind the pair of bucket seats, was equally recognisable to the rear. But the Brescia was sturdy, stable and reliable, the perfect foundation for Amherst to exploit.

The engine and gearbox, together with three cross-shaft members, were fitted in such a way as to stiffen the chassis frame, and this rigidity, the 610kg (12cwt) weight, 2m (6ft 7in) wheelbase and 1.15m (3ft 9 in) track all combined to make for first-class handling and road-holding – prerequisites for hill-climbing.

Basic wire wheels were fitted with 710 x 90 tyres all round. The rear brakes were initially cast-iron shoes, but later fitted with Ferodo linings, and applied by a hand-operated lever fitted to the outside of the cockpit on the right-hand-side. The foot brake operated a band brake on the transmission, and the Brescia would not be fitted with front brakes as standard until 1926. The gear lever utilised a gate shift and was also fitted to the outside of the cockpit on the right. The clutch, mated to the gearbox by a short dumb-bell shaft, would cause Amherst much angst over the following two years. It comprised six steel discs and seven thicker, cast-iron discs, and was operated by two coil springs attached to the clutch pedal lever under the floorboards.

A Brescia feature preferred by Amherst was the accessibility of the engine. By now the basic design, with a bore and stroke of 69 x 100mm giving a capacity of 1,496cc, comprised four cylinders and 16 valves, operated by a single overhead camshaft. The classic water-pump design common to many Bugattis was already present, driven from a transverse drive off the vertical shaft drive for the valve gear, while the system for lubricating the crankshaft was still more distinctive. Oil was pumped to a pressure filter and on to a gallery pipe which squirted the oil into holes drilled in the crankshaft webs, and so into the bearings. Amherst later called it 'spit-and-hope' lubrication.[2]

This was the raw material with which Amherst set to work ahead of the 1923 season. His initial search for more speed focused on increasing the Brescia's compression ratio. This measures the difference between the combined volume of the cylinder and combustion chamber when the piston is at the bottom and top of its stroke. Essentially, the higher the compression ratio, the more mechanical energy an engine can squeeze from its air-fuel mixture. Amherst went about this by fitting stronger valve springs and high-compression pistons, and by ordering the same alcohol-based fuel, RD2, which Vauxhall's famous engineer Harry Ricardo had helped to develop for its 3-litre TT cars.

On a limited budget, Mays was obliged to drive the Brescia to events rather than tow it on a trailer. Amherst therefore arranged to switch the car quickly between standard road-going and competition specifications. For example, he divided the fuel tank in two, fitting pairs of pipes and taps, so that two-thirds of the tank held ordinary fuel and the other third RD2. Similarly, to compensate for the extra crown height of the high-compression pistons, Amherst fitted a pair of packing pieces, some 8mm (0.3in) thick, beneath the base of the cylinder block, so that the normal compression ratio was restored for road use. Thus, when Mays and Amherst drove the Brescia to an event, they would travel in standard-compression mode on ordinary fuel, then, having reached the hill-climb, they would switch over to alcohol fuel, take out the packing pieces and be competition-ready in a trice.

Initial trials on the flat, straight roads around Bourne were encouraging, as Mays saw peak revs increase from 4,000 to 5,000rpm. Amherst also came up with a highly effective way of tuning the carburettors:

We used a straight length of road with a white concrete surface. Initially I would set them up for a rich mixture. Ray would then drive the car with me in the passenger seat looking backwards and watching the exhaust. Any black smoke could easily be seen over the white road, in which case I leaned the mixture until the smoke disappeared.[3]

Amherst's next idea delivered such impressive results that it was to become something of a Villiers trademark in the years ahead. As he explained to journalist Mike McCarthy in 1983:

In those days everyone thought the cam opened the valve and the spring shut it. If you think about it, the valve is stationary both when it is fully closed and when it is fully open. This means that it has to accelerate and decelerate each time it opens and closes, so the spring must hold it against the cam when it's decelerating as well. Once you've grasped that you can design the cam and spring to do their job. I also extended and rounded off the nose of the cam to give some overlap to allow the mixture a chance to get into the cylinder.[4]

He then drew the cam profiles on postcards and cut them out. In old age Amherst was interviewed for *Bugantics*, the magazine of the Bugatti Owners' Club, by a friend, Donald Parker, who learned how the job was completed:

A shaft was then turned up in case-hardening steel with the lobe sections left as discs and they were indexed to show the maximum opening position. And now you won't believe this . . . but it really is true . . . the job was completed by hand filing. 'Surely that must have been a heck of a job,' I said. He replied, 'No . . . if you use the right files and techniques . . . you see I had been trained in engineering at Oundle'.[5]

Others have queried whether Amherst may have been exaggerating at this point, but in all the interviews he gave in the last 20 years or so of his life, he consistently stuck to his story of hand filing the Brescia's new camshaft. As he told McCarthy, 'I was quite good with my hands in those days.'[6]

All this development and testing had eaten heavily into the months before the 1923 British sprint and hill-climb season got under way. The first event that Mays planned to enter, the Southsea speed trials, was now so near that Mays had to collect the completed camshaft in person and take it to Southsea on the train. In a scene that would be repeated many times over the coming years, he and Amherst worked through the night to fit it, and at 5 o'clock on the morning of the speed trials they pushed the heavily-modified Bugatti up and down the Southsea promenade until its engine finally burst into life, now delivering 6,000rpm.

This was far in excess of anything the competition had to offer, and Mays comprehensively set FTD – even though the Brescia's engine gave up two-thirds of the way down the course. Amherst's renewed partnership with Mays had won first time out, and he had delivered his friend with a 50 per cent increase in engine speed. However, he had not yet found a way of providing it in a reliable and consistent form.

Once back in Lincolnshire, testing on the Bourne Fen road and experiencing the heady speeds at 6,000rpm, they were able to replicate the problem. Fortunately, it turned out to be nothing more than fuel starvation. The standard fuel lines could not deliver sufficient fuel at the enhanced engine speeds, and by drilling larger passages in the carburettors and fitting bigger bore fuel lines, Amherst was able to provide Mays with a more consistent, longer-term, performance improvement, and acceleration all the way to 90mph (145kmh).

Mays therefore looked to April's Angel Bank hill-climb, in England's West Midlands, with growing confidence; even in a 1½-litre car he felt he could win the event outright.

Then a much more serious problem emerged: the big end bearings were showing signs of overheating and cracking. Mays, the great negotiator, swung into action, arranging with the managing director of Richards Whitemetal Factory, situated not far from Angel Bank, to fashion new bearings at no cost. The boss of Richards was persuaded of the PR benefits of advertising that only their bearings could withstand the extraordinary revs of the Bugatti. A night shift was laid on and new bearings were made, but examination of them after a brief test on a country road outside Birmingham revealed the same cracks. So two more sets of bearings with different clearances were tried, but after five days and nights with little sleep for Amherst, Mays, or the gallant staff of Richards, the problem remained.

Almost 60 years later, the nightmare still made a deep impression on Amherst, as he explained to Parker: 'Our worst failures were with the big ends . . . we tried all the variables with different types of white metal and clearances and the problem nearly defeated us.'[7] Finally, exhausted through lack of sleep, it dawned on him that the problem was not with the material of the bearings at all, but with their lubrication. Bugatti's method of squirting oil into holes drilled in the crankshaft webs and on into the bearings might work at 4,000rpm, but not at 6,000rpm.

Amherst explained: 'Studying the matter at great length it occurred to me that the jet of oil which was aimed at the slot on the crank web would, at high speed, vaporise and bounce out. What was required was some way of trapping it in.'[8]

Thus were born Amherst's 'rat traps'. On the sixth consecutive night shift, four small, triangular metal boxes were fashioned and screwed to the crankshaft webs so as to trap the oil from the jets. Mays was concerned they may fly off the moment the engine was started, but they held, the big ends were properly lubricated and he was back in business, screaming up the hill at Angel Bank in 27.8 seconds to win the event outright. The ingenuity and perseverance demonstrated by Amherst and the night shift at Richards Whitemetal Factory in the week leading up to the 1923 Angel Bank hill-climb proved critical to the subsequent success of Mays and the little Brescia, as the 'rat traps' were still doing an effective job at the end of the following year.

A week later came the hill-climb at Kop Hill, and Mays took the 1,500cc class win, though the overall FTD was set by his friend

Humphrey Cook in his 3-litre TT Vauxhall, *Rouge et Noir II*. These results were repeated at Aston Clinton the following month and at Madresfield in July. Cook's Vauxhall, sister of the car in which Matthew Park had set FTD at Shelsley the year before, would come to be of great significance to Amherst in the years ahead.

In spite of all Mays's class wins, and a second FTD at Angel Bank in July, there were many disappointments along the way, particularly in connection with the Bugatti's clutch assembly. It reached the point where, before each event, a reamer had to be passed through each bolt hole in turn, and new bolts fitted.

As the summer of 1923 wore on, so Mays's attention came to focus still more on his chief target for the year, Shelsley Walsh, scheduled for the second Saturday of September. He and Amherst recalled the lessons learned the previous summer at South Harting, and calculated the gear ratios needed to keep the Brescia near its peak 6,000rpm all the way up the hill. The new gears arrived at Eastgate House on the Thursday before the event, and the car was only completed at midnight on the Friday.

Amherst's Herculean efforts in the run-up to Angel Bank demonstrate what a grafter he was, but he was particularly glad to be so busy in the run-up to Shelsley. Back home in Speen, his father Ernest had entered the final weeks of his life and was beyond help.

On ordinary fuel and standard valve springs, Mays and Amherst gently motored the Brescia through the night in the direction of the Malvern Hills, arriving at the Abbey Hotel in Great Malvern in time for breakfast. In the hotel car park they fitted the stronger springs and switched to alcohol fuel. Then they headed over to Shelsley, 'announcing our arrival,' recorded Mays in *Split Seconds*, 'with a brief joyous burst of speed that sent the exhaust note up to a lovely scream as we entered the paddock.'[9]

The competition was fierce. In addition to season-long rival Humphrey Cook, Vauxhall's works driver Matthew Park was back with his own 3-litre TT, the car in which he had set FTD of 53.8 seconds on the hill the previous year. Malcolm Campbell was giving Shelsley a try in a 4.9-litre Indianapolis Sunbeam, while Mays's chief rival in the 1,500cc class was Archie Frazer Nash in one of his own creations.

Mays roared up the hill in 52.6 seconds and beat Frazer Nash to the 1,500cc class prize by a comfortable two seconds. His advantage over Park turned out to be much narrower – just 0.1 seconds – but when Cook spun his Vauxhall in the Esses, Mays knew he had achieved his ambition and set FTD at Shelsley.

There was more to come. At that time only a single blast up the hill was officially recorded, but Mays also participated in a team event and was thus able to apply the lessons of his official attempt in a second run. Though this second time was not officially recognised by the stewards, the spectators certainly considered his 51.9 seconds to be special, since it beat Chris Bird's official course record of 52.2 seconds.

Mays had driven the narrow course superbly, but Amherst's many enhancements to the Brescia had played their part, too. At Britain's premier hill-climb, the little car had won its class, set overall FTD and, at least as far Mays and Amherst were concerned, broken the Shelsley record. No car of such a small engine capacity had ever held it before.

A season in which much frustration and many late nights had been experienced ended in success. When Mays perused the daily and the motoring press after Shelsley, he noted 'the resultant publicity would bring in its train the financial support without which I should not have been able to continue motor racing'.[10] During the year he had also learned how to generate publicity even when he was not winning; at the Skegness speed trials back in May – another event won by Cook in the TT Vauxhall – he and Amherst had raced their little Bugatti against a De Havilland bi-plane!

Even Bugatti themselves got in on the act. When Mays and Amherst visited the Bugatti stand at October's Motor Show in London, they found a Brescia advertisement proclaiming their successes. They were also handed a letter from Le Patron himself, Ettore Bugatti. In it he congratulated them on their record with the Brescia, and the Shelsley win in particular, and invited them to come down to Molsheim with the car.

This was an immense honour, but one which, agonisingly, Mays felt unable to accept, since he was out of money and was meant to be working for his father's company. By coincidence, Humphrey Cook, never one to turn down the opportunity of some Continental touring, was wandering around Olympia that day, and on hearing of Mays's plight, agreed to drive him and Amherst to Molsheim in his 30/98 Vauxhall sports four-seater, provided the trip also took in Paris and the French Riviera.

Mays and Amherst could hardly believe their good fortune, though the journey would prove to be a less than happy one for Cook. His luggage fell off the back of the car en route, the Vauxhall was dented in Turin while serving as a grandstand for locals trying to catch a glimpse of Mussolini being granted the freedom of the city, and on one wet day a severe bump in the road led to Mays's head ripping a gaping hole in the car's canvas hood.

At Molsheim, Ettore Bugatti was disappointed that the Englishmen had not brought their heavily-modified Brescia with them, but he still proved an exceedingly generous host. On the basis they would bring the car out for him to inspect, he would arrange for Amherst to stay and oversee its rebuild in the Bugatti works, and he would provide them with a second Brescia, all at a price Mays felt he could afford. Indeed, when Thomas Mays learned of the esteem in which *Le Patron* held his son, he gave Ray paid leave and bankrolled the second trip to Alsace.

This time, the journey was made in convoy, Cook leading the way in his 30/98 Vauxhall, and Mays and Amherst following in the little Brescia. In contrast to the first trip it all seemed rather uneventful until in the Vosges Mountains, the last obstacle separating them from their overnight stay in Strasbourg, disaster threatened. The temperature dropped suddenly and the group were caught in a heavy snowstorm. Worse, Cook got himself stuck in a snowdrift and since the Bugatti had no headlights, Mays and Amherst had no option but to press on over the top and down into Strasbourg. Through the peaks the cold was so severe that the Brescia's oil pipes iced up and the lubricant seized solid. Neither Mays nor Amherst was adequately dressed for the conditions. Fortunately, salvation was at hand in the form of a local blacksmith, who lent them a blowlamp. The oil pipes were freed up, Mays and Amherst were able to resume their journey and they made Strasbourg before the last vestiges of daylight faded, Cook following on some time later.

In Strasbourg's market square the next morning, Mays and Amherst repeated the task they had performed on so many Saturday mornings, removing the cylinder packing and switching the Brescia's fuel supply over to RD2, before heading over to Bugatti's home. If *Le Patron* had any lingering doubts about what Amherst had achieved with the Brescia, they were swiftly removed as, with stopwatch in hand, he watched Mays put the car through its paces on the Molsheim–Strasbourg road. In fact, he was so impressed that he decided to test-drive the car himself on the way over to the Bugatti works, frightening Mays to such an extent that he was glad when the last drops of RD2 ran out. And so Amherst settled down to enjoy a fascinating spell as Ettore Bugatti's guest in Molsheim, while Mays returned to England to begin a new round of meetings with suppliers and sponsors, raising the funds needed to support a twin-car 1924 campaign.

Amherst was aware of the sensitivities of his host. Ettore Bugatti was 42 years old, the head of an increasingly successful and famous marque, and focused heavily on the development of his Type 35 Grand Prix car. Amherst was not yet 23 and an unknown foreigner, yet he was responsible for the quickest Bugatti sprint car yet, and here he was, explaining to *Le Patron*'s workforce how to extract more than 50 per cent more revs than standard from their 1½-litre engine.

It is clear that Amherst rated Ettore Bugatti highly. In a letter to a friend, John Millar, more than 50 years later, he expressed frustration that Bugatti historian Hugh Conway down-played the great man's knowledge of engineering. He had personally watched *Le Patron* forge the first tubular front axle for the Type 35, and told Millar he was a brilliant designer, with more engineering knowledge than many a PhD. It was only in the mid-1970s that Amherst in turn learned how impressed *Le Patron* had been with his work. Bugatti expert David Sewell unearthed a letter Ettore had written in September 1924 to one of his famous women drivers, Elizabeth Juneck, congratulating her on her first outing in the Type 35. In the letter Bugatti praised Mays's successes with the Brescia and listed the 1½-litre records he had secured at Shelsley Walsh, South Harting, Caerphilly, Aston Clinton, Spread Eagle, Kop and Angel Bank.

Bugatti was a good host to Amherst, and one day invited him to join him and his friends for an afternoon's boar hunting in the wooded hills above Molsheim. Amherst had never hunted boar before and was advised to react quickly when he got an animal in his sights. Regrettably, when he did fire, what he thought was a boar turned out to be the felt hat of one of Bugatti's friends – Amherst focused on cars rather than wildlife thereafter.

During his stay, Amherst shared a house with Meo Constantini, the Bugatti racing department manager, who was a fine driver in his own right and would go on to win the Targo Florio in 1926. On one occasion Constantini asked the young Englishman to accompany him on a test drive. First, he disconnected the front brakes, then braked hard from speed and fought to control the car as it swapped ends. Then he disconnected the rear brakes, braked again from speed, and brought the car to a halt in a straight line. Intriguingly, front brakes would not be fitted to Brescias as standard until 1926, while Amherst and Mays remained so focused on improving acceleration and top speed that they did not get around to thinking about adding front brakes until well into their season of running two cars.

Once the rebuild of the older car was completed, Amherst drove it back to Bourne, where Mays was much impressed with its new, streamlined bonnet line. As they waited impatiently for news from Molsheim about the new Brescia, they put their minds together on what to call their brace of Bugattis – 'old' and 'new' would hardly do.

In a London restaurant one night they saw a couple at a nearby table enjoying a bottle of Cordon Rouge champagne and noted its distinctive label, with gold lettering over the red sash which evoked

France's highest civilian honour, the *Légion d'honneur*. Mays had long since proved to himself the adage, 'If you don't ask, you don't get', and whisked off a letter to the famous Reims-based company, G. H. Mumm & Co, requesting permission to name the older Brescia after its champagne. Mumm not only agreed, but sent three cases of Cordon Rouge to Eastgate House. Mays was less successful with Martell, which agreed that the new car be called *Cordon Bleu* after its cognac, but stopped short of dispatching any brandy to Lincolnshire. Nevertheless, 44 years before Gold Leaf Team Lotus, non-motor trade sponsorship had arrived in British motor racing.

Still the quest for further advantage went on. Having seen the benefits of using tailored gear ratios at Shelsley Walsh, Mays gave careful consideration to each of the hill-climbs he would compete in, and ordered gears specific to each event. The dismantling and reassembly of gearboxes would become a weekly task at the peak of the forthcoming season.

When news finally reached Mays that *Cordon Bleu* was ready for collection, he and Amherst journeyed by train to Strasbourg to pick up the car. It was specially kitted out with brackets and boxes attached to the chassis frame so that they could bring back spare parts and accessories. The day after returning to Bourne, the two men drove the cars to nearby Peterborough, where specialist paint firm Brainsby's finished them in Mays's favourite blue-battleship grey, and applied the *Cordon Rouge* and *Cordon Bleu* transfers.

There was no time for Amherst to turn *Cordon Bleu* into full *Cordon Rouge* specification, so for now the younger car was fitted with lights and mudguards, so that she could compete in sports-class events, while Mays entered *Cordon Rouge* in the racing classes. Yet at one of the early meetings of the 1924 season, the Aston Clinton hill-climb in May, the writing was shown to be already on the wall for the two little cars, and a clear challenge was laid down which would influence Amherst's direction for the rest of the decade and assure his fame as an automotive engineer known the world over.

Mays and Amherst took only *Cordon Rouge* to Aston Clinton, and found that, in addition to the usual competition, they were up against American Dario Resta, driving the same type of 2-litre supercharged Sunbeam with which England's Henry Segrave had won the previous year's French Grand Prix. The magic resonance of supercharging comes through loud and clear in the pages of *Split Seconds*. Mays writes: 'Up till now my little Bugattis had proved almost unbeatable at hill-climbs – even by racing cars of any capacity. However, the Sunbeam I feared, because the word "supercharger" symbolised a sort of magical superiority in my mind.'[11]

Mays did his best, setting a new outright Aston Clinton record in *Cordon Rouge* to take the 1½-litre class win in 44.6 seconds, but Resta cut two seconds off this to set FTD, and also took the South Harting FTD two weeks later. Driving back from Clinton, Mays recalled, 'Amherst and I thought, talked and dreamed of nothing but superchargers.'[12]

Another class win in the following month's Blackpool speed trials restored the pair's confidence and they took both *Cordon Rouge* and *Cordon Bleu* to the Spread Eagle hill-climb in Hampshire with renewed optimism. Competition was again strong. In addition to his TT Vauxhall, Cook was now campaigning a new 1½-litre Aston Martin, so narrow it was nicknamed *Razor*. Also present were two men who within a couple of years would each hold the world land speed record: Welshman Parry Thomas was in his Leyland, while Malcolm Campbell, like Mays, had two entries, with a Ballot to complement the Indianapolis Sunbeam.

Mays and the two Brescias utterly dominated. *Cordon Bleu* was entered for six sports-class events and Mays won the lot. He also won all six racing-class events in *Cordon Rouge*, setting a final mark almost three seconds lower than the old course record, at 39.6 seconds. Campbell was over a second away in the Sunbeam. The Spread Eagle organisers, the Hampshire Automobile Club, even had to request Mays for some of their trophies to be returned.

Next up was the annual pilgrimage to Shelsley Walsh. The day did not begin propitiously, as *Cordon Rouge*'s transmission was playing up and required attention in the paddock. Amherst had by now wrung a consistent 6,500rpm from *Cordon Bleu* for his friend to exploit, and Mays raced up the hill to set a new course record of 50.8 seconds, more than a second inside his unofficial time of the previous year. In *Cordon Rouge*, he knew he was going faster still as he reached the Esses, only for the transmission problem to return and lose him speed as he headed up the final straight. Remarkably, his time was only one-hundredth of a second slower than the one he had set in *Cordon Rouge*, but before Mays and Amherst could celebrate an extraordinary 1–2 in the premier hill-climb event on the calendar, news came through that Cyril Paul, in a 2-litre Beardmore, had beaten both Brescia times and lowered the hill record to 50.6 seconds.

There was little time to see to *Cordon Rouge*'s gearbox and clutch maladies, as 'The Welsh Double' was scheduled for the following weekend. This was a pair of back-to-back events organised by the South Wales Automobile Club, comprising a speed-trial over a mile of Porthcawl Sands on the Saturday and, on the Sunday, the Caerphilly hill-climb, at which Mays and what was now known as *Cordon Rouge* had won the 1,500cc class for the last two years running.

FTD at Porthcawl fell, as it had on Colwyn Bay's Promenade when the speed-trial fraternity had last visited Wales, to John Joyce, works driver for AC. Joyce was hitting a rich vein of form, and in the remaining months of the 1924 season would set a further four FTDs. As Amherst mused on the lessons on supercharging doled out on hill-climbs by Dario Resta's Sunbeam, and at Brooklands by the blown Fiats, he also took due note of the AC's competitiveness.

On the following day, Mays duly completed his hat-trick of 1,500cc class wins at Caerphilly, setting a time of 63.2 seconds in *Cordon Bleu*. This was not enough to prevent his former supplier of carburettors for *Quicksilver*, Bertie Kensington-Moir, taking FTD in a Bentley, and does not begin to describe the tribulations Mays faced that day. *Cordon Rouge* continued to misbehave, stripping a gear on the start line, and worse was to come on his second run in *Cordon Bleu*. As he lined up for an open left-hander on the loose-shale road surface he felt a sudden lurch and saw out of the corner of his eye his left-hand rear wheel bounding along beside him. The moment was caught on camera and has become one of the most popular images in the National Motor Museum's picture library at Beaulieu. In a cloud of loose stones and dust, Mays managed to wrestle his three-wheeler to a halt, but the Brescia's rear axle-shaft had finally given up the unequal struggle of trying to cope with all that extra power Amherst had generated. More time and money had to be expended, designing, ordering and fitting revised axles to both cars.

By this time, nearing the end of his second season of working on the little Bugattis, even Amherst was beginning to run out of ideas on how to make them go faster and finally turned his attention to improving their braking. Mays sent *Cordon Bleu* over to a firm called British Wire Products to be fitted with its Whitehead front brakes. He persuaded the managing director to fit them for free *and* give him cash into the bargain, but either he was on particularly silver-tongued form that day, or he was exaggerating in *Split Seconds* when claiming Mr Whitehead agreed to give him £500, as this is almost £22,000, or over US$29,000 in modern-day terms.

Nevertheless, *Cordon Bleu* was in the ultimate Villiers specification when she was driven up to the start line for the Holme Moss hill-climb in Yorkshire on 27 September 1924. Not only was she proudly displaying brake drums on all four corners, but Amherst had made modifications to both her pistons and valves, so that she now revved to an extraordinary 6,900rpm. Indeed, so fast was the Brescia that day that Mays lowered the Holme Moss course record by nearly 4 seconds.

However, as Mays completed his last major competitive outing in *Cordon Bleu*, he found that its throttle had stuck open and that he needed to climb still more of Holme Moss if he were to avoid the spectators blocking the road ahead. He careered up a bank to his right and eventually wrestled the car to a halt, switching the fuel supply off as he leapt from the cockpit, but the engine still screamed away until the carburettors finally emptied. When he and Amherst got the car back to Bourne, they found the crankshaft, valves and pistons all severely damaged.

As a footnote to that eventful Holme Moss hill-climb, it should also be recorded that Mays's new course record in the Brescia did not survive the afternoon, and that it was he who beat it, driving a borrowed TT Vauxhall. Its sister car, Cook's *Rouge et Noir II*, would re-enter the lives of Mays and Amherst frequently in the years ahead.

The damage done by *Cordon Bleu*'s sticking throttle was a sad end to a glorious campaign, but the car was to play its part in a more unfortunate episode yet. At the season's end Mays sold *Cordon Rouge* to an accomplished driver and Bugatti agent named F. B. Taylor, but, once repaired, *Cordon Bleu* went to a far less experienced man, a Cambridge undergraduate friend of Mays named Francis Giveen.

Over the winter Mays gave the young man some coaching in performance driving on Toft Hill, near the Bourne–Stamford road, but on one occasion Giveen exited a bend too fast, rolled the Bugatti and lay trapped under it. Remarkably the Brescia's little windscreen bore the weight of the car and Giveen emerged unscathed, pronouncing himself ready for the forthcoming hill-climb season.

He was anything but. On 28 March 1925, at the Essex Motor Club's event at Kop Hill, near Princes Risborough in Buckinghamshire, Giveen ran wide and mounted a spectator bank, breaking the leg of a visiting Vauxhall worker. Had a cold wind not already encouraged the bulk of a huge crowd to make their way home before Giveen's run, the consequences, in terms of loss of life and injury, could have been catastrophic.

As it was, the authorities felt obliged to intervene. Hill-climbs and sprint-events on the public highway had never been legal, but now the RAC announced that, 'for the present' they would no longer issue permits for such events. In fact, the ban was never lifted and a way of life for the British motor racing enthusiast had come to an end. At a stroke the private course at Shelsley Walsh became host to Britain's only hill-climb of any consequence, while Brooklands would remain the only circuit in the country until Donington Park opened in 1933. Even beach racing came under threat. As Mays recorded in *Split Seconds*, 'From every point of view this was a sad day for me.'[13]

Yet, over 25 years after he parted with *Cordon Rouge* and *Cordon Bleu*, Mays knew how important they had been to his career: 'Amherst and I had acquired a wealth of information about the racing game, and still more about the high revving, high compression type of engine and all that goes with it . . . much useful data can now be traced to the experimental work in these two Bugattis'.[14]

Of course, the Brescia provided Mays and Amherst with a wonderful basis for those experiments – light, sturdy, and with inherently sound road-holding capabilities – and it was extraordinarily generous of Ettore Bugatti to support the two men as he did. Equally, *Le Patron* recognised talent when he saw it, and the great success of *Cordon Rouge* and *Cordon Bleu* brought his marque to the attention of a much wider British audience.

Overall, Mays set 14 major hill-climb FTDs and took more than 100 class wins in his time with the Brescias. He was a fine hill-climb and sprint driver, but he could never have achieved anything like this without his great friend's ingenuity, development work and perseverance. Over the course of Amherst's two years working on the cars, he raised their engine speed from a little over 4,000rpm to 6,900 and their power from around 45bhp to almost 80. Most remarkably of all, given that the Brescia in standard form was hardly a heavyweight to begin with at some 610kg (12cwt), Mays claimed *Cordon Rouge* weighed only 442kg (8.7cwt) when he set the last of those class wins at Holme Moss.

This is an extraordinarily impressive record, a point not lost on Mays. In an article for *The Light Car and Cyclecar* the following year entitled 'Lowering hill-climb records', he wrote: 'For this extraordinary increase in rpm I was very much indebted to my friend Amherst Villiers, whose help in designing special camshafts, working out compression ratios and so forth was absolutely invaluable.'[15]

Indeed, in later life Amherst viewed his work on the Brescias as the most pleasing of all his motor racing projects, telling journalist Brian Palmer: 'I think the little Bugatti was the most rewarding because we got those high revs and we were so far ahead of everybody else, though I confess we had difficulty in holding it together until the end.'[16]

Chapter 5

First Forays into Supercharging

The 'magical superiority'[1] which Raymond Mays recalled about Dario Resta's Sunbeam at the 1924 Aston hill-climb had less to do with sorcery and more to do with forced induction.

Essentially, with a normally aspirated engine, when the piston moves down, a vacuum is created and air is sucked into the combustion chamber at atmospheric pressure. Here it is mixed with fuel and ignited by the spark plug. More power can be delivered by a bigger bang, but this requires not only more fuel but also more air for it to burn. Hence the supercharger, which drives compressed air into the combustion chamber at above atmospheric pressure. No vacuum is needed, so the piston and therefore the engine do not need to be bigger; a larger explosion delivers more power from the same-sized engine.

Supercharging became an early feature of aero engines, since it overcame the performance degradation caused by the lower air pressure and density at altitude. The motor sport world was swift to see its advantages, too. As early as 1908 Lee Chadwick designed a supercharged car and entered it in the inaugural American Grand Prize in Savannah, Georgia. In Europe, Fiat used a Wittig supercharger on its Grand Prix cars in 1922, but switched to a Roots-type blower the following year, scoring a 1–2 at Monza to record the first win in a major race by a supercharged car.

Indeed, Amherst consistently recounted across three interviews during the 1970s and 1980s that it was the Fiats' performance in the 1923 JCC 200-mile race at Brooklands, a year before Resta won at Aston, which first alerted him to the merits of supercharging. Neither car, driven by

Malcolm Campbell and Charles Salamano, finished the race, but they dominated its opening laps and Amherst was most impressed.

One way or another, he and Mays jointly concluded that, after two years of great success with *Cordon Rouge* and *Cordon Bleu*, 1925 should be the year of the blower. They could have chosen to supercharge the little Bugattis, but these were surely at the limit of their development potential. Besides, selling them and receiving works backing from another car manufacturer would generate much-needed funds for the forthcoming year. After two seasons with French Bugatti – three if Mays's initial 1922 campaign is included – the two men agreed that if the manufacturer could be British, then so much the better.

Their reasoning took them to Thames Ditton in Surrey, home of AC. The original Autocarriers Limited, manufacturers of three-wheel vehicles, had moved there in 1911 and, under the management of S. F. Edge, become increasingly successful at motor sport. Selwyn Edge was arguably Britain's first motor racing hero, and a superb self-publicist. Born in 1868, he enjoyed success as a cyclist and became an early advocate of the motor car. Unhappy with the effects on his hand and arm of using a tiller to steer his Panhard-Levassor, he commissioned a manufacturer of coin-weighing machines, Montague Napier, to make him a steering wheel. Soon, Napier was making cars for Edge to sell and race. In 1902, Edge drove a Napier to victory in the Gordon Bennett race, run from Paris to Innsbruck, and he was one of the racers whom Hugh Locke King and Henry Holden turned to when developing their plans for Brooklands. Edge in turn exploited the circuit as soon as it was open, generating enormous publicity for Napier by attempting to lead three cars to run for 24 hours at an average of over 60mph (97kmh). All three cars beat the target, that of Edge's exceeding 65mph (unlike the other two, he drove single-handed the whole way), thereby comfortably breaking the 100kmh mark, too.

After parting company with Napier, Edge was obliged to spend some years away from the motor industry, but upon his return in 1921 he acquired a controlling interest in AC and set about building its reputation at Brooklands and on the many hill-climbs and sprint-events around the country. With works driver John Joyce behind the wheel, AC began to enjoy success with a number of 1½-litre, overhead-camshaft, single-seater designs. Of particular importance to Edge was the one-hour speed record for 1,500cc cars. In November 1922 Joyce became the first to put the record beyond the 100mph barrier, and regularly improved upon it, taking it to 104.19mph (167.67kmh) two years later.

By this time, Joyce and the AC were among Mays's most respected sprint rivals. As early as March 1924 they had recorded a 1,500cc class win at Kop Hill, and through the late summer and autumn Joyce had come more and more to the fore, with outright FTDs at Colwyn Bay, Porthcawl, Ringinglowe Road and Brighton.

To Amherst and Mays, AC ticked all the boxes. It was British, it was successful and, in Selwyn Edge, it was managed by a man with a sense of the value of publicity every bit as acute as that possessed by Mays himself. Indeed, it may be assumed that the meeting between the two men at which it was agreed that Mays would campaign an AC in 1925 was some encounter.

The outcome of that meeting was that Edge would provide Mays not only with a 1,500cc AC racing car for Amherst to supercharge, together with spare parts and some financial support, but also a 2-litre sports car for daily use. The deal was sealed by Edge offering Mays an existing works car with which to participate in the Saltersford hill-climb, some two weeks after the throttle-sticking excitement at Holme Moss. Mays duly trounced the opposition, breaking the hill record by nine seconds. Since Joyce was winning the Bexhill speed-trial the same day, and would also win the following weekend's hill-climb at Kop, it seemed that Mays and Amherst's choice of AC for 1925 had been a wise one.

In retrospect, the question must be asked as to how much due diligence went into establishing whether the AC's engine could withstand the additional pressures of supercharging? It seems that in the spirit of mutual goodwill established between Amherst and Mays on the one hand, and Edge and his chief engineer Sidney Smith on the other, this vital issue was overlooked.

There is no question that Amherst undertook what research he could. He visited Frenchman Auguste Rateau, who was well-known for his aero engine supercharging work a decade earlier. Perhaps influenced by the success he had seen Fiat enjoy with the switch to Roots-type superchargers, Amherst searched for such a blower, acquired one from an Oxfordshire farm, and began experimenting.

The origin of the Roots supercharger lay in an 1854 attempt by Francis and Philander Roots, two brothers from Connersville, Indiana, to create a more efficient water wheel for their woollen mill. While rotating a shaft to turn the pair of impellers, one of the men found he could generate sufficient wind power to blow his brother's hat off, and the first commercial applications of their invention were not as a water wheel, but in blowing air into furnaces and mine shafts – quite literally, a blower. A century and a half later there is still a Roots factory in Connersville today.

Variations on the theme developed, with two- and three-rotor options, but Amherst decided upon the simpler twin-lobe form for his first superchargers, drawing the mixture from a carburettor round the inside of the rotor casing and discharging it under pressure to the induction pipe. The three-rotor option deals more effectively with the 'pulsing' effect of twin rotors, but Amherst's approach had less revolving weight and, quite simply, had less that could go wrong.

He had two opportunities to see the results of his findings. Humphrey Cook watched his friend Raymond Mays set about gaining an advantage for 1925 through Amherst's supercharging work, and decided to follow suit. His TT Vauxhall, *Rouge et Noir II*, was now three years old, and he had not enjoyed anything like as successful a hill-climb and sprint season in 1924 as he had the previous year. He arranged for Amherst to design a supercharger and installation for his car, too, though in this case Vauxhall would carry out the work, using Amherst's drawings.

Given that AC's base at Thames Ditton, south-west of London, lay more than 100 miles from Bourne, Mays conceded that the conversion work on the AC could not be carried out at Eastgate House. Amherst had decided to use a Memini carburettor, as fitted to the supercharged Fiats, and so Mays made an arrangement with its London operation that the work would be carried out there. Similarly, he contacted the manager of the Grosvenor Hotel, where he had stayed during his early days in the Grenadier Guards rather than at their Chelsea barracks, and negotiated a special rate on a room for him and Amherst, who was often to be found late at night, lying on the floor of the hotel lounge, surrounded by engineering drawings.

Back at Memini's, work commenced on both the engine and the latest AC chassis, which had already been developed further from the car which had won back the one-hour record for 1½-litre models the previous November. Much work had gone into improving its weight distribution and road holding. The chassis frame had been lowered and lightened, the seats pushed back over the rear axle, and revised shock absorbers fitted. *The Light Car and Cyclecar* also referred to improvements to the engine, calling it 'one of the most powerful engines of its capacity which employs atmospheric induction'.[2]

Interest in Amherst's developments mounted. The lack of sprint and hill-climb meetings since Giveen's antics in March only heightened the anticipation; if great things were expected of AC's normally aspirated car, what would his supercharged version be capable of?

The first clues came in a gushing article in *The Light Car and Cyclecar* in mid-May, two weeks before Shelsley Walsh:

One of the prettiest and most promising little racing cars that has ever been built is now nearing completion . . . Whilst differing externally in a considerable number of respects from the standard type of A.C., the car, which is now almost ready, and all the modifications to which have been made under the direction of Mr. C. Amherst-Villiers [sic] and Mays himself, still bears a pronounced resemblance to previous and existing A.C. racers, although, from its radiator to its beautifully streamlined tail, it is entirely individual.[3]

The car had, indeed, a very neat and purposeful design, perhaps the best looking of all Amherst's cars in this initial guise. The narrow body was built, as usual, by Mays's friends at Brainsby's in Peterborough. The most notable feature was, of course, the supercharger. Fitted with high-tensile, steel-forged rotors, it was mounted horizontally and projected beyond the modified radiator, driven directly from the camshaft at engine speed. Sitting beneath the blower was a pair of oil pumps, one sucking oil from a tank in the tail of the car and delivering it to the engine, the other returning it from the sump to the tank.

Naturally, Amherst had provided one of his special camshafts, chain-driven off the rear of the crankshaft, and designed revised pistons made of a heat-treated alloy. The dash-mounted magnetos, each supplying its own set of four spark plugs, were another of his modifications. With two plugs per cylinder and the relatively low speed of the magnetos he hoped to improve reliability. However, the bronze cylinder head and aluminium cylinder block casting were of standard AC specification, and this would prove to be the car's Achilles heel.

The Light Car was most struck with Amherst's rear suspension, claiming that the broadly-splayed springs 'should ensure complete immunity from rolling', and also noted a revised front axle and pedal-operated brakes on all four wheels.[4] In truth, Amherst and Mays were less confident about the coming season than their friends in the press. Bench-testing the engine demonstrated that the detachable cylinder head seemed incapable of withstanding the pressures inflicted on it by the supercharger. Scraping the cylinder head and fitting new ring joints allowed the engine to run at full power – about 5,500rpm at 10lb boost pressure – for longer, but water still found its way into each cylinder bore.

A new cylinder head was considered out of the question. Mays's budget did not allow for it, and to miss Shelsley Walsh was unthinkable. Instead Amherst came up with a less expensive alternative. He hoped that by using revised copper rings, and scoring a groove around the cylinder head bores for the rings to squeeze into under pressure, a tighter seal would be created.

Minimal testing back at Bourne proved inconclusive, and even the usual last-minute drive through the night towards Malvern created fresh concerns in the minds of Amherst and Mays, as a strange knocking sound, emanating either from the AC or the lorry carrying it, accompanied them on their journey.

Even the warm-up in the paddock brought fresh dramas. They found that the magneto advance-retard control had fouled against the bonnet. Repairs of a sort were conducted, but in the time available the bonnet was not refitted. Initially all seemed well. Mays later recorded: 'She ran fast and well on the lower slopes. Reaching the famous "S" bend safely, I changed gear and gave full throttle between the "esses".'[5] A photograph catches the moment, Mays applying a touch of opposite lock as he exits the Lower Ess.

A split-second later, his run was effectively over. When he went to dab the throttle on his approach to the Upper Ess, there was no response, and he found himself trundling up the finishing straight with sufficient time to identify individual faces in the crowd. When he returned the car to the paddock, Amherst found the advance-retard switch disconnected and the ignition fully retarded.

Mays's spirited drive on the lower sections of the course ensured his time was not a total disgrace – he managed 57 seconds dead – and if the car had simply held together round the Upper Ess and on to the finish line, the 1925 campaign of Amherst and Mays with the AC might be recalled more fondly. The winner was future land speed record hero Henry Segrave, wearing lounge suit, tie and – most unusually for the time – helmet, and his FTD was only 53.8 seconds, while Joyce, in the works AC, was a mere two seconds quicker than Mays.

Thus consoled, the two friends took their AC to Brooklands. Their reputation from the *Cordon Rouge* and *Cordon Bleu* days, and the due respect paid to Amherst's supercharger, meant that Mays found himself bottom of the handicap and leaving the Railway Straight start line last of all. On the first lap he overtook several cars and maintained

4,900rpm (about 107mph/172kmh) on the Byfleet Banking. But on his second lap Mays felt the revs drop away and he coasted up the finishing straight and into the paddock to retire. There, Amherst removed the plugs and saw the telltale signs of water in the cylinders. Again, the cylinder head had failed to cope with the rigours of supercharging.

Clearly the season was not delivering the anticipated results and it was time for a frank meeting with Edge and Smith. They concluded that a combination of bigger retaining bolts and less boost would provide greater reliability. After due consideration, Amherst and Mays felt this was a retrograde step. Why go to all the trouble of designing and fitting a supercharger, and then run it on such low boost that any competitive advantage was surrendered? The only alternative was for Amherst to design a more durable cylinder head, and for Mays to find a way of funding it.

Since this would require the car to go back into the workshop, a curtailed racing programme was agreed for the balance of the season. Reasoning that the AC in its current specification could participate safely in short-distance speed trials, Mays would compete at Skegness and Pendine. Then, with Amherst's new cylinder head fitted, they would race in September's Junior Car Club 200-mile race at Brooklands.

One of the regulations for the JCC 200 throws up a most unfortunate feature of the two men's season: each driver had to be accompanied by a riding mechanic. For this one race Mays's AC would need a two-seater body. When the works AC was previewed in *The Light Car and Cyclecar* in March of that year it was noted that 'a two-seater body is fitted at the present time, but it is possible that a single-seater may be built later in the year'.[6] Amherst's revisions had included the fitting of a single-seater body, yet when preparations began for the JCC 200, he found that the twin-seater body and larger fuel tank required would necessitate an extension to the chassis frame, requiring more time, more cost and, crucially, more weight.

In fairness, when Amherst and Mays first sat down to consider their 1925 campaign, Brooklands may not have been on their minds.

Only when hill-climbs and sprints on public roads were banned in the wake of Giveen's accident at Kop Hill did their plans have to change, and by then, presumably, Amherst's short-chassis, single-seater design was already set.

To make matters worse, the plan to take in a couple of sprint events ended in failure. Even the half-mile course at Skegness proved too much for the little AC. This time the cylinder head coped, but clutch slip meant Mays was pipped to the line in his heat by Maurice Harvey's Alvis. An early issue of *The Brooklands Gazette*, the forerunner of *Motor Sport*, recorded that 'in the finals neither of these cars behaved quite well'.[7] Two of the AC's gearbox selectors became bent and again Mays was unplaced.

He and Amherst wondered whether they should even bother with the 600-mile round-trip to South Wales for the Pendine speed trial, and events proved they should not have. Mays led away in his heat, but as he changed into third 'suddenly came the same awful "rough" feeling and loss of power. Water! Once more off with the ignition switch and a glide to the finish – last again!'[8]

Short of money, and denied the publicity of success that would have enabled him to generate some, Mays decided to take the S. F. Edge route and go record-breaking. Englishman Ernest Eldridge was not only the current holder of the world land speed record, but he had also taken a car of his own design, fitted with a 1,500cc Anzani engine, to the new track at Montlhéry near Paris and beaten Joyce's one-hour record in the AC, raising it to 107.62mph (173.19kmh). Mays and Amherst reasoned that while they were waiting for Brainsby's to produce the chassis subframe and two-seater body for September's JCC 200, they could be winning the one-hour record back for AC.

At a distance of more than 80 years, and sitting behind a laptop rather than the wheel of a potent racing car, it is easy to question their judgement. Why not focus exclusively on Amherst's new cylinder head and the one-hour record, and forget about the expense, risk and weight of a chassis extension and new body? And why, when the car had not yet managed 10 miles in an event without giving trouble, did they think it was going to be capable of racing Europe's finest over 20 times the distance? It appears that, weighed down by the AC's numerous problems, their objectivity was suffering.

At least Amherst had the consolation of knowing his supercharger design for Humphrey Cook was taking shape at Vauxhall's racing department. Work was also progressing well with his new cylinder head. Fashioned in bronze, it had two inlet valves and one exhaust valve per cylinder. Revisions had also been made to the aluminium block. This time, surely, the car would deliver on the potential of its supercharger.

Tests on the roads around Bourne boded well, Mays recalling that 'the engine felt entirely different, smoother and much more powerful'.[9] The next step involved several hours' gentle running on the bumps of Brooklands, and this proceeded so satisfactorily that Amherst advised Mays to drive a series of laps on full throttle.

Amherst stationed himself with stopwatch and notebook to record lap times, while friends took up position on the Railway Straight to record the car's speed over the half-mile.

After a few laps averaging 90mph (145kmh), Mays opened the AC up and went progressively faster as he tried different lines on the banked bends. Several of his laps were clocked at over Eldridge's record, and his top speed down the Railway Straight was recorded at 116mph (187kmh) – and this in the first real trial of any meaning, without making any adjustments to the car.

The test was brought to an abrupt end when the steering column bracket snapped, and Mays had a nasty moment bringing the car back under control, one hand on the wheel and the other holding the column in place. Nevertheless, when Amherst left for London to instruct Memini's on making a stronger steering column bracket, he and Mays were in better spirits than for many months. His new cylinder head had done its job, and they were back in business. It was only after he left that Mays spotted some moisture on the outside of the aluminium engine block – it had developed a crack.

What impact this would have had on the one-hour record attempt will never be known, as Brainsby's chose this moment to call Mays and tell him that unless the car was brought back to Lincolnshire immediately, they would not be able to fit the chassis subframe, larger fuel tank and twin-seater body in time for the JCC 200. Again, rather than cut his losses and focus solely on the one-hour record, Mays headed for Bourne with the car, there to be met by Amherst.

The car was sent over to nearby Peterborough for Brainsby's to have its chassis extension and new bodywork fitted, while Amherst stayed at Eastgate House to examine the engine. His prognosis was positive. The new head and his other revisions had withstood the Brooklands tests, and the crack could be fixed by two small aluminium plates, one inside the block and one outside it, smeared with white lead and held in place with four bolts. Their last shot at glory, the JCC 200, was still feasible.

Preparations for the race were underway elsewhere, too. Hot favourites were the Darracqs of Henry Segrave, Giulio Masetti and Caberto Conelli. Humphrey Cook would not be driving the TT Vauxhall supercharged by Amherst; he would instead be at the wheel of a new Aston Martin.

Brooklands itself was going through a unique makeover. Back in 1906, when Hugh Locke King had consulted with Britain's early racing drivers about how his circuit should look, it was Selwyn Edge who, imagining ten cars abreast, had recommended a width of 100ft (30m). But even Brooklands' famous handicapper, A.V. Ebblewhite, had never managed to contrive such close racing. Now, the Junior Car Club had devised an interesting way of exploiting the circuit's great width. As drivers raced off the Byfleet Banking, they were not to take the slight right-hand kink at the Fork and stay on the Outer Circuit. They were to race up the finishing straight, staying to the left-hand side of a series of flags, and sweep round a 180-degree right-hand hairpin marked by a barrel, then race back down to the Fork and take that as a left-hand hairpin, to rejoin the Outer Circuit. This detour would be a severe test of brakes and transmission, and would add about 600yd (550m) to the lap. The 1925 JCC 200 would therefore be 65 laps long rather than the usual 73.

As the day of the race drew near, the AC's patched-up engine and twin-seater body were reunited, and Amherst and Mays commenced testing on the roads around Peterborough. A profound sense of dismay came over them. The car was simply not as responsive as before. There could only be one reason for this – the weight of the chassis extension and two-seater body. A line from *Split Seconds* seems extraordinary, but it does sum up how distracted Amherst and Mays had become by all their troubles with the car. Mays writes: 'In our struggles over the last few months we had somewhat overlooked this very important consideration of weight.'[10]

A visit to a weighbridge confirmed their worst fears. The revised car weighed in at 21cwt (1,067kg), some 7cwt (356kg) more than in single-seater trim. The changes required to make the car eligible for the JCC 200 race had put 50 per cent on its weight, and this was before the larger fuel tank was filled and Amherst climbed aboard. Mays knew now that there was no realistic chance of defeating the Darracqs, but he still hoped to complete the race and put the AC back into single-seater trim for an attempt at the 1,500cc one-hour record before Brooklands closed for its usual winter repairs.

Practice for the JCC 200 started at Brooklands with no sight of Amherst, Mays or the AC. Many drivers were complaining about the rough state of the finishing straight, and *The Light Car and Cyclecar* reported that Humphrey Cook's Aston Martin 'had suffered severely in this respect during the first few days of practising, his front wheels bouncing several inches off the track and giving the impression that the car must be very difficult to hold when the brakes are in action'.[11]

The same magazine published pen portraits of each of the competitors, and noted that 'Raymond Mays will go down in history as one of the men who managed to extract more power from a 1,500cc Bugatti than anyone else. The other man was Amherst Villiers.'[12]

These men of history eventually reached Brooklands in time for the final practice session, the day before the race. The AC had lost its sleek appearance of earlier in the year. It *looked* 50 per cent heavier. Worse was to come when they finally got out on the track; the car was overheating severely. Amherst concluded that the car's weight, and the heavy acceleration exiting the two hairpins, required greater water capacity than the car possessed, and dashed off to have a second radiator made. He arrived back at the circuit in the early hours of the morning and he and Mays worked through the night to fit the new radiator to operate in series with the existing one. In the time available, aesthetics were no longer a consideration; the sides and top of the original oval radiator could be seen behind the new one, which did at least sport the distinctive AC logo. A second water tank was added too, fitted in the space between the fuel tank and rear suspension, and hooked up to the pair of radiators by two large hoses.

The newly named *Motor Sport* was unimpressed.

> *In contrast to the peaceful demeanour of the Darracqs, Raymond Mays' A.C. was being coaxed into some semblance of good temper, like a petulant child. Additional feeding arrangements in the shape of an auxiliary radiator and yards of rubber hose stretching from front to rear of the car gave it the appearance of an experimental effort. This, combined with the frantic antics of the mechanics, accounted for Mays'* [sic] *long odds with the 'bookies'. He was quoted at 'twenties'.*[13]

It took until 10 o'clock on race morning to ensure the two radiators were working, and to fit the auxiliary water tank into a space between the fuel tank and rear suspension. An animated crowd witnessed the fitting of the hoses. Mays recalled, 'We just had time to warm up the engine, fit the racing plugs, have a brandy and ginger ale and go straight to the start line.'[14]

Thus fortified, the first lap went well for him and his riding mechanic Amherst, both of whom were wearing the same type of peaked helmet Segrave had sported at Shelsley Walsh. They lay fifth as they crossed the finish line, and two significant threats were already out. One of the favourites, Caberto Conelli in the Darracq, had broken his rear axle at the start, and Humphrey Cook demonstrated he was still uncomfortable with that first hairpin, suddenly slewing right under braking, sliding through the flags dividing the two flows of traffic, and ending up overturned against the railings on the far side. It took six marshals to lift the car from Cook, who emerged bruised and shaken, and his mechanic, who required several days' hospital treatment.

Little did Amherst know it, but his first forays into supercharging were ending almost simultaneously. Cook was so upset by his Brooklands accident that, for a time at least, he quit racing, and, without reference to Amherst, sold his Vauxhall to Jack Barclay. Barclay chose to remove the supercharger and race the car at Brooklands in original TT specification. Amherst was far from impressed.

Worse, as early as lap two, he was learning that the massive amount of work expended on the AC would be in vain, Mays visiting the pits to change the plugs. He and Amherst did not race much further before the temperature needle shot off the dial. They returned to the pits, removed the radiator cap, and found no water. A photograph published in *The Light Car and Cyclecar* captures the scene an instant later. The bonnet is off the car, and the two men, still wearing their helmets, are kneeling each side of the engine, checking the hose connections and looking for leaks, apparently oblivious to the pool of water around them. Then they found the gaping hole in the auxiliary water tank, punctured on the rough Brooklands road surface by a shock absorber arm.

'We were beaten,' wrote Mays in *Split Seconds*, 'and to describe our feelings after months of almost superhuman efforts is impossible. Utterly dejected and with nothing to fight for, our exhaustion became very apparent.'[15]

Worse was to come. When the two men returned to Eastgate House and examined the effects of the water leak on the engine, they saw that part of Amherst's new cylinder head had melted. Out of money, there was no way of repairing the engine and converting the AC back into single-seater trim for an attempt on the one-hour record before winter repairs began at Brooklands. The game was up. Dejectedly, the two men returned the AC and the 2-litre road car to S. F. Edge. Britain's first-ever motor sport hero knew something about the highs and lows of the racing game, and had some prescient words for them: 'I am sorry. You two have tried hard and I don't think your efforts will prove in vain.'[16]

Remarkably, Amherst had still not had his fill of the AC. He bought it from Edge and turned it into a single-seater for Tim Birkin, the Villiers-Birkin Special. Again, success eluded the car, but Amherst's first supercharged engine finally found its true home when it was fitted in a speedboat of Birkin's. The irony was not lost on Mays; as a racing car engine, water had proved its downfall, yet when it sat in the stuff, it was highly effective.

Mays had bigger problems to worry about. Invoices were pouring into Eastgate House for all the development work on the AC, and he had no choice but to forget about a 1926 motor racing campaign, and buckle down instead as an employee in his father's company, raising the money to clear his debts. It meant that he and Amherst would have to go their separate ways. 'It was,' he wrote, 'a severance I felt deeply.'[17]

Amherst made his way back to London to ponder the lessons learned from his challenging year. Certainly, he knew now that when he next turned to supercharging he would have to devote at least as much effort to the engine itself as to the blower and its installation. Perhaps he realised, too, that last-minute solutions and all-night sessions in garages, which had worked far more often than not on the Brescia Bugattis and would again in the future, were not a cast-iron guarantee of success. There are clear signs that when he next supercharged a racing car for Raymond Mays, he knew that an optimal power-to-weight ratio was more important to success than outright power.

At least the year ended on a high. On 16 December, at St Margaret's, Westminster, Amherst gave away his elder sister, Barbara, in marriage to Brigadier General Sir Hill Child. Amherst's uncle, Viscount

Wimborne, made Wimborne House available for the reception, and a wonderful time was had by all. And though Amherst had failed to help his great friend Raymond Mays deprive Ernest Eldridge of the one-hour record for 1,500cc cars, he had teamed up with a rather famous individual in an attempt to snatch Eldridge's outright world land speed record.

Chapter 6

BLUEBIRD

Away from purpose-built circuits such as Brooklands and Montlhéry, and the hill-climbs, sprints and beach races, the other main form of competitive motor sport at this time concerned the setting of speed records, and the chief focus here lay on the records for the mile and the kilometre. One man came to enjoy particular prominence across the entire motor sport spectrum in the inter-war period, yet is forever associated with the world land and water speed records, and Amherst was influential in his early successes on land. His name was Malcolm Campbell.

Born in 1885 and educated, like Amherst's father Ernest, at Uppingham School in the East Midlands county of Rutland, Campbell spent his school days doing whatever he had been told not to, and reading the adventure yarns of Rider Haggard, most notably *King Solomon's Mines*. 'The story fired my imagination to an extraordinary degree,' he wrote later. 'It was this particular book which left me with a real longing for adventure.'[1]

Such a young man would never find it easy to settle down, but after character-building spells in Germany and France, he gave insurance a try and became a highly adept Lloyd's broker, with a penchant for developing creative types of business. The income from his libel insurance policy for newspaper editors made him prosperous, and Campbell first sought to slake his thirst for adventure by building his own plane. He soon learned he was rather better at motor racing.

In 1911 he bought the Darracq that the then current land speed record holder, Victor Hémery, had driven to victory two years earlier in the

Vanderbilt Cup. The night before Campbell first raced it at Brooklands, he mused on what to name his new mount. A play about fairies by the Belgian writer Maurice Maeterlinck, originally named *L'Oiseau Bleu*, was enjoying great success in the West End. Campbell liked the name, thought it might bring him luck, and named the Darracq *Blue Bird I*. Thus was born one of the most evocative names in the history of British automotive and nautical endeavour, and by the end of the 1911 Brooklands Easter Meeting, Campbell had won two races. By the end of the year, Maeterlink had won the Nobel Prize for Literature.

In an echo of how Amherst would spend the early years of the Second World War as an ATA pilot, Campbell served with the Royal Flying Corps during the Great War, ferrying new aircraft out to St Omer and, at considerable personal risk, returning in planes 'Unfit for Further Flying Service'. He won the first post-war British motor race when Brooklands reopened for business in April 1920, and was in the crowd there in May 1922 when 'Cupid' Hornstead's world land speed record of 124.10mph (199.72kmh), set just four days before the assassination of the Archduke Ferdinand in June 1914, finally fell. The man behind the wheel was Kenelm Lee Guinness, a member of the famous brewing family, and equally successful as a racing driver and businessman. Products from his company, KLG Spark Plugs, were fitted to most British performance cars and military aircraft of the time, and he amassed a fortune when he sold the company to a forerunner of today's Smiths Group plc, spending some of it on a steam yacht, the *Ocean Rover*. The vessel became Guinness's favoured mode of transport when he took his motor racing team to circuits near the Atlantic or Mediterranean coasts of Europe.

Guinness's record-breaking car was a Sunbeam, designed by the company's chief engineer, Breton-born Louis Coatalen. It was a single-seater, fitted with a narrow radiator cowling, and powered by a shaft-driven, 350hp V12 engine, based on Sunbeam's 'Manitou' aero engine of the First World War. In truth, Brooklands was already an inappropriate venue for a record attempt in such a vehicle. The *Association Internationale des Automobiles Clubs Reconnus* (AIACR), the forerunner of today's Fédération Internationale de l'Automobile, required the record to be based on the average time set over two runs of the measured distance, made in opposite directions, and there were concerns about whether Brooklands's Railway Straight was long enough, since driving 'the wrong way' up it meant easing off for the steep Home Banking before the completion of the mile. Guinness did indeed set a new record speed of 133.75mph (215.25kmh), but it was the last time the record would be broken on a closed circuit.

Two years later, on a narrow, tree-lined stretch of road in the town of Arpajon, near Paris, Englishman Ernest Eldridge used a vast Fiat fitted with a 21-litre aero engine to beat Guinness's time and set a new record of 146.01mph (234.98kmh), and this was the last time the record would be broken on a public road.

A significant point had been reached in the quest for speed. Over the course of Amherst's life, the world land speed record had risen over 80mph (130kmh), or approximately 125 per cent. Circuits and public roads could no longer play host to record attempts; beaches and the still wider expanses of deserts would provide the stage going forward. Designers had begun to pursue two distinctly different ways of developing a car capable of pushing the record higher. Some felt that the larger the aero engine, the quicker a brutish machine could be propelled over a timed mile. Others felt that a lighter, more streamlined approach was required. The targets were the same for both schools. The landmark 150mph barrier (approximately 241kmh) was tantalisingly close, and beyond that, the 'three miles in a minute' record could be secured by paring just four further seconds from the time required to travel the mile.

Malcolm Campbell was obsessed with both targets and, initially at least, with the Sunbeam. He later wrote of the moment he first clapped eyes on it: 'I regarded the Sunbeam as a real racing machine. It was so big, and so powerful, that it seemed as if it could be made to travel just as fast as a man dared drive it.'[2]

He knew that he dared drive it faster away from the confines of Brooklands, and no sooner had Guinness set his record than Campbell plagued Coatalen for permission to give the car its full head at a more appropriate venue. He was lent the Sunbeam for a record attempt on the beach at Saltburn in Yorkshire, but though he got it up to 138mph (approximately 222kmh), the record eluded him because stopwatch timing was not acceptable to the AIACR. He also learned of the car's tendency to 'crab' at high speed.

Anything but discouraged, Campbell now bought the car from Sunbeam, and took it over to Fanø island in Denmark for another record attempt. Again, the timing apparatus was considered unfit for purpose and, much worse, the car's continued crabbing caused a tyre to fly off and kill a young spectator.

Absolved of blame for the boy's death, Campbell remained convinced that once the venue and timing equipment were up to the job, he would not only beat Eldridge's record, he would also breach 150mph (241.40kmh). However, his eye was already on the next barrier – three miles in a minute. The Sunbeam was clearly incapable of 180mph (289.68kmh), and he knew he would need a purpose-built vehicle to attack this higher target.

It was this realisation, and his fierce ambition to be the first man to attain it, that took him to Amherst's door. When Campbell was not obsessing about the land speed record, he was still racing at Brooklands and competing in hill-climbs and sand races, and he had taken note of the advantage Amherst had given Raymond Mays in *Quicksilver* and the Brescia Bugattis. He had also observed with interest Amherst's first experiments at supercharging with the AC and Humphrey Cook's Vauxhall. When Campbell first introduces Amherst in *My Thirty Years of Speed*, he calls him 'a very clever designer who was particularly interested in racing-type engines and, more particularly, in superchargers'.[3] Equally appreciative of Amherst's skills was Campbell's chief mechanic, Leo Villa, who considered that *Cordon Rouge* and *Cordon Bleu* 'had put up outstanding performances at most of the classic hill climbs'.[4]

Campbell was delighted when Amherst agreed to a dual assignment. He would carry out what was by now his stock in trade, the designing of new camshafts for the Sunbeam and for Campbell's latest racing car, a Targa Itala, and he would also take a close look at what untapped potential was left in the Sunbeam. Villa was particularly impressed with how Amherst acquitted himself on the Itala. He fitted the new camshaft and, following tests at Brooklands, 'found the car's all out performance much improved'.[5]

Amherst was less impressed with how Campbell exploited the Itala's advantage, recording in a 1985 interview that he 'was a fascinating person but had no ethics whatever . . . he won race after race with it because he was very clever. He didn't let it all out at once so as to fool the handicappers.'[6]

As for Amherst's second task, his conclusions about the Sunbeam were just as forthright. He advised Campbell that a very different design of car would be needed to achieve three miles in a minute. Campbell records, 'These conversations were the actual beginning of the "Blue Birds", which were built later.'[7]

The first thing to settle upon was the engine. More than ten years after the start of the First World War, Amherst and Campbell felt they needed something with greater performance than the war-surplus aero engines which had driven most recent land speed record cars, and they managed to procure a Napier Lion engine, similar to that which had powered Captain Henry Biard's Supermarine Sea Lion to victory in the 1922 running of the Schneider Trophy, the famous seaplane race, regularly contested by America, Britain, France, Germany and Italy.

The Napier Lion had two merits. First, it weighed only 915lbs (415kgs) and delivered more than 500hp at 2,200rpm, so for its time it offered an enviable power-to-weight ratio. Second, its 12 cylinders were arranged in three blocks of four, the outer pair set at an angle of 60 degrees, sitting each side of the vertical central block, and this enabled Amherst to set about designing the most streamlined record-breaker yet.

Meanwhile, Campbell focused on finding a new site for a further record attempt with the modified Sunbeam. Pendine, the Welsh village on the Carmarthenshire coast which regularly hosted sand race meetings, provided him with an answer. Its seven miles of flat, open sands were frequently streaming wet, but they were firm and offered plenty of space for Campbell to get the Sunbeam up to full speed before entering the measured mile, and to slow down and turn around beyond it. The RAC arranged for official timing apparatus that satisfied the requirements of the AIACR, and in September 1924 Campbell recorded an average speed of 146.16mph (235.22kmh), fractionally beating Eldridge's 15-month-old record.

For good measure, he returned to Pendine the following summer and became the first man through the magic 150mph barrier, with a new record of 150.76mph (242.63kmh). The effect was extraordinary. The previous year, Campbell's achievement had been witnessed only by his small team and a handful of villagers. Now, he may have travelled less than 5mph faster – a margin of a little over 3 per cent – but he was the only man on the planet to have driven at over 150mph, and the press lauded him. Campbell lapped up the attention, but knew that the publicity meant only one thing: more rivals would enter the competition to be the fastest man on earth.

Sadly, Kenelm Lee Guinness would not be one of them. While Campbell was first breaking the record at Pendine in September 1924, Guinness and his co-driver Thomas Barrett were racing in a Sunbeam in the San Sebastian Grand Prix, on the north coast of Spain. They slid off in the wet and suffered a violent accident. Both men were thrown clear of the somersaulting car, but Barrett was killed instantly and Guinness's injuries were so serious that he never drove competitively again.

In his place, two other British drivers whom Campbell knew well from regular competition at Brooklands stepped up to the challenge. Their names were Henry Segrave and John Parry Thomas, and their approaches were very different. Segrave was supported by Sunbeam, for whom Coatalen designed a simple, light car based on current racing-car principles, capable of utilising the relatively confined environs of Southport Sands on the Lancashire coast, and powered by a 4-litre, supercharged V12 engine. This new Sunbeam enabled Segrave to pip Campbell's record in March 1926, and raise the bar to 152.33mph (245.16kmh).

Parry Thomas, on a tighter budget and without works backing, relied on the huge aero engine approach. He acquired from the estate of the late Count Louis Zbrowski (the man behind the original *Chitty-Bang-Bang* cars) a brutish car fitted with a chain-driven, 27-litre Liberty aero engine, known as the *Higham Special*. The car's design may have bordered on the obsolete, but Parry Thomas fettled it up and renamed it *Babs*. A month after Segrave had snatched the record from Campbell, Thomas took the car to Pendine and recorded an extraordinary 169.30mph (272.47kmh). The next day, he went even faster, raising the record to 171.02mph (275.24kmh).

In spite of the intense competition, Campbell decided that record breaking and motor racing were not enough to fuel the 'real longing for adventure' which had first been inspired by *King Solomon's Mines*.[8] He had been much impressed by the way Guinness had travelled to some overseas races in his yacht, the *Ocean Rover*, and when KLG told him he was planning to recuperate from his San Sebastian injuries on a voyage to the Cacaos Islands, 400 miles off the coast of Columbia, to search for buried pirate treasure, he was only too keen to join the expedition. Leaving Amherst working on the design of the first *Bluebird* land speed record car, Campbell set sail. As described in *My Thirty Years of Speed*, the venture, including night-time visits to the team's camp by a ghostly presence and a desperate sprint from a jungle fire started by Campbell, reads as though it were lifted straight out of a Rider Haggard tale. But no treasure was found, and on the voyage home Campbell's thoughts returned to *Bluebird* and the 180mph target.

Amherst had been hard at work, producing what the doyen of motor sport writers, Bill Boddy, has described as 'the first of the modern, specialised cars to go after the Land Speed Record.'[9] British motoring weekly *The Motor* was particularly impressed when *Bluebird* was unveiled in November 1926: 'The first impression one has of the car is its great length, accentuated by the narrow, perfectly streamlined single-seater body and the very small amount of ground clearance . . . The greatest originality has been displayed in the construction of the whole vehicle, from the front wheels to the point of its streamlined tail.'[10] *Motor Sport* was equally complimentary, calling the car 'a wonderful piece of work . . . designed in accordance with airship practice, all the lines being carefully calculated to give the least possible wind resistance at the colossal speeds that are anticipated.'[11] The low ground clearance to which *The Motor* referred was achieved by Amherst slinging the chassis frame under the rear axle, which had the effect of bringing the centre of gravity lower than the wheel hub centres.

At the time, Campbell reckoned he had spent some £8,000 (almost £350,000, or more than US$470,000 in today's terms) on having the car designed and built, and Amherst had done his utmost to manage costs. For a start, he did not charge for his work on the Itala, the Sunbeam or *Bluebird*, though Campbell did give him an engraved gold watch after he visited the Itala works to explain his camshaft developments. He also brought in Joseph Maina, designer of the car's complex, three-speed epicyclic gearbox on a free-of-charge basis, and arranged for the chassis, made of 3 per cent nickel steel and strengthened by four enormous, machine-forged cross-members, to be constructed by Vickers. The car itself was built at Guinness's KLG Spark Plugs factory, the Robinhood Engineering Works in Putney Vale, near where the old London to Portsmouth road (now the A3) dissected Richmond Park and Wimbledon Common.

Upon his return from the Cacaos Islands, Campbell was disappointed by the slow progress of the build. In part this was caused by the arrival of Joseph Maina at the Robinhood works; all work on the car was suspended while he supervised the installation of the gearbox.

Another reason was the extensive testing which Amherst had insisted upon at each stage of *Bluebird*'s manufacture. As *The Motor* recorded, 'First the raw material, then the forgings, then the partly machined and, finally, the completed components were all tested in Messrs. Vickers' laboratory by the very latest apparatus, so the very best of everything may be said to have gone into the building of the car.'[12] This approach would actually reap dividends for Campbell. Not only was it safer – unlike Parry Thomas, and American challengers such as Frank Lockhart and Lee Bible, each of whom would be killed in pursuit of the land speed record, Campbell would die in his bed – but the development potential engineered into *Bluebird* by Amherst was something that would be exploited for years to come.

Regardless, the impatient Campbell moved the car and construction team to his home at Povey Cross, near where Gatwick Airport is situated today. Work continued flat out as the end of the year approached, resumed after the shortest of breaks for Christmas, and the team reached Pendine on New Year's Eve intent on breaking Parry Thomas's record. The car sported a neat streamlined body and, for its time, a particularly small frontal area. This had been achieved through reducing the radiator size by fitting over the steering column a ten-gallon tank for the bulk of the cooling water, and accentuated by the louvred bodywork that covered the chassis dumb-irons. *Bluebird* was finally ready for action. But, by this time, Amherst had abruptly left the team.

The longer he lived, the more fatalistic Amherst would grow. In a 1974 interview with Eoin Young, he said, 'When I'm poised on the brink of some new achievement, fate steps in and turns over to the next chapter. This sort of thing has been happening all my life and it really is infuriating.'[13] Similarly, after interviewing Amherst nine years later, Mike MacCarthy wrote, 'He has "had more rugs pulled from under him", to quote one of his pet phrases, than most folk have had hot dinners.'[14]

Since the split with Campbell is the first significant instance in Amherst's long life of a chapter ending prematurely and a rug being pulled from under him, it is important to establish what lay behind it. There is little consensus in the public record. In his autobiography, *My Thirty Years of Speed*, Campbell himself was most complimentary about the role Amherst played in the development of the *Bluebird* record cars, but by the point he describes the run up to the record-breaking run at Pendine, all reference to Amherst has ceased. Similarly, in her biography of her husband, Lady Dorothy Campbell mentions 'the assistance of Mr. Amherst Villiers' in 'the conception of the "Blue Bird", destined to be probably the most famous racing car of all time',[15] and then makes no further reference to him, or to Maina, whatsoever.

At least Leo Villa writes of Amherst's departure in his books. In *My Life with the Speed King* he states, 'To add to Campbell's worries, something misfired, and Amherst Villiers terminated his engagement quite abruptly.'[16] Then he takes credit for finding Amherst's replacement, explaining that Maina, 'a very competent designer and engineer, was a friend of my family and had recently completed the design of the epicyclic gearbox for its inventor, W. S. Forster Brown.'[17] Villa claims he arranged for Campbell to meet with Maina and Forster Brown, and it was agreed that, on the basis the gearbox would be used on *Bluebird*, Maina 'would finish the design that Amherst Villiers had left incomplete'.[18] This version, and chronology, of events are mirrored in Villa's earlier book, *The Record Breakers*.

Leo Villa was chief mechanic, first to Malcolm and then to Campbell's son Donald, for some 45 years. He did occasionally criticise both men mildly, but loyalty to them played a strong part in his published writing, and his claims regarding Amherst and Maina can be refuted absolutely.

When an argument broke out in the correspondence pages of *The Motor* in February 1928, as to who was responsible for which parts of the modified *Bluebird* which Campbell was about to drive in excess of 200 mph, Amherst explained in some detail that it was he who had proposed bringing Maina on to the project, and even quoted a letter Maina had written to him: 'We note that you have definitely decided, on Captain Malcolm Campbell's behalf, to use the gear in the car which you are building for him to attempt the world's record, and that you have already approved the general design.'[19]

Amherst's own version of the events leading up to his departure from the *Bluebird* project, whether as related in private conversation to friends such as Hugo Spowers or historians such as Doug Nye, or in the interviews with Young and McCarthy, remained consistent. McCarthy wrote,

Maina had a large house in Hampstead, complete with drawing office facilities, so Villiers handed over all the drawings. Then one day, coming up from Povey Cross, Campbell told Villiers, 'Maina has all the drawings, and everything is under control, so we won't be needing you anymore.' Villiers was stunned, to say the least, by the off-hand way Campbell dismissed him and his efforts, for which he never received a penny. From that day on, Villiers never spoke to Campbell, and another rug had been pulled from under him.[20]

Young recorded Amherst's comments on his departure from the Bluebird project thus:

Villiers arranged a deal with a man named Joseph Maina, who had designed an epicyclic gearbox and was prepared to donate it to the Bluebird programme for the publicity the record attempt would achieve for his transmission. Since neither Campbell nor Villiers had drawing offices, Villiers decided they should work from Maina's premises in Hampstead. However, after six months Villiers discovered that Campbell had made an arrangement for Maina to take over the complete car. The page was being turned on another of the Villiers chapters.[21]

More than 80 years later, how does one filter through the silences, claims and counter claims and establish the truth? Fortunately, there is an arbiter who can guide us through the minefield. Steve Holter has been fascinated with speed records in general and the Campbells *père et fils* in particular since childhood. He not only met Amherst, but also Lady Dorothy Campbell and Leo Villa when writing his seminal book on Donald Campbell, *Leap into Legend*. As such, his views on the reasons for Amherst's departure, and on whether he jumped or was pushed, are fascinating:

If you speak to five people on the same subject and they all tell you the same thing, you know they've spoken to each other. On the other hand, it's quite natural for people who have gone their separate ways and not spoken since to have different opinions and interpretations of the same events.

I'm 99 per cent certain that Amherst walked, and that Maina was on board before he left. There would have had to be at the very least drawings of the gearbox for Amherst to have completed his design of the chassis and the gearbox installation. Amherst was on the project throughout the construction at the Robinhood Works, and moved with the team down to Povey Cross. I'm convinced the chassis was complete and the bodywork was being worked on before he left.

Malcolm Campbell's problem was that he was a perfectionist, yet he had no idea how anything worked. He would hover over people's shoulders, ask questions, and query whether something would work even if he didn't understand the answer. Leo Villa was faced with it all the time, but out of loyalty never referred to it in his books. But Amherst found that atmosphere very frustrating – the constant interference, the constant questioning of his ability, the constant changing of minds, only for Campbell to disappear off on that treasure hunt . . .

And I think Campbell was unrealistic about what was involved in actually preparing the car for the record attempt. Amherst told me, 'He thought he could come back from the Cacaos, slide the seat forward, wind up the windows and drive off and set the record. He didn't seem to realise we needed him there for the detailed layout of the cockpit, the positioning of the steering wheel, the peddles and so on.'[22]

Holter believes the diametrically opposed design mentalities of Amherst and Maina only added to the tension:

Amherst didn't necessarily stretch the boundaries; his philosophy was to keep it simple, because that made it easier to develop. But that gearbox of Maina's . . . sure, there was a challenge matching a low revving aero engine to the gear speeds required, especially when coming down through the gears after the measured mile, but that thing almost broke Campbell's wrist![23]

Indeed, Amherst's tart comment to Holter was that 'that gearbox gave Campbell everything he deserved',[24] and it is notable that one of designer Reid Railton's first actions on taking responsibility for the

FREE TRADE CANDIDATE

ERNEST VILLIERS.

Printed and Published by King, Thorne & Stace, 4 and 5 Jubilee Street, Brighton.

*Amherst's father
Ernest Villiers, seen
here in the run-up to
the 1906 General
Election. He had the
most impolitic of
political careers.*
(County Archivist of
East Sussex)

*Amherst's mother
Elaine did a rare
thing for a woman of
her background: she
married for love.*
(County Archivist of
East Sussex)

ABOVE: *Oundle's 1917 School House rugby team. Amherst stands at top right; Raymond Mays, the young man who drove many of the racing cars Amherst developed, sits in front of him.* (Oundle School)

LEFT: *Oundle's famous headmaster F. W. Sanderson was a major influence on Amherst.* (Oundle School)

OPPOSITE BOTTOM: *Quicksilver's aluminium bodywork glows in the sun, moments before Mays puts Amherst's developments to good effect and wins the 1921 Inter-Varsity speed trial.* (Bourne Civic Trust)

ABOVE: *Eastgate House, in Bourne, Lincolnshire: home to Raymond Mays throughout his life, and to many of the racing cars Amherst developed in the 1920s and '30s.* (Author's collection)

ABOVE: *Amherst works on Mays's Brescia Bugatti at the Madresfield speed trial in June 1922, two years before the pair named it* Cordon Rouge. (Bugatti Trust)

LEFT: *Amherst, slide rule in hand, working on developments for* Cordon Rouge *at Eastgate House.* (Bugatti Trust)

OPPOSITE TOP: *In an outbuilding at Eastgate House, Amherst ponders his refinements to a piston, while Mays looks on.* (Bugatti Trust)

OPPOSITE BOTTOM: *At the Caerphilly hillclimb in 1924, Mays learns the hard way that the rear axle of* Cordon Rouge *has not kept pace with Amherst's developments.* (National Motor Museum, Beaulieu)

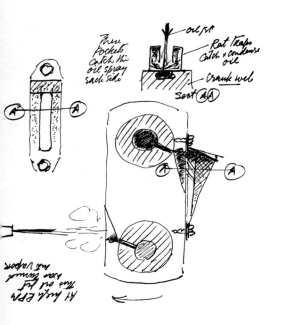

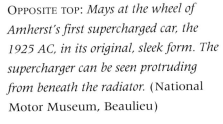

LEFT: *How Amherst's 'rat traps' overcame the problems of Bugatti's 'spit-and-hope' lubrication at high revs.* (Bugatti Trust)

OPPOSITE TOP: *Mays at the wheel of Amherst's first supercharged car, the 1925 AC, in its original, sleek form. The supercharger can be seen protruding from beneath the radiator.* (National Motor Museum, Beaulieu)

OPPOSITE BOTTOM: *With bonnet removed to stop the AC's advance-retard control from snagging, Mays hussles out of the Lower Ess at Shelsley Walsh in 1925. Moments later the control snapped altogether and he was left to trundle up to the finish.* (Bugatti Trust)

LEFT: *Amherst's 1920s watercolour of Mays in* Cordon Rouge *became the basis for this poster half a century later.* (Eoin Young)

ABOVE: *Mays in the bloated, heavy two-seater version of the AC, shortly before the 1925 JCC 200 race at Brooklands.* (Bourne Civic Trust)

LEFT: *Amherst (left) and Mays are about to discover that their all-night work fitting a second radiator and yards of ancillary hosing is in vain, and that the AC's engine has been terminally damaged by the leaking water they are kneeling in.* (National Motor Museum, Beaulieu)

RIGHT: *Speed king Malcolm Campbell commissioned Amherst to design his first* Bluebird *land speed record breaker.* (National Motor Museum, Beaulieu)

BELOW: Bluebird *in the fog at Campbell's Sussex home, Povey Cross.* (Getty Images)

ABOVE: *Campbell trialling* Bluebird *on the sands at Pendine in January 1927, a month before he finally raised the world record to 174.88mph (281.45kmh).* (Getty Images)

LEFT: *Jack Kruse commissioned Amherst to develop the world's first supercharged Rolls-Royce.* (Jan Kruse)

ABOVE: *Amherst at Brooklands, testing the supercharged Rolls-Royce Phantom, chassis number 31HC.* Autocar *wrote, 'But the noise . . .'* (LAT Photographic Digital Archive)

BELOW: *The completed car, with unique engine/blower unit housed in the cabinet on the near-side running board.* (Tom Clarke)

OPPOSITE: *31HC in 1932, after Amherst removed the engine/blower unit and had a sleek James Young sedanca coupé body fitted.* (Tom Clarke)

RIGHT: *Almost 60 years later, Amherst is reunited with 31 HC's engine/blower in a Sussex barn.* (Rolls-Royce Enthusiasts' Club)

BELOW: *Mays streaks ahead in the Vauxhall Villiers at the start of the 1928 Southport 100 race. In the middle of the pack, Amherst adjusts his goggles and sets off on one of his rare outings as a racing driver.* (LAT Photographic Digital Archive)

ABOVE: *Back at Southport in 1929, Amherst (right) makes late adjustments to the* Vauxhall Villiers, *still sporting its original Vauxhall radiator. Peter Berthon stands behind him, while Mays (left) prepares to climb aboard.* (National Motor Museum, Beaulieu)

OPPOSITE TOP: *Amherst works on the engine/ transmission unit of the* Villiers Supercharge. *The supercharger sits on the chair behind him, while Berthon and Tom Murray Jamieson can just be seen in the shade.* (Getty Images)

RIGHT: *Amherst conducting the tests that would lead to the* Villiers Supercharge *being fitted with twin rear wheels.* (National Motor Museum, Beaulieu)

ABOVE: *Another image from the same test, with Berthon standing in front of the car, now sporting its sinister-looking intercooler, Amherst leaning over the engine, and Mays in the cockpit.* (National Motor Museum, Beaulieu)

LEFT: *The man who insisted on the supercharging of the 4½-litre Bentley by Amherst, Sir Henry 'Tim' Birkin, and the Hon. Dorothy Paget, who bankrolled Birkin's team of Blower Bentleys during 1930.* (Stanley Mann)

third record-breaking incarnation of what was originally Amherst's *Bluebird* was to design a new transmission.

Holter also detected some resentment on Amherst's part as to how he was treated at Povey Cross. As a fellow Shelsley Walsh competitor of Campbell's, Amherst's great friend Raymond Mays was frequently invited to parties there, but Amherst only stayed to work on the Itala and *Bluebird*. Amherst never thrust his family background on those around him; nevertheless, it rankled with him that while others with a less privileged upbringing partied at Povey Cross at weekends, he effectively used the tradesman's entrance during the week.

So, for a number of reasons Amherst felt obliged to walk away from the *Bluebird* project when success was tantalisingly close. Almost five decades later, Holter could still sense his disappointment: 'Amherst had clearly wanted to be in it right to the death. The most galling thing for him was that he didn't participate in the final success.'[25]

Ultimately, it is no coincidence that the first time a rug was pulled from under Amherst's feet was the first time he undertook a major project without Raymond Mays. The division of labour in their working relationship was clear from the outset, and reflected their relative skills: Amherst did the development, Mays figured out how to pay for it – or preferably, not pay for it – and did the driving. Conversely, with *Bluebird*, Amherst felt that he did the design and tried to deliver the build, with Campbell first looking over his shoulder, then the other side of the world, and then returning home and demanding where his record-breaking car was. None of this is to be critical of Campbell. Simply, Amherst found it much harder to work for him than with Mays, and eventually felt obliged to walk.

As we shall see presently, Amherst's 'next chapter' would prove to be a fascinating and lucrative project, but it is harder to see what Campbell gained from losing him. The 1927 *Bluebird* confirmed that Amherst was a fine designer, but in fact all his previous automotive work, from *Quicksilver* via *Cordon Rouge* and *Cordon Bleu* to his early supercharging projects, should have demonstrated that his real skill lay in development, and Campbell would be in sore need of this capability over the next 15 months or so. On the other hand, Joseph Maina's work, wrote Leo Villa, 'had one great drawback. He would never use a straightforward shaft or lever if he could dream up an elaborate hydraulic arrangement, all valves and connections, to do the same task.'[26]

The problems this approach caused manifested themselves as soon as Campbell first took *Bluebird* out on to the streaming wet sands at Pendine on 2 January 1927. He discovered the clutch was hard to engage, and found the location of the gear lever, between his legs, made it difficult for him to change gear. He stalled *Bluebird* at high speed and the car had to be rescued from sinking in the sand. There was no alternative but to make a humiliating return to Povey Cross and rectify the transmission problems. A month after calling *Bluebird* 'a wonderful piece of work', *Motor Sport* was unimpressed: 'Campbell is nothing if not enterprising, but one wonders just what induced him to start out for hitherto unattained speeds with a gear box so tremendously unorthodox in design.'[27]

Soon after those words appeared in print, the team returned to Pendine. On 1 February Campbell equalled Parry Thomas's speed on his first run down the measured mile but suffered a puncture on the return leg. Three days later, after local schoolboys had cleared the beach of the seashells thought to be responsible for the tyre problems, Campbell set an average speed for the two runs of 174.88mph (281.45kmh) and the record was his once more.

The great risks Campbell ran, and the inherent safety of Amherst's design, were brought into sharp focus the following month when John Parry Thomas brought his old-fashioned, chain-driven *Babs* back to Pendine in a bid to reclaim the title of 'fastest man on earth'. The right-hand-side driving chain snapped, flailed through its guard and decapitated the popular Welshman.

The news of Parry Thomas's death reached Henry Segrave while he was crossing the Atlantic on his way to Florida for a record attempt on the expanses of Daytona Beach, 23 miles long and 500yd wide at low tide. This had been made possible by the decision of the American

Automobile Association to take membership of the AIACR, which thus allowed records set in the United States to be recognised internationally. This development, and the RAC's decision, in the wake of Parry Thomas's accident, to ban further record attempts at Pendine, meant that no further world land speed records would ever be set in the United Kingdom. So it was that the 174.88mph (281.45kmh) mark set by Campbell in Amherst's *Bluebird* would serve as the British land speed record for more than 40 years.

In the hold of the ship carrying Segrave to the United States was a new Sunbeam, powered by a pair of old Matabele aero engines linked together by a dog clutch and enveloped by a long shell of a body to minimise wind resistance. As such, the '1,000hp Sunbeam', as it became known, certainly looked fit for purpose, and so it proved as Segrave not only captured the '3 miles per minute' crown, but also exceeded 200mph, setting a new record of 203.79mph (328.98kmh). This was more than a 16 per cent increase on Campbell's mark, and Segrave returned to England to a hero's welcome.

In truth, the '1,000hp Sunbeam' was something of a legend in its own lifetime. It may have been aerodynamically efficient for the time, but the Matabele engines actually delivered only 400hp each, and at a great price: the Sunbeam weighed almost a third more than *Bluebird*. Campbell, therefore, continued to believe in the inherent soundness of Amherst's design approach – a single-engine, more compact and lighter car – and argued that, provided he could obtain a more powerful engine, he could use *Bluebird* to regain the record. He procured an updated version of the Napier Lion aero engine, now similar in specification and power output to the one which had enabled Flight Lieutenant Sidney Webster to win the 1927 Schneider Trophy. Aerodynamic developments included fitting fairings behind the front wheels and in front of the rear ones, and placing a pair of surface-mounted radiators along the tail of *Bluebird* so that it could be shrouded with a bulbous nose – although Amherst argued in *The Motor* that 'advantage might be gained by provision of a wedge shaped nose which would part the air with less disturbance'.[28.]

Nevertheless, as Amherst also wrote, 'the general arrangement of the chassis, including such parts as rear axle, brakes, springs, clutch, engine mounting' were all as he had originally set out when, in February 1928, Campbell thundered up and down Daytona Beach in the revised *Bluebird* at an average of 206.96mph (335.72kmh), to regain the record from Segrave.[29.]

Here, we must take our leave of *Bluebird*, as each successive record set thereafter by Campbell – his ninth and final mark was 301.13mph (488.48kmh) in 1935 – owed less and less to Amherst's original design, and more to designer Reid Railton and the prodigiously powerful Rolls-Royce R-type engine. Suffice it to say that Campbell, like Segrave, was knighted for his great prowess at breaking both land and water records, but died on New Year's Eve 1948, burned out at the age of 63. Segrave was killed in 1930, aged just 34, on Lake Windermere in the English Lake District during a world water speed record attempt. Guinness never really recovered from his appalling accident at San Sebastian and committed suicide at his home in 1937. He was buried at Putney Vale Cemetery, next door to his Robinhood Engineering Works.

As for Amherst, Maina may have got the lion's share of the credit for the first *Bluebird* land speed record car at the time, but history has been kinder. A dispassionate examination of the available evidence demonstrates that Amherst can deservedly be credited with designing the bulk of one of the first land speed record cars to focus on efficiency rather than brute force, and for playing his part in the legends that are Malcolm Campbell and *Bluebird*. Even the 1935 *Bluebird*, in which Campbell became the first man to breach 300mph, contained vestiges of Amherst's original chassis design of nine years earlier. However, as he explained to journalist Brian Palmer in 1985, once he had left the *Bluebird* project, Amherst never spoke to Campbell again. 'You know, life's funny,' he said, 'there are some awfully nice people around and some that, frankly, could do with an overhaul.'[30]

Chapter 7

THE FIRST SUPERCHARGED ROLLS-ROYCE

Jack Frederick Conrad Kruse was born in September 1892, in the Essex town of South Weald, the eldest son of a banker. Upon leaving school, he went to work for Lord Northcliffe, the future Viscount Rothermere, and was promoted swiftly to become private secretary to the great newspaper magnate. As a Second Lieutenant in the Royal Naval Division in the First World War, Kruse saw action at Gallipoli and, if that experience was not wretched enough, the ship on which he was evacuated was torpedoed on the way home. When peace came he was demobbed with the rank of Captain, and he set up a variety of businesses in England and Holland before rejoining Amalgamated Press as a director of the newly formed *Continental Daily Mail*.

On a business trip to the United States in 1922, Kruse met and fell in love with the woman who would become his second wife, a widow named Annabel Wilson, who was heiress to her father's hotel chain. The couple married and moved to England, where in due course they set up home at Sunning House, situated by the women's golf course at Sunningdale in Berkshire. Annabel had the house redesigned in Hispanic style, and the couple threw lavish parties there.

With his various business interests and his wife's capital, Captain Kruse also acquired a property in North Yorkshire as a country retreat, where he could indulge his passion for touring cars. He added a four-car garage, tennis court and nine-hole golf course to the house, and found the rough hillside roads of the area ideal for test-driving his latest purchases, which were usually fitted with Barker's bodies. The coachbuilder's showroom manager, Frank

Manning, was a frequent visitor and sold Kruse a pair of Rolls-Royce Silver Ghosts.

In September 1925 Kruse acquired one of the new Rolls-Royce Phantom cars, a 7.7-litre, 6-cylinder model that, in terms of acceleration and a top speed of some 80mph (approximately 129kmh), established itself among the top echelons of high-performance touring cars. Kruse's Phantom, chassis number 31HC, was sent to Barker's, which returned it to him fitted out in resplendent style, with silver-plated wheel hubs, steering column and levers, and a torpedo body augmented with a small rear deck area.

In search of greater performance, Kruse checked out Bentleys too, buying a 4½-litre Vanden Plas tourer, and a pair of 6½-litre models, but he never really got on with Bentleys and would come to be openly critical of both the company and its products. He went on to acquire a number of what would now be considered classic Continental cars, including a pair of SSK Mercedes, half a dozen Lancias and even more Alfa Romeos. Rolls-Royce was the marque closest to Kruse's heart, and in the winter of 1926 he determined upon a unique way of providing one with enhanced performance. He commissioned Amherst to supercharge his Phantom, 31HC.

It is not known how Kruse met Amherst. It may even be that Malcolm Campbell, known to have frequented parties at Sunning House, introduced them, or tipped off Kruse that Amherst had suddenly become available. Kruse would have been familiar with Amherst's work on the Brescia Bugattis and on *Bluebird*, and would have followed the all-English supercharging efforts on the AC and Vauxhall with great interest.

For Amherst, everything about the new commission was a breath of fresh air. Where on *Bluebird* there had been budget constraints and interference, now there was a lucrative and totally blank canvas. As he later related to his friend Donald Parker, Kruse's brief was simple: 'Do something with my P1. Have some fun. Do something exciting.'[1]

Amherst geared up for the project in thorough fashion. He formed a company and opened a design office on Sackville Street in London's West End, hiring Charles Lowe as his office manager. For a workshop, he rented the ground floor of a mill over the River Colne in the village of Stanwell Moor, which today lies immediately south-west of Heathrow Airport's Terminal 5. The mill offered easy access to the straight road running beside the Staines reservoirs, ideal for short bursts of speed on test drives.

Even when he had been working at Eastgate House with Raymond Mays, Amherst had never enjoyed such resources before, and he now began to think laterally about having some fun and doing something exciting with Kruse's Phantom.

One consideration was to address a criticism made of the supercharger: that it leeched the power of the engine of which it was meant to be enhancing the performance. A second factor demonstrates the influence aeronautic engineering was already having on Amherst. Many years later, in a letter to his friend Sir Peter Masefield, he explained that, by this time, he was already giving thought to using a supercharger driven by its own dedicated engine to pipe compressed air to each of an aircraft's several engines. He was also giving thought to producing a small, high-quality, four-seater car, to be driven by a low-capacity, supercharged engine. Though this vehicle would never see the light of day, its image in his mind's eye, together with that of a central blower supercharging multiple aero engines, played a crucial role in determining his blueprint for Kruse's car. He decided to design and build a separate engine to drive the supercharger.

This engine was a 4-cylinder, 625cc, short-stroke, overhead-camshaft unit which developed 10hp and peaked at 8,000rpm when the Roots-type blower was engaged. The combined engine/blower unit weighed only 200lb (91kg), had its own ignition and starter, and was contained within a neat chest fitted to the left-hand-side running board of the car. Hydraulically damped steel tubes passing across and underneath the chassis helped to even out the weight distribution, a process completed by mounting two spare wheels to the opposite running board.

Amherst then turned his attention to the Rolls itself. He took the Phantom's engine to pieces, reassembled it with his own camshaft, pistons and valves, and fitted a dry-sump lubrication system which was fed from a 5-gallon tank suspended by the gearbox. He revised the carburettor so that it could take the 10lb per square inch output from the supercharger, and added a blow-off valve to prevent the supercharger rotors being damaged in the event of a backfire. The dashboard also got the Villiers treatment, with a separate choke and Ki-Gass pump to inject raw fuel into the inlet manifold in order to start the little engine, an accelerator lever fitted to the steering column to control its speed, and an altimeter for Kruse to refer to when touring in the Alps.

Amherst first took 31HC to Brooklands for a shake-down test in the early autumn of 1927. Devoid of much of its bodywork, and with the engine/blower unit exposed for all to see, the car made for an extraordinary sight. An *Autocar* reporter at the track was less than impressed. He wrote, 'Unfortunately, his plugs did not like the supercharger. The gauze on the air intake clogged up, the radiator shutters refused to stay open, and so the water boiled like anything, and the inlet valves seemed to have an abhorrence of seating properly. All these, though, are comparatively minor and curable troubles. But the noise . . .'[2]

In 1927 the proverb, 'all publicity is good publicity' still lay almost half a century away, and Amherst took umbrage at this criticism, instructing his manager, Charles Lowe, to respond. Three weeks later, Lowe's letter to *Autocar* concluded thus:

It should be remembered that there exists a great difference between a racing car openly competing in a public event, and an experimental model using the track for research purposes, as intended.

We do not expect any extreme privacy to be accorded at Brooklands, but suggest, in the interests of progress, that Press reports should be impersonal and strictly confined to fair criticism, rather than ridicule, which is known to be destructive.[3]

Amherst need not have worried. Within a few months, he had overcome these teething problems – albeit without addressing the car's fearsome noise – and Barker's had completed the modifications to the bodywork he had requested. The car was now decked out in matt olive green and fitted with a vast pair of Carl Zeiss headlamps, which the driver could change to amber in the event of fog and could also dip by means of another lever. The aero-deck had been retained, and the rear passengers were afforded some scant protection from the slipstream by means of an auxiliary screen, which could be raised and lowered on hydraulic rams.

Captain Kruse was away on the day Amherst delivered the car to Sunning House, but in 2001, John Kruse, Jack's son who was a young boy at the time, recounted to Rolls-Royce historian Tom Clarke what happened next. Amherst took Mrs Kruse and John 'on a hair-raising dash to Bagshot and back. With rain beginning to fall heavily and the hood down, John Kruse can remember looking up at the dashboard to see 110mph indicated. Not an occasion or a figure that a 10-year-old could ever forget.'[4]

Just how much Amherst made from supercharging Jack Kruse's Rolls-Royce Phantom is a matter of debate. The chauffeur of a subsequent owner understood the total project cost to have been £16,000 – over £700,000, or US$945,000 in today's money – although a 1939 edition of *Motor Sport*, which raised the Kruse Phantom in an article about a later supercharged Rolls-Royce, claimed £10,000. Whichever total is correct, this presumably includes the cost of the car itself (about £2,000) and Barker's work. An alternative reference point is provided by Rolls-Royce's response to the third owner of the car, Charles Diamond, when he asked them for the cost of removing the engine/blower unit and restoring the Phantom's engine to its original specification. They quoted £1,700 (the modern equivalent is about £76,000, or slightly over US$100,000).

Regardless, the most extraordinary aspect of Amherst's remuneration for the Phantom project was that he also came to acquire from Kruse a beautiful Bugatti Type 35, registered YP9453, clad in distinctive maroon paintwork, instead of the more common

French Racing Blue. His consistent explanation in later interviews with car magazines, spread across more than 11 years, is that Kruse gave him the car. As he explained to Brian Palmer in *Thoroughbred & Classic Cars* in November 1985, 'He asked me round to lunch then gave me a key saying he'd bought a Type 35 Bugatti which his wife thought too fast for him and that he was giving it to me.'[5]

Even allowing for Kruse's great wealth, the gift of a Bugatti, in addition to a generous fee, seems excessive. Perhaps Amherst accepted the Bugatti in part-payment, or bought it with his fee. After all, Raymond Mays records in *Split Seconds*, 'Amherst purchased a second-hand 2-litre Grand Prix Bugatti' – note 'purchased', not 'was given'.[6]

We shall never know the precise financial arrangements behind the first supercharging of a Rolls-Royce. Suffice it to say that Amherst was rewarded handsomely. On which basis it may seem fair to conclude that Kruse was happy with the car, but, restless spirit that he was, he sold it within 15 months of receiving it from Amherst. The new owner was the Hon. Dorothy Paget.

Paget was born in 1905, the younger daughter of politician and yachtsman Lord Queenborough. She inherited a fortune from her maternal grandmother, and used it to indulge her twin passions of horse racing and gambling. Her career as a racehorse owner was expensive but successful, with over 1,500 winners, the most famous of which was Golden Miller, winner of the Grand National and five consecutive Cheltenham Gold Cups. Her stable of thoroughbred cars was almost as impressive, and though she had a strong aversion to men (it was noted when she embraced Golden Miller after one particular win that the horse was the first male she had ever kissed – and he was a gelding) she still hired one of Britain's leading racing drivers, Sir Henry 'Tim' Birkin, to coach her in the art of performance driving. She even raced at Brooklands under the pseudonym of 'Miss Wyndham'.

Birkin was one of several 'Bentley Boys' to have been offended by Jack Kruse's frequent criticisms in the motoring press of British car manufacturers, and of Bentley in particular. For Birkin, the final straw came when Kruse rebuked Bentley for withdrawing from the 1928

Tourist Trophy race, to be held on the country roads around the Northern Irish town of Ards. The inference was that Bentley could win on the 'superior track' of Le Mans, but could not cope with rougher road conditions. Kruse and Birkin slugged it out on the correspondence pages of *The Motor* for months to come.

Thus, when Birkin learned that Paget had acquired his rival's supercharged Rolls-Royce, he became keen to experience at first hand what Kruse had commissioned as a solution to the apparent inadequacies of British touring cars. Birkin arranged to test-drive 31HC at Brooklands, and recorded an average speed, according to different accounts, of somewhere between 94 and 108mph (151 and 174kmh). Even allowing for the banked nature of the track, this was a formidable average speed for such a heavy car. Amherst recounted to Tom Clarke that if he had had more time, he would also have modified the Phantom's rear axle, to make the car capable of still higher speeds. Whether the tyre technology of the late 1920s could have coped with an even faster 3-ton motor car is unknown.

Paget kept 31HC no longer than Kruse, and sold it to the newspaper owner and journalist Charles Diamond. Diamond had been born in Ireland but emigrated to England, and founded the *Catholic Herald* in 1884, which espoused the Republican movement in Ireland so strongly that when he wrote an article in 1919 entitled *Killing is no Murder*, he was imprisoned for incitement to murder.

In the 1970s, writer Eoin Young interviewed Diamond's former chauffeur, Reginald Power, who relived fond memories of long trips to France and Germany in the car:

> *I had it up to 94 or 96mph once in Germany but it weighed nearly three tons and with that weight you couldn't expect much in the way of acceleration. We used to get 12–14 miles to the gallon, but with the blower on you could only guess at the fuel mileage. Paget's chauffeur told me it did 7–8 to the gallon with the blower going and he had done more miles on the Continent than I had. I only put the supercharger on when we were on hills or when the 'old man' felt like blowing the cobwebs away.*[7]

In 1932 Diamond hit financial problems and sold the Phantom for only £250 (about £12,500, almost US$17,000 in today's money) . . . to Amherst. He immediately decided to remove the engine/blower unit and substantially alter the body, thereby demonstrating that, glorious though his grand design had been, it was hardly a working proposition as an everyday car. His latest ideas were turned into reality by coachbuilders James Young. The new look comprised an elegant sedanca coupé body decked out in black, with light grey doors and rear quarters, and long, flowing running boards. It was an extremely attractive car, and remained Amherst's primary choice of transport until shortly before the Second World War. Mechanically, he maintained the developments he had made to the Phantom itself, and went on tweaking the car to his satisfaction, fitting revised pistons in 1935. As for the engine/blower unit, he kept this in the hangar he retained at Heston Airport, west of London.

In May 1938 Amherst decided finally to sell the old Phantom. The splendidly named London car dealer, Bunty Scott-Moncreiff, advertised it in *The Motor* as the 'recent property of famous engineer' for £385 (a little over £18,500, or US$25,000 today). Four years later, as Amherst made preparations for his move to North America, he gave away the little engine and supercharger to an aircraft mechanic contact of his named Davis. And there, with the world in conflagration and much more important issues to worry about, Amherst lost all remaining contact with the extraordinary car he had been close to for more than ten years.

Captain Jack Kruse had other things on his mind, too. The Wall Street Crash had impacted heavily on his and Annabel's wealth, and they were forced to part with much of their extensive property portfolio. Annabel developed a debilitating illness, and Kruse formed a friendship with a Russian woman who lived in the Pyrenees. By the late 1930s his remaining businesses had collapsed and, leaving his last car, a Buick saloon, with his son John, he moved to Nice to be with his Russian friend. When the Germans invaded France, Kruse tried first to make for England and then for Spain, but turned back and was interned in Grenoble, where he died, aged only 50, in February 1943. Annabel had succumbed to her illness two years earlier. Two lives had burned brightly, but briefly.

In old age Amherst found himself thinking about the Phantom and the little engine and supercharger again. When, in May 1979, *Autocar* devoted a celebratory issue to the 75th anniversary of the Rolls-Royce marque, Eoin Young wrote an article about 31HC, and recorded that Amherst 'has made efforts to trace his fantastic Phantom, but it seems to have completely disappeared, a victim of the war perhaps, or the knacker's yard'.[8] Five years earlier, Young had written an article about Amherst for Australia's *Sports Car World*, informing its readers, 'the Rolls-Royce has disappeared and Amherst would very much like to meet up with it again. Surely a Roll-Royce with such an amazing engine specification doesn't just vanish?'[9]

In fact, the Phantom had been in Australia for at least 25 years by then, including a stint towing gliders at the Horsham Flying Club in Victoria, and was to spend so long 'down under' that it became known as 'Sheila'. But still Amherst wondered about the little engine and blower, to the point of obsession. Then, extraordinarily, in the summer before his 90th birthday, word reached his friend Donald Parker that a small engine incorporating a supercharger was thought to exist on a farm east of Hastings, on the Sussex coast. The description seemed to fit the bill, so one day Parker picked up Amherst in his Rolls-Royce Silver Wraith, and the pair motored down and started asking questions.

Parker told the readers of the Rolls-Royce Enthusiasts' Club *Bulletin* what happened next:

After a few enquiries we found the farm and tracked down the farmer, who led us to a barn wherein stood on trestles an engine – the engine. Instead of looking dirty, damaged or corroded it was pristine . . . The farmer described how it had been given to him by a former employer who always thought it had been built for a Birkin Bentley to attack the Brooklands outer circuit record. Nice idea.[10]

Amherst was overjoyed. In a letter to his friend, Sir Peter Masefield, he explained that the unit had not been run since he had last seen it, because no one realised its water and oil were drawn from the Phantom engine. He thought it was in marvellous condition but would need restoring.

He knew exactly what to do about this last point. He bought the engine and blower from the farmer and brought them back to his Kensington home. Out went the sofa, and in came a Black & Decker 'Workmate'. Amherst rigged up a simple metal frame over this, and then set about dismantling and restoring the unit.

Parker was most impressed when he paid a visit to Amherst to examine the device: 'Aluminium was used wherever possible. It was finished like costume jewellery, totally elegant – something you could never throw away. I am glad it has survived and that it has made Amherst happy.'[11] The find did indeed make Amherst happy, and at a time when the last years of his life would be filled with great stress because of a forthcoming breach of contract case, it acted as a great relief to him.

The final twist in the tale of the first supercharged Rolls-Royce came in 1998, seven years after Amherst's death. The Guernsey-based car collector Peter Channing purchased the Phantom and brought it back from Australia. Knowing that the engine/blower unit had been located, he formed the ambition to refit the device to the car, and contacted Amherst's daughter Janie to make her an offer for it. She chose not to part with it, and in 2004 it still sat on the Black & Decker 'Workmate' in the corner of Amherst's old living room.

Eighty years on, what are we to make of the world's first supercharged Rolls-Royce? For Jack Kruse, it was a rich man's indulgence. He encouraged Amherst to explore the very edge of creativity simply because he could, and yet he sold the car after little more than a year. The sheer impracticality of the design was confirmed when Amherst removed the engine/blower unit after acquiring 31HC for himself.

For Amherst, at least at the time, the Kruse project was enjoyable and lucrative, and a great change from the frustrations of *Bluebird*.

But in hindsight it had a significant impact on the automotive project with which Amherst is most associated – the Blower Bentley – and is important to Amherst's overall standing as an automotive engineer for three reasons. First, after the doomed AC venture and the aborted work on Cook's Vauxhall, 31HC was Amherst's first successful supercharging project. He demonstrated quite clearly that he could design and implement a reliable forced induction system to significantly increase the performance of a car.

Second, 31HC was the car that brought most of the leading players in the Blower Bentley story together. Dorothy Paget came to own the Phantom while it was still fitted with its blower, and Tim Birkin manhandled it around Brooklands at speeds in excess of 100mph. Thus, when Birkin proposed to Bentley that the supercharging of its 4½-litre model was the only way to compete with Mercedes at Le Mans, and to Paget that she should bankroll his team of Blower Bentleys, there was only one man they thought of turning to when it came to delivering the work – Amherst.

Finally, an automotive application of aeronautic engineering principles in the development of a dedicated engine/blower unit may have been a highly creative flight of fancy, but in his modifications to the Phantom's camshaft, pistons, valves, carburettor and lubrication system, Amherst also confirmed he could handle the practical implications of supercharging. It is the breadth of his work on Captain Jack Kruse's Rolls-Royce Phantom that is truly intriguing – if W.O. Bentley had permitted Amherst to similarly optimise the engine of his 4½-litre model for supercharging, then the legend of the Blower Bentley may have been based on rather more racing success than is actually the case.

Chapter 8

THE *VILLIERS SUPERCHARGE*

While Amherst had been busy on *Bluebird* and Jack Kruse's Rolls-Royce Phantom, Raymond Mays had endured much frustration. Saddled with repaying his debts from the unfortunate season with the AC, he spent 1926 working for his father, and was restricted to a single competitive outing. Harold Clay offered him his TT Vauxhall for the September Shelsley Walsh meeting, and Mays made the most of the opportunity. With Amherst as passenger, he roared up the hill in 49.4 seconds, the first time he had breached 50 seconds. A splendid photograph of the pair shows them grinning from ear to ear as they clip the apex at the Bottom Ess.

A mill-owner from Macclesfield in Cheshire, Basil Davenport, who had been enjoying success at northern competitions in a much-modified hill-climb special known as *Spider*, had decided to try his hand at Shelsley. *Spider* was such an odd-looking contraption, with its engine poking out from both sides of extraordinarily narrow, tatty bodywork, that a policeman at the first Shelsley meeting of 1926 had actually tried to bar him from the paddock on the grounds that it could not possibly be competing. Davenport proved that looks can be deceptive by beating Mays's time and lowering the course record to 48.8 seconds. He would be Mays's chief hill-climb competition over the next few years.

By the end of that year, Mays had cleared his AC debts. He had also met the man who would in due course become even more important to him realising his motor racing ambitions than Amherst. At the time Peter Berthon was a young cadet at RAF Cranwell, just a few miles from Bourne, and would shortly be invalided out of the service because of injuries sustained during a forced landing.

Mays had a car and manufacturer support lined up for 1927. The UK arm of Mercedes Benz lent him a 2-litre Targo Florio, with which he won several speed trials and came second to Davenport in both Shelsley Walsh meetings. Amherst still helped out when his other commitments permitted, advising on stronger valve springs for the Mercedes, and a mechanism for permanently engaging the supercharger, rather than just on full throttle as originally designed.

Amherst also agreed to accompany Mays and Berthon to the Blackpool speed trials on the Lancashire coast. On the journey north the truck carrying the Mercedes had a puncture and Amherst jumped out to change the wheel. Unfortunately the jack broke and trapped his hand under the wheel. He was in agony, so Mays rushed him to a nursing home in Grantham. Amherst was lucky to emerge from the accident with only the tip of the third finger of his right hand missing. In the many years ahead it would affect neither his engineering nor painting, but the pain he experienced that afternoon changed him in other respects. He had been raised a 'hunting, shooting, fishing' type of young man, but now he concluded that if his finger could hurt that much, then in all conscience he could no longer hunt wildlife.

For 1928 Mays declined the offer to race for Mercedes on the Continent and therefore needed to make alternative arrangements. Simultaneously, Amherst, still the tenant of a design office in Central London's Sackville Street and a workshop in the old mill in Stanwell Moor, found himself without a major project. When Mays wrote, suggesting they team back up again, it made eminent sense to him, particularly once he knew that the car which Mays had in mind was the ex-Humphrey Cook TT Vauxhall.

From Amherst's point of view, the car was unfinished business. Neither Cook nor its current owner, Jack Barclay, had ever raced it with his supercharger, and it still rankled with him that Cook had sold it to Barclay without letting him know it was on the market. Further, if he was going to work free-of-charge again for his old friend, at least Mays could agree to the car advertising Amherst's technical prowess; it would be called the *Vauxhall Villiers*. On that basis, the two friends agreed a deal with Barclay, and Amherst and Mays became joint owners of the car, and the unused supercharger, for the princely sum of £275 (the modern equivalent would be a little over £12,000, or less than US$17,000).

Before describing what Amherst did to justify the car's new name, it is necessary first to learn a little about the TT Vauxhall as originally designed. It was a handsome car: consideration of effective channelling of the airflow over it had resulted in a small square radiator, fluted bonnet lines and distinctive cones rising in front of the driver and passenger. The chassis, designed by C. E. King, was notable for its ladder frame sweeping over front and rear axles, and the four-wheel braking system; the 12in front and 16in rear drums were controlled by compressed air and operated by a lever on the steering column.

The 3-litre, 4-cylinder, mainly light-alloy engine was the work of internal combustion guru Harry Ricardo, and employed twin overhead camshafts to operate four valves per cylinder. The crankshaft revolved on ball bearings, with roller bearings for the big ends. The flywheel was mounted in the middle of the crankshaft, to reduce torsional vibration, and the deep barrel-shaped crankcase, cylinder block and main bearings were formed into a single, rigid unit.

Power output was said to be 129bhp at 4,500rpm, and had been achieved in part by severely cutting away at the aluminium pistons to minimise friction with the cylinder walls. Performance was also enhanced by the special fuel created by Ricardo, comprising a mixture of fuel and alcohol; this was the RD2 fuel which had been used to good effect by Amherst on *Cordon Rouge* and *Cordon Bleu*.

Wet sump lubrication was employed, operated by a pair of piston-type pumps, one to spray oil on to the crankshaft and the other for the rocker shafts. A twin-choke Zenith carburettor drew warm air from the bottom of the crankcase and provided mixture to the outer pair of cylinders from one tube and the inner two from the other.

Standard Vauxhall multi-plate clutch and gearbox internals were used, but they were mated with the engine inside new castings and this initially created much additional work for Amherst when he needed to get at the gearbox or clutch – either the entire engine/transmission unit or the rear axle had to be taken out, since a cross member of the ladder-frame chassis ran beneath the gearbox and prevented tipping the unit up. In due course, the cross member was cut in two and fitted with a bolt. Undoing this and tilting the engine casing up made it much easier to work on the transmission and saved many hours of work. Refitting the huge coil clutch spring was another regular challenge; once it sprung out and grazed Amherst's nose on its way to leaving a hole in the garage roof.

Vauxhall built three of the cars. In original form, they were capable of 115mph (185kmh), in spite of weighing 22cwt (1,118kg). The intention had been to enter them for the 1922 Grand Prix season, only for the formula to be switched to a 2-litre capacity. Indeed, if it were not for the fact that the RAC chose to run the first post-war Tourist Trophy under the old formula, it seems unlikely that the cars would ever have run as a works team.

As it was, in June 1922 they lined up for the TT race on the Isle of Man, against three of the previous year's Grand Prix Sunbeams and a trio of prototype Bentleys. Sunbeam's Jean Chassagne won the 302-mile (510km) race in a little under 5½ hours, and the sole surviving Vauxhall, the No. 2 car driven by the running shop foreman Osborne Payne, came home third some 19 minutes later.

Fortunately, the TT Vauxhalls soon recovered from their inauspicious debut, and only a month later, Matthew Park used the No. 1 car to set FTD at Shelsley Walsh in 53.8 seconds. He managed to knock more than a second off this a year later, but it will be recalled that this was the event at which Mays pipped him to FTD by a tenth of a second in *Cordon Rouge*.

In due course, all three TT Vauxhalls made their way into private hands. Park's car was acquired by Harold Clay, and borrowed by Mays to go second quickest at Shelsley in 1926. The No. 3 Vauxhall was the car lent to Mays by Peter Gurney at the eventful Holme Moss hill-climb two years earlier. The machine about to be unleashed on British motor sport as the *Vauxhall Villiers* was the No. 2 car, which Payne had taken to third place on its debut. Mays was about to become the first, and very probably the only man to drive all three TT Vauxhalls in competition.

In the spring of 1928 Amherst's mother Elaine took an extensive apartment on London's Kent Terrace for 'the season', overlooking the western perimeter of Regent's Park. Handily positioned between Sackville Street and Stanwell Moor, this suited Amherst admirably. Conversely, Mays's father Thomas was unwell, so Mays and Berthon were expected, at least during the week, to be in Bourne taking care of his business. It therefore made sense for Amherst to take the newly acquired car and supercharger to Stanwell Moor for reassembly.

As would be the case on the Blower Bentley, the supercharger on the AC had been fitted horizontally beneath a modified radiator. On the Vauxhall, it was mounted vertically and behind the radiator. Embossed 'AMHERST VILLIERS' in large lettering at its base, it was driven off the front of the crankshaft and flanked by a pair of Zenith aero carburettors. Amherst also fitted new pistons with thicker crowns, and replaced the original coil and battery ignition with a pair of magnetos.

Enveloped in a new, two-seater body painted in the usual Mays blue-grey colours, this, then, was the specification of the *Vauxhall Villiers* when Mays first tested it on the road running by the Staines reservoirs near Amherst's workshop. The two men tweaked the car over several days, grateful that the engine and supercharger noise echoing off the banks of the reservoirs did not attract any interest from the nearby Staines police station.

Mays pronounced the *Vauxhall Villiers* ready for the May Shelsley Walsh meeting, but it suffered engine failure soon after leaving the start line and Davenport, now running *Spider* on homemade alcohol fuel brewed in a disused henhouse, lowered the course record to 46.8 seconds and ran out winner by a massive 3.6 seconds. Third was the impressive May Cunliffe – one of Britain's finest women racing drivers, she drove her recently-acquired 2-litre Grand Prix Sunbeam up the hill in 51.2 seconds.

The *Vauxhall Villiers* was on better form for the second Shelsley meeting of 1928, which was brought forward to July. Mays was not entirely happy with his time of 48 seconds, for he knew that he had lost time through excessive wheelspin at the start and some tail-sliding on his way up the hill, and was not surprised to have to cede FTD to Davenport again. But Davenport's time, another hill record in 46.2 seconds, was disconcerting. How was he to be defeated?

Fortunately, that year's sand racing events proved more successful. At Skegness, Mays used the *Vauxhall Villiers* to set FTD in the speed-trial, and won the longer circuit event, with Berthon as passenger, in the Bugatti which Amherst had acquired from Jack Kruse. In June the three men took both cars to Southport for the annual speed trials and 100-mile race, at that time the longest race in Britain held outside Brooklands.

In the mile-long Southport speed trials, Mays, in the *Vauxhall Villiers*, comfortably beat Davenport in the unlimited class, but just missed out to Jack Dunfee's Sunbeam. The 100-mile race was likely to prove even more challenging. Twenty-four drivers were to line up in three ranks to race on a 2-mile track comprising two straights linked at one end by a wide-radius sweep and at the other by a sharp hairpin that was expected to rut up considerably. Odds-on favourite was Malcolm Campbell in a 1½-litre Delage. Rank outsider was Amherst, who had elected to try his hand as a racing driver, at the wheel of his Bugatti.

A picture of the start shows Mays roaring away in the *Vauxhall Villiers*, sand spraying up from the rear wheels, while Amherst is back in the pack, both hands off the steering wheel, still adjusting his goggles. Perhaps he was wise; Berthon, riding as mechanic to Mays, lost his goggles early on and spent most of the 100 miles with his eyes tightly shut.

Down the back straight on lap one, Mays was leading, but gradually Campbell gained the upper hand and was a lap up by half distance. He seemed destined to win when the *Vauxhall Villiers* went on to three cylinders and Berthon, his attentive listening to the engine perhaps aided by his lack of vision, recommended Mays to continue but only at reduced speed. The logic of his advice became clear when Campbell was forced to retire with 11 laps remaining, his rear axle having broken on the bumpy sand. Mays was left with a handsome lead over May Cunliffe, who had her father riding as passenger in her Sunbeam. Tragically, he was killed when she took the hairpin too tightly and overturned, and Mays was left to win the Southport 100 in joyless circumstances. Amherst's brief adventure as a racing driver left him fourth overall, and second in the 2-litre class.

So the *Vauxhall Villiers*'s first season had met with some success and some reliability issues, but the main lesson was that somehow Amherst would have to give the car a greater power-to-weight ratio if Mays was to win Shelsley again. This was easier said than done – at the end of its seventh season of racing, much of it at bumpy Brooklands, the car's chassis frame showed signs of cracking. The solution was to bolt deep plates to each side member, which dealt with the cracks and made for a more rigid chassis, but increased the weight.

Over the winter of 1928 the car was taken back to Amherst's workshop, and plans put in hand to find more performance. His future brother-in-law, Desmond Fitz-Gerald, Ireland's 28th Knight of Glin, was one who paid a visit to review the work at Stanwell Moor. His diary entry for 27 October reads: 'Amhurst [sic] and I motored over to his works to see the racing Vauxhall he is building with the Villiers supercharger fitted. It is one of the most beautifully fitted jobs I have ever seen.'[1]

Progress, in fact, was slower than anticipated since, unlike the previous spring, Amherst found he was no longer between projects. Tim Birkin had presented him with one of the most exciting challenges imaginable – the supercharging of the 4½-litre Bentley, to take on Caracciola and Mercedes at Le Mans. Mays was magnanimous about this development. In *Split Seconds* he writes, 'I would never have dreamt of standing in Amherst's way at what was obviously a turning point in his fortunes.'[2]

Nevertheless, Amherst's Blower Bentley work meant that, in May

1929, when Mays drew up at the Shelsley Walsh start line in the *Villiers Supercharge* – now clad in white bodywork, his grey-blue colours transferred to the seats – the only new development on the car was its Clayton-Dewandre brakes, with a vacuum servo cylinder on each wheel. It was not enough. Mays managed to improve on his July 1928 time by 0.2 seconds, Davenport failed to match his by the same margin, and that still enabled the northerner to take his sixth consecutive Shelsley FTD by 1.4 seconds.

Shortly afterwards, Amherst came free of his Bentley work, and turned his exclusive attention to the Vauxhall, redesigning its pistons, valves and cooling system, fitting stiffer valve springs and a new radiator, and increasing the supercharger's boost pressure. Back up on the Bourne Fen road, Mays's favourite testing ground, the car was now delivering more than 250bhp, and revving in excess of 5,500rpm. This increased power gave Mays a new challenge: excessive wheelspin from a standing start. And this was on a straight road; combined with the car's stiffer chassis, more bhp would mean more fish-tailing out of Kennel Bend and the Esses. How could the tyres be made to grip the road better?

Amherst instigated some standing-start experiments. First, he noticed that Mays was leaving long black strips of rubber on the road. But, as he progressively lowered the pressures of the rear tyres, so the tyre marks shortened and Mays shot away all the quicker. Taken to the extreme, excessively low pressure tyres simply ripped themselves from their wheels, but Amherst knew he was on to something, and searched for another way of increasing the rear tyres' contact point with the road surface. He calmly concluded that the solution was twin-rear wheels. As was to happen so often throughout their partnership, this meant that he and Mays had much last-minute work on their hands if they were to be ready for the September 1929 Shelsley Walsh. With practice runs now allowed on the day before the Saturday event, Thursday was spent in Birmingham, fitting the new twin-rear wheels.

On the Friday morning, the Shelsley paddock was agog at the sight of the uniquely-shod *Vauxhall Villiers*. Amherst stationed himself at various points on the hill as Mays, with Berthon riding as passenger, took three practice runs and familiarised himself with the new slingshot effect off the start line, the revised cutting points on the bends required to allow for the wider wheels, and the extra adhesion accelerating away from the Esses.

On the Saturday, as usual, the competition for FTD was the exclusive preserve of Basil Davenport and Raymond Mays, and both were down for late runs. Davenport shot up the hill in 47 seconds dead, 0.8 seconds short of his record, but still the fastest yet. Then it was Mays's turn in the *Vauxhall Villiers*. Even with his four low-profile rear wheels, the tail slid out at Kennel Bend and the outer rear wheel grazed the bank on the exit, but still Mays recorded 46.2 seconds.

As Simon Taylor recorded in his centenary celebration, *The Shelsley Walsh Story*, 'an era was about to end, and another begin'.[3] Davenport would never set FTD at Shelsley again; on his second run his engine cried enough at the Esses. Mays, in his jubilation, went faster yet, taking FTD and lowering the hill record to 45.6 seconds. It was the first of five official Shelsley Walsh records for him, and he would make FTD there a further 19 times, the last of them in 1950.

Amherst had, at a stroke, made it *de rigueur* for hill-climb cars to be clad in twin-rear wheels. At the first Shelsley meeting of 1930 he was amused to see cars which could not possibly benefit from them, and which could only be slowed by the additional weight and drag, nonetheless fitted with them. The ultimate compliment was paid to him in June 1936, when Hans Stuck arrived in Worcestershire with the awesome 550bhp V16 Grand Prix Auto Union. It, too, was sporting twin rear wheels.

Mays found that his name was currency again. At the following month's Motor Show at Olympia – the one at which Amherst slapped an injunction on Bentley – his meeting with the sales manager of India Tyres led to a £250 retaining fee (the modern equivalent is more than £11,000, or almost US$15,000) and free tyres for the 1930 season, as well as a valuable PR campaign with the Vauxhall the following winter.

Going into 1930, the car was now entering its ninth season of competition, and Amherst set about his most ambitious development programme with it yet. It would be needed. The July Shelsley Walsh meeting had become a round of the European Hillclimb Championship. Some of the Continental giants – men such as Rudolf Caracciola and Hans Stuck – were expected, so competition would be even stiffer and times were expected to tumble, especially since the Midland Automobile Club had chosen to mark the occasion by resurfacing the course.

When the old car reappeared, it had a new name; henceforth, it would be known as the *Villiers Supercharge*. Its appearance had radically altered, too, and it was barely recognisable as a TT Vauxhall anymore. The front dumb-bells were encased in streamlined bodywork, the radiator was shorter, squatter and slightly inclined, and new, low-line bonnet and tail-mounted fuel tank fitted. The most sinister looking change was the intercooler jutting out though the right-hand side of the bonnet, necessitated by the need to lower the temperature of the hot mixture between the supercharger and the inlet manifold. It took the form of a long aluminium tube with inner and outer walls between which the mixture passed, cooled on its way by the fins surrounding both walls. More than one Shelsley wag commented on its similarity to a machine gun.

Under the bodywork were many more developments. New bearings for the crankshaft were lubricated by a revised, pressure-fed oil system. A revised cylinder block had been fashioned in a new, lighter metal, and revised connecting rods fitted. Blower pressure was increased still further, and the engine could now rev to 6,000rpm. Mays quite rightly considered this to be an extraordinary speed for a 3-litre engine with a stroke of 130mm, claiming that it 'represented a piston-speed of nearly 500ft per sec., or half the speed of a small-bore rifle bullet!'[4] Little wonder an intercooler was needed.

The core team of Mays, Amherst and Berthon, had, by now, been augmented by Amherst's star employee from his supercharging business, Tom Murray Jamieson. Even so, the reassembly of the car ahead of Shelsley was the usual last-minute job, so much so that the practice day was missed altogether. They set off for Worcestershire in the early hours of the day of the meeting, Amherst and Mays in the *Villiers Supercharge* and the rest of the team aboard Mays's road car, but they had only travelled as far as Stamford – some 15 miles from Bourne – when they threw the towel in; the car simply wasn't capable of a competitive performance.

Leaving it in a lock-up garage, they pushed on for Shelsley and arrived in the early evening, to be greeted with the news that Hans Stuck, on his first run in his 3½-litre Austro-Daimler, had shattered Mays's record of ten months previously by 2.8 seconds, and had set precisely the same time – 42.8 seconds – on his second. There was time for a pleasant meal with Stuck and his compatriot Caracciola, who had just broken Shelsley's sports car record, and a quick look at the Austro-Daimler. Its power output, some 200bhp, was not as great as the *Villiers Supercharge*, but the car weighed barely half that of its English rival. Where on earth were 3 seconds to be found?

On the late-night journey back to Bourne, at least Amherst could console himself with thoughts of the car which set 7th fastest time of the day. It may not have been the *Villiers Supercharge*, but it was a TT Vauxhall – the ex-Matthew Park, ex-Harold Clay, No. 1 car – and it was fitted with one of Amherst's superchargers. Its owner and driver was David Brown, future owner of the Aston Martin and Lagonda marques, and the nature of his business relationship with Amherst will be explored in Chapter 10.

The team used the eight weeks before the September Shelsley to good effect. In a practice run on the hill the day before the event proper, Mays got the *Villiers Supercharge* within 0.2 seconds of Stuck's remarkable time. Surely, in the white heat of competition, adrenaline alone would enable him to find more than a fifth of a second? Heavy rain prevented him from finding out. He did indeed set FTD, but it was 'only' 48.4 seconds, almost 4 seconds outside Stuck's record. Mays also had another rival to watch out for; Dick Nash, at the wheel of an ex-Frazer Nash supercharged special called *Terror*, was the only other driver to beat 50 seconds.

Again Amherst could look fondly upon another car which had

performed creditably. Third fastest time of the day had gone to Alex Spottiswood, in 50 seconds dead. He was driving the ex-Jack Kruse Bugatti Type 35, sold to him earlier in the year by Amherst.

Over the winter of 1930/31, Amherst focused on his business and, in particular, the supercharging and race-tuning of an Austin Seven Ulster, which led directly to him losing Murray Jamieson to Austin (see Chapter 10). Mays, meanwhile, used the *Villiers Supercharge* in extensive PR activity with India Tyres, including some film work which was shown in Gaumont cinemas up an down the land. When this work extended beyond Christmas, Mays was able to acquire a 4½-litre Invicta sports car. Jamieson designed some modifications to its engine, and Mays was successful with the car in the sports class at the 1931 Shelsley Walsh meetings, and at Brooklands. With the *Villiers Supercharge*, however, results were mixed. Mays came second to Nash at the July Shelsley, but set FTD again in September, although heavy rain prevented him from seriously challenging Stuck's record.

Oddly, Mays also decided to take the *Villiers* to Brooklands for the Mountain Championship race. The old car now weighed in excess of 30cwt (1,524kg) compared with the 22cwt (1,118kg) of the original TT Vauxhall, and had not appeared at the circuit for more than four years. During that time it had been developed exclusively as a sprint and hill-climb car. It was decided that Amherst should join Mays and Berthon at the circuit to establish how the *Villiers Supercharge* would cope with lengthy running on the bumpy track. Unsurprisingly, regardless of alterations to tyre pressures, wheel balances and shock absorbers, the test was not a success. When the car vibrated so violently on the Byfleet Banking that Mays and Berthon momentarily lost vision altogether, the team concluded that it would be best for them and the *Villiers Supercharge* if it remained focused on hill-climbs and sprints.

The 1932 season was not a vintage one for the car. Now in its 11th season of competition, it had reached the limit of its development potential, and Amherst, the architect of the myriad developments undertaken over the previous five years, was devoting more time to his business.

In June 1932, he was on hand once more to support Mays at Shelsley Walsh. This was the occasion when the BBC held its first ever outside broadcast of a motor sport event, prompted, at least in part, by the guaranteed ferocity of the sound the *Villiers Supercharge* would make on its way up the hill. It was also the meeting at which Ettore Bugatti sent his son Jean over to see how he would fare in a rare, four-wheel-drive Type 53, but Jean hit the bank at Kennel Bend so hard during practice that he never found out.

Radio listeners as far away as Australia heard Mays set a time of 44.6 seconds in the old *Villiers*. Nash missed out by not completing his first run and hitting both banks exiting the Esses on his second. But a surprise was in store. The fifth Earl Howe, Francis Curzon, had only taken up motor racing four years earlier, at the age of 44, but he demonstrated how good a driver he had become by winning Le Mans the previous summer with Tim Birkin. Here at Shelsley, he upheld Bugatti honour by taking his Type 51 up the hill in 44 seconds dead.

Worse was to come for Mays and the *Villiers Supercharge* at the September meeting: warming the old car up on a public road a few miles from Shelsley, he broke the crankshaft. Amherst helped to tow the car into the paddock, and once again he found some consolation through his interest in another car competing on the hill. A customer of his, Ron Horton, had recorded a time of 44.8 seconds in his *Horton Special*, good enough for third place overall and a class win. The *Horton's* chassis was a one-off, developed by Robin Jackson in his Brooklands workshop and powered by an early 1,100cc Alta engine. Poking out from under the radiator, just as on the 1925 AC and the Blower Bentley, was an Amherst Villiers supercharger. Mays, too, was consoled when he took the Invicta up the hill in 45.6 seconds, the fastest Shelsley climb by a sports car yet.

The performances of the *Horton Special* and the white Invicta gave advanced notice of a parting of the ways. Amherst was spending more and more time on his business, and was starting to focus on aero engine development. He therefore wanted to be released from his responsibility for the *Villiers Supercharge*. Meanwhile, his great friend's success with the white Invicta had generated such interest that Victor Riley readily agreed to the supercharging of his 1½-litre racing car for Mays to drive in 1933. With design and development input from Jamieson and Berthon, and financial support from Humphrey Cook, the *White Riley*, as it became known, was made ready in record time and would have a highly successful season, leading directly to the formation, a year later, of English Racing Automobiles Ltd (ERA). With Cook's assistance, Mays bought out Amherst's interest in the *Villiers Supercharge,* and the old car entered its final season in front-line British motor sport – its 12th – without the man it was named after. It would do him proud.

The May 1933 Shelsley Walsh meeting was run in pouring rain, so once again there would be no serious attempts on Stuck's record, but Mays set FTD again in 44.8 seconds. It was the fourth time that Mays had driven the car initially known as the *Vauxhall Villiers*, and latterly the *Villiers Supercharge*, to Fastest Time of the Day at Britain's premier hill-climb.

The Shelsley meeting of 30 September 1933 enjoyed splendid autumn sunshine, and an air of expectancy hung over the hill. Surely, this was the day when Hans Stuck's three-year-old record of 42.8 seconds would finally fall. Many eyes were on a young American, Willard Whitney Straight, who had impressed in May at the wheel of a 2½-litre Maserati. Mays's hopes rested chiefly on the *White Riley*, but he had also brought along the old *Villiers Supercharge* one last time. As he recorded in his autobiography, 'I could not resist entering that good old car for Shelsley, in addition to the new Riley, because I always wanted to prove that she could beat Stuck's record, and also because for sentimental reasons I did not like going to Shelsley without her.'[5]

Mays realised the promise of the *White Riley* by racing up the hill in 42.2 seconds, finally getting under Stuck's time, but he did not hold the record for long, as Straight posted a time of 41.4 seconds, the first time Shelsley had been climbed in under 42 seconds. On his second run Straight went faster still and left the record at a breath-taking 41.2 seconds.

By then, Raymond Mays had had his final competitive run in the *Villiers Supercharge*, and a marvellous one it was at that. Again, in his own words:

> *That lovely note of the Villiers rose in crescendo as the twin wheels spun off the mark. The good old car fairly hurled herself up the famous gradient, but after the Riley she felt a bit cumbersome and heavy. We reached the finish after an exciting run in 42.4 seconds – not quite fast enough to beat Whitney . . . [but] . . . at long last it had been proved that the good old Villiers could just better the Austro Daimler's magical time.*[6]

It was a wonderful way to bow out. Mays went off to start his ERA adventure, and the car was sold to Sid Cummings, who continued campaigning it until 1937. After the Second World War Tony Brooke found its engine in an old Bugatti, fitted it into an unused TT Vauxhall chassis discovered in the possession of a former Jack Barclay mechanic, and gradually brought it back to something approximating its 1929 specification. In 1964 he took it up Shelsley Walsh quicker than Mays ever managed in it, albeit on a *much* better road surface. The car was subsequently acquired by former Vintage Sports-Car Club president Julian Ghosh, and today, in its original red Vauxhall racing colours, it resides in the museum at Brooklands, where its former owners, Humphrey Cook and Jack Barclay, had raced it.

Peter Berthon, Tom Murray Jamieson and Humphrey Cook all played their part in the legend of the *Villiers Supercharge*, and all would support Mays at ERA. The only one who did not was Amherst Villiers, the man the Vauxhall was named after. He had first met Raymond Mays when a 14-year-old schoolboy. Together they had given up their summer holidays in 1917 to produce munitions in the Oundle workshops for the war effort. At Cambridge Amherst had given his friend the archetypal 'unfair advantage' over his Inter-Varsity rivals with his developments to *Quicksilver*. The stepped increase in performance delivered by Amherst on Mays's Brescia Bugatti was so great that *Le Patron* himself invited them out to Molsheim and gave them a second car for free. Together they cut their supercharging teeth through that challenging year with the AC. And together, on the *Villiers Supercharge*, they transformed a car rendered obsolete by a rule change before it had turned a wheel into something so potent that it was still breaking records at one of Britain's most important motor sport events in its 12th season.

The partnership had been based on a highly effective division of labour: Amherst the developer, frequently showing an originality of thought of which his friend could only dream, and Mays, the consummate driver and wheeler-dealer. Was there anything else at the heart of the association? Clearly, Amherst and Ray were great friends and would remain so. But it is an established fact that Raymond Mays was a homosexual, and he and Amherst spent so much time together in the 1920s – regularly living under the same roof at Eastgate House, and sharing a room at the Grosvenor while developing the AC – that it is legitimate to ask if they were lovers.

Amherst was twice married, and the father of two children. He was happily married to their mother, his second wife Nita, for more than 20 years. Even before her death in 1968 there were girlfriends, and there were more after. Indeed, towards the end of his life he told motor racing historian Doug Nye, 'I am not looking forward to my interview with God. I've fucked too many women!'[7] So it seems most unlikely that he and Mays were involved in a gay relationship in the 1920s. Even if they were, Amherst would hardly have been the first young man of his background and time to have experimented in this way.

Regardless of what lay at the heart of their relationship as young men, their working partnership on *Quicksilver*, *Cordon Rouge*, *Cordon Bleu* and the *Villiers Supercharge* delivered enormous success. Even their trials with the AC were not in vain; as S. F. Edge had forecast, the lessons learned served them well when it came to supercharging the Vauxhall. It is fascinating to imagine what effect Amherst would have had on ERA and BRM, or indeed whether history would have judged him a greater success if he had remained focused solely on performance cars.

The fact remains that the partnership between Amherst and Raymond Mays was now over, and the two men would not work together again for almost 30 years. Amherst was displaying that same independence of thought which had driven his father through his short Parliamentary career, and his mother to marry for love rather than money. He was off to try his hand as a businessman, straddling the automotive and aeronautic fields.

Before we learn how he got on, it is necessary to examine the motor racing legend with which he is most associated – the Blower Bentley.

Chapter 9

THE ENIGMA OF THE BLOWER BENTLEY

Not unlike Amherst watching the scintillating opening laps of the Fiats at Brooklands in 1923, or Raymond Mays pondering his defeat to Dario Resta's Sunbeam at Aston the following year, so Tim Birkin's supercharging epiphany came at the Nürburgring, during the German Grand Prix of July 1928.

He was racing a 4½-litre, normally aspirated Bentley, and his performance attracted much positive comment, the Mercedes chairman even claiming that his lap times were so consistent that people could set their watches by him. This was, in truth, faint praise, since the supercharged, 7-litre SSK Mercedes had just finished first, second, third and fifth, while Birkin had trailed home eighth, and felt that he, too, needed a supercharger if he were to redress the balance.

The following month, the Tourist Trophy was given a new lease of life, run for the first time since the 1922 event which had witnessed the competitive debut of the car which became the *Villiers Supercharge*. Now the race was to be hosted at Ards, named after the town through which the circuit ran, Newtownards in Northern Ireland. The works Bentleys chose not to participate, on the grounds that the handicapping was unfair – the action which stung Jack Kruse into criticising the company in the correspondence pages of *The Motor* – but Birkin was to race his own Bentley.

The revived Tourist Trophy had attracted massive pre-race publicity, and though Amherst had no personal involvement in it, he decided to take a break from his work on the *Villiers Supercharge*, and lead a party of friends and family over to Ireland. The plan was to drop in on various society contacts and take in not only the TT, but also the Dublin Horse Show. Among his party was his younger sister Veronica. While visiting Kilruddery House near Dublin, home of the Earl and Countess of Meath, Amherst and Veronica met the heir to Glin Castle in County Limerick, the future 28th Knight of Glin.

Known in motor racing circles as Desmond Fitz-Gerald, he had raced and entered a wide range of cars at Brooklands. Until recently he had run a car business with another Brooklands driver, Alastair Miller. Fitz-Gerald was most taken with Veronica, and when he learned that his feelings were reciprocated, he used the back seat of Amherst's car to propose to her. The following January they were married, Amherst giving his sister away in a ceremony at St Peter's Church, in London's Eaton Square.

Over the years, Veronica's choice of husbands (she married a second time in 1954) would prove important to Amherst, but in August 1928, his main focus was on attending the TT. His friend Tim Birkin won his class in his 4½-litre Bentley, but managed only fifth overall on handicap. First and second places fell to a Lea-Francis and an Alvis, both of them supercharged, and Birkin became all the more keen to benefit from Amherst's expertise in supercharging.

Sir Henry Ralph Stanley Birkin had been nicknamed Tim by his sister Ida, after the children's comic book character Tiger Tim. He was born in July 1896 into a family whose great wealth had been generated in the lace industry. However, fortune deserted the family in other respects: elder brother Thomas was killed in the First World War while serving in Salonika, Ida lost her life to tuberculosis in 1923, and four years later younger brother Archie died in a wretched motorcycle accident on the Isle of Man, hitting a fish cart during practice for the TT in the days when the roads were closed only on race day. Little wonder that Tim's father did not care for his choice of career as a racing driver.

Tim Birkin had endured an eventful war, first with the 7th Sherwood Foresters, then with the Royal Warwickshire Regiment, and finally as a Captain in the RFC, contracting malaria while serving in

Palestine, and as he famously recorded in his autobiography, *Full Throttle*, he was not inclined to settle down, finding 'the view of my future life, as I then beheld it, a very dull and confined one; it was bounded by the four walls of an office, which afforded none of the excitements of the career I was leaving . . . motor racing provided the energy, adventures, and risks most like those of the battlefield.'[1]

A small, slight man with a pronounced stutter, Birkin may have appeared the antithesis of a motor racing hero, but wrote, 'once I am in the car, when there is no need to talk or to concentrate on anything but the race, all my awkwardness disappears; I feel at home, I feel as happy as a king.'[2]

His early racing was at the wheel of a French car, a DFP, which had benefited from some work carried out by a British distributor named Bentley and Bentley, one of the proprietors of which was Walter Owen ('WO') Bentley. When Birkin married Audrey Latham in 1921, he vowed to give up racing, and spent much of his time in the Norfolk coastal town of Blakeney where they had honeymooned. He became a crack shot – once bagging 47 birds from 50 shots – and a fine sailor, but made more rapid progress over the water when he inherited his sister's 30ft racing launch. Ida had first fallen ill while working in a Nottingham hospital during the war, and subsequently spent time in Switzerland, convalescing in the mountain air and enjoying her speedboat on Lake Geneva.

After her death, Birkin arranged for the *Ida* to be fitted with a 6-cylinder, Louis Coatelen-tuned, Sunbeam engine, but since he owned several boats and hydroplanes in Blakeney, it is by no means certain that it was this vessel which subsequently used Amherst's supercharged AC engine.

What is clear is that when Birkin returned to motor racing after he and his wife divorced in 1927, one of his earliest ventures was with Amherst. This was the last roll of the dice for the old AC, which Amherst returned to single-seater mode and entered at Brooklands as the *Villiers-Birkin Special*, without success.

For the next three years, Birkin largely raced Bentleys. Their founder, W.O. Bentley, was some eight years Birkin's senior, and had enjoyed a gentle upbringing in the north London suburb of St John's Wood, becoming entranced by the steam locomotives heading north on their way from King's Cross. His love of trains led him to a gruelling five-year apprenticeship at the Great Northern Railway locomotive works in Doncaster, Yorkshire, at the end of which he and his brother acquired the DFP dealership.

WO took to developing and racing a 2-litre DFP, and breaking class records in it at Brooklands. The aluminium pistons he fitted to it were a notable breakthrough, proving more reliable than either light steel or cast iron variants. This led him to serve with the Royal Naval Air Service during the First World War. One company he worked with was Gwynne, which was manufacturing French Clerget rotary engines under licence, and struggling with their pistons distorting in the airstream after as little as 15 hours of service. WO later wrote, 'this was an expensive way to gain air supremacy over the Western Front',[3] and soon the car-makers Humber had been switched to the manufacture of two WO-designed rotary aero engines, the BR1 and BR2, which served with distinction in the Sopwith Camel.

Even before the Armistice, WO's mind had turned to developing his own car, and though he returned to the DFP dealership he had run with his brother, and arranged for some of the components of his pre-war record-breaker to be fitted to Birkin's first racing car, he was soon working on a 3-litre design of his own, to satisfy the sports car market which he felt had been ill-served before the war.

Though the car took some time to appear, vital publicity was generated when three prototype Bentleys finished second, fourth and fifth in the 1922 Tourist Trophy, the race in which the TT Vauxhalls had first appeared. Bentley lifted the team prize, and WO himself was at the wheel of the fourth-place car, finishing only six seconds behind Osborne Payne's Vauxhall after 5½ hours of racing.

The names of Bentley and Le Mans first became linked two years later, when John Duff and Frank Clement won the great race in a 3-litre model, and though Bentley Motors was in such poor financial health by 1926 that diamond millionaire Woolf 'Babe' Barnato had to bale it out, racing success continued. The 3-litre was therefore an obvious choice of car for Tim Birkin as his return to motor racing gathered pace the following year.

Tim and his brother Archie entered the Bentley for the Brooklands Six Hour race in May and, assisted by Clement when Archie's driving proved somewhat erratic, they finished third. Precisely one month later Archie was dead, killed on the stretch of road still known to motorcycle fans today as Birkin's Bend, and Tim, now the sole surviving child of Sir Thomas Birkin, gave Le Mans a miss two weeks later. He did not, therefore, witness the famous win by Sammy Davis and Dudley Benjafield, who valiantly nursed home a car badly damaged in a six-car pile-up at White House corner, or the debut of the 4½-litre Bentley, which led convincingly until becoming involved in the mêlée.

The performance of the new car at Le Mans, and its win later that summer in the Grand Prix de Paris, a 24-hour race held at France's own banked circuit, Montlhéry, made the 4½-litre Bentley's weapon of choice for 1928. Birkin, now very much one of 'the Bentley Boys', drove with distinction in a 4½-litre at the Brooklands Six Hour Race, covering the greatest distance, winning his class and finishing third overall. Then he and the veteran French driver Jean Chassagne performed heroics at Le Mans, recovering from a three-hour delay to finish fifth, while Barnato, partnered by Bernard Rubin, secured the first of his unique sequence of three wins from three starts.

Yet by that autumn, after being outclassed at the Nürburgring and in the TT, Birkin was demanding that the 4½-litre Bentley be supercharged by Amherst. WO fundamentally disagreed, famously arguing in his autobiography, 'To supercharge a Bentley engine was to pervert its design and corrupt its performance . . . I always held that the supercharger applied to the Bentley engine was, by its nature, a false inducer.'[4]

WO also had concerns about the financial and production implications of going in with Amherst. Regulations demanded that if the supercharged car were to race at Le Mans, 50 production models would have to be built – no light undertaking. However, WO no longer controlled the company that bore his name, and Barnato decreed that Birkin would have his wish: the 4½-litre would be supercharged by Amherst.

Unfortunately, the arrangement between Amherst, Birkin and Bentley Motors was riddled with compromise. As Amherst later recalled, 'WO never really liked the idea of an outside engineer coming in, of course, but it was more or less thrust down his throat and he had to accept it because of financial pressure.'[5] Nevertheless, Amherst's involvement in the project, as laid out in his October 1928 agreement with Bentley Motors, was restricted to the design of the supercharger and various ancillaries, and provision of the first four units.

Moreover, WO was adamant that Bentley would not race the Blower themselves, but would campaign the Speed Six, a performance version of the 6½-litre model which had been in production since 1926. It would be left to Tim Birkin to race a team of Blowers, and he rented a pair of factory units in Welwyn Garden City, in Hertfordshire, and began to build a workforce which, at its peak, numbered some 30 people.

The man brought in as works manager at Welwyn was Clive Gallop, who was well known to both Birkin and WO. Before the First World War, he had worked for Peugeot and raced its cars, and it was his familiarity with the French company's 3-litre engine which prompted WO to make him an early employee of his fledgling company. But Gallop had also supported Birkin at the beginning of the decade when he raced the DFP, and later worked with Count Louis Zbrowski on his *Chitty-Bang-Bang* cars, which very much belonged to the old school of mating a vast aero engine to a rudimentary chassis. By 1928, Gallop still raced occasionally in his own right, but a serious accident in that first Ards Tourist Trophy race encouraged him to quit racing and take up Birkin's offer to become his works manager.

Amherst was not a fan of Gallop, telling Mike McCarthy in a 1983 interview:

He was a very tiresome man because he was one of those people who knew everything and wouldn't listen to anyone else. To me, you're learning all the time, and you've got to keep a very open mind. Anyway, Gallop became the 'expert' and Tim swallowed all his guff . . . The dry sump lubrication system went out the window, of course, and instead of the cars being designed and built properly from the beginning it all went off half-cocked. It's amazing to me how much the cars did achieve, in fact.[6]

A further challenge was the lack of supercharging expertise at Bentley. Nobby Clarke had first met WO during the First World War. He was recruited as Bentley Motors' first mechanic, and subsequently promoted to foreman and then service manager. He managed Bentley's pits at Brooklands and Le Mans, and continued as service works manager long after Rolls-Royce's acquisition of Bentley, finally retiring in 1958. As such, his opinion is to be respected, and some 35 years after Amherst developed the supercharger for the Blower Bentley, Clarke told the author of *The Other Bentley Boys*, Elizabeth Nagle, 'The trouble with superchargers was that we knew nothing about them at the time. Nothing about the effect of pressures, or the effect of overloading – all the problems related to them. We'd no idea how they would behave; we were only on the fringe of knowing something about blowers, and the results proved it.'[7]

A notable example of this is described by Michael Hay in his definitive book on the Blower Bentley.[8] It was not until Barnato himself drove his own Blower, the ninth of the production cars, to the south of France and back that he suggested lowering its compression ratio, and the company found this improved the car's acceleration. Bentley had stumbled upon a paradox of forced induction; its greater volumetric efficiency (the ratio between the volume of fuel/air mixture entering the cylinder, and the cylinder's actual capacity) means that more mixture can be ignited, producing a bigger bang, so that, as Hay notes, more power is generated by lowering the compression ratio. He also records that the service record for Barnato's car dates this change in compression ratio to March 1931, some two years after Amherst's involvement with Bentley ended.

Amherst, armed with four years of valuable experience of superchargers and their implications for an engine's lubrication and ventilation, was effectively shut out of both the Bentley and Birkin camps, neither of whom had anything like as much knowledge of blowers. He was particularly concerned about the standard Bentley crankshaft, telling Eoin Young during their 1974 interview, 'I couldn't understand how the centre bearing could remain in, because here were these two big weights with the centre connecting rods coming round and nothing but the poor little centre bearing to hold it straight.'[9] He actually drew his counter-balanced crankshaft, which weighed almost half as much again as the standard one, one Saturday afternoon in Birkin's London apartment.

'Half-cocked' or not, the project began in earnest when Bentley gave Amherst a set of blueprints of the 4½-litre engine, and he set to work. Hay has identified that the earliest of his Blower drawings is dated December 1928, and the latest March 1929. The crankcase was modified to take the counter-balanced crank, the cylinder block stiffened, and the connecting rods shortened and stiffened to allow for stronger, flat-top pistons.

The supercharger itself was another of Amherst's Roots-type blowers. As initially drawn by him, it had smooth inner and outer casings, but since, at the increased temperatures generated at speed, expansion of the former was restricted by the latter and risked fouling the rotors, later units had a single casing which was ribbed to permit more consistent heat dissipation. This is interesting, as period photographs of the AC's supercharger appear to show a ribbed casing, and visitors to the Brooklands Museum today can clearly see the blower on the *Villiers Supercharge* has one. A photograph of Amherst working on that car's engine at Eastgate House also shows the detached blower sitting behind him on a chair, clad in a ribbed casing. It has not proved possible to date that image precisely, but the presence of Tom Murray Jamieson in the background indicates that it post-dates Amherst's involvement with the Blower Bentley.

In Amherst's own brochure, 50 copies of which were printed to coincide with the launch of the production Blower Bentley at the London Motor Show of October 1929, a section is devoted to 'Silence'. In it, Amherst writes that 'careful design of the air passages and ports, and the use of double-walled rotor cases, enables us to avoid pneumatic noise.'[10] However, on racing cars such as the AC and *Villiers Supercharge*, and, as the roving *Autocar* reporter noted at Brooklands, on Jack Kruse's unique Rolls-Royce, Amherst had not given a thought to noise. Now that his supercharger was to be fitted to 50 road-going production Bentleys, and he was trying to develop his supercharging business, silence was a selling point. But reliability at racing speeds was a much more important criterion, and it seems that post-Blower Bentley versions of the Vauxhall's supercharger followed the revisions made to the unit on the Bentley.

The position of Amherst's supercharger on the Bentley, thrust boldly out beyond the radiator, is also intriguing. It follows Amherst's practice on the AC, but is quite different from the arrangement on the *Villiers Supercharge*, where the blower is situated under the bonnet, at right angles to the engine/transmission unit. It may be that Amherst wanted to follow the arrangement on the AC, and clearly the blower's position in the airstream could only help to dissipate the great temperatures generated by supercharging. As it was, cooling on the Birkin cars was always marginal, and their bonnets were noted for their many louvres and slots. But it seems WO gave Amherst no option. Young reports, 'When the two men met, WO made it clear that he didn't want the blower under the bonnet cluttering up his clean engine room. It had to be mounted out in front.'[11]

Today, it is generally thought that Amherst received no payment from Bentley for his work. Indeed, in those fatalistic interviews of the 1970s and 1980s, this is exactly what Amherst claimed. After interviewing him in 1974, Eoin Young wrote, 'The contract also called for the Villiers trade name to appear on all the superchargers (in accordance with his agreement to forego royalties) and in the Bentley catalogue.'[12] In 1983, he told Mike McCarthy that WO 'told me that he wasn't going to pay me because the publicity from having my name on the blower would be enough'.[13] And two years later, in the interview with Brian Palmer, Amherst claimed that WO 'said there would be no question of royalty . . . the superchargers would not go under the bonnet but be out in front and that I would get a lot of publicity from this and that would be enough.'[14]

In fact, 12 months after the agreement between Amherst and Bentley Motors had been drawn up, he had cause to take the company to court, and papers from that action relate that Amherst *was* paid for his design and production work, and that a further payment was made when the company standardised upon his design, a point defined as Bentley fitting Amherst's blower to a further six cars, over and above the original four. What is not known now is how much he was paid.

In recounting the run up to the 1929 season, Michael Hay records, 'At some point during this period, Villiers fell out with those around him, and left the project.'[15] As we have seen, Amherst did indeed have a low opinion of Clive Gallop, and clearly bridled against the restrictions imposed on him by W.O. Bentley, whom he scathingly referred to in later life as 'Old Pussy Face'.[16] But he never fell out with Birkin, who, when asked three years later by Alvis to race for them at Le Mans, replied that he would, provided that their car was supercharged by Amherst. Amherst was still assisting Birkin in June 1929, when the pair took the first Blower Bentley – Bernard Rubin's famous YU3250 – out on the Barnet bypass for its first test.

It seems far more likely that Amherst simply completed his contractual obligation to Bentley by delivering the four superchargers, supported Birkin in the run up to the Blower's first competitive outing, the Brooklands Six Hour Race of late June, and then returned to Eastgate House to crack on with the raft of engine, supercharger and twin rear wheel developments on the *Villiers Supercharge* which enabled Raymond Mays to break the hill record at Shelsley Walsh in September.

Birkin retired from that first race in the Blower, but recorded in *Full Throttle* that after it,

> *the supercharger was approved; it had only just been fitted, and meant an increase of 100 h.p. – 35 of which it required for itself – and a far swifter acceleration. To transmit the higher power of a supercharger involves much redesigning of engines, but the difference in speed between [a] 'blown' and 'unblown' Bentley is a difference between 125 and 108 m.p.h. and more than worth the trouble.*[17]

Formal approval of Amherst's supercharger completed his arrangement with Bentley Motors, and he passed all his drawings to the company. Among them was the drawing of the blower's front casing, showing how the words 'AMHERST VILLIERS SUPERCHARGER MARK IV' were to be embossed on it. Approval also marked Bentley's commitment to developing the 50 production models, and this meant that Birkin could look forward to going head-to-head with the supercharged SSK Mercedes at Le Mans the following year with his own team of forced-induction cars.

As for the balance of the 1929 season, the Birkin Blowers were no more successful than they had been on their debut. Birkin managed third place, and Rubin eighth, in July's Irish Grand Prix in Dublin's Phoenix Park. At the following month's Tourist Trophy, held again at Ards, Birkin, with the redoubtable WO on board as riding mechanic, set the second highest average speed, but could only manage 11th on handicap, and neither of his team-mates, Bernard Rubin and Beris Harcourt-Wood, finished. In the season-closer, the 500 Mile Race at Brooklands, Birkin fought an enthralling duel with Kaye Don's Sunbeam at average speeds in excess of 120mph (193kmh), but the Bentley spewed out so much oil on to his goggles and windscreen that he had to make several pit stops and, 80 miles from the finish, the exhaust system that WO had advised was not up to the job caught fire and forced him into retirement.

Still, the irrepressible Birkin recorded in his biography that 'the year went out to the fanfare of British superchargers, and hopes were high for the future'.[18] The reason for his high hopes came in the rather large form of the woman to whom he had been giving high-performance driving lessons. Opinions vary as to how good a student the Hon. Dorothy Paget was. Michael Hay relates that a correspondent with the *Daily Telegraph* described her as 'one of the finest woman drivers of fast cars with whom I have ever come in contact', while hill-climb ace and noted motoring journalist and broadcaster John Bolster said 'she nearly caused a massacre by giving her Mercedes Benz full boost on the start line at Shelsley – in reverse!'[19]

Regardless of her personal prowess behind the wheel, and her utter aversion to men in general, Paget respected Birkin as a racing driver of the highest quality, and had experienced Amherst's supercharging wizardry in person after buying Jack Kruse's Phantom. She therefore decided to broaden her sporting ambitions beyond horse racing, and to sponsor Birkin's team. With proper funding finally in place, he was able to rebuild all three of his existing Blowers – one as a single-seater for Brooklands, and the other two on shorter chassis to improve their handling on road courses – and to add a fourth road car. He also arranged for all but the single-seater to be clad in the classic Vanden Plas body with which we associate the Blower Bentley today.

Back at Bentley Motors, extensive lubrication problems with the first production models were causing great tension ahead of the October 1929 London Motor Show. There was a real fear that a running car, with which to give demonstration runs to members of the press, would not be ready in time. In the end Bentley was obliged to borrow the engine from the Birkin car that had been crashed by Harcourt during the TT.

Amherst was an eager visitor to the Motor Show on 16 October. He was keen to start exploiting the opportunities presented to his business by Bentley launching the production version of the Blower, and his brochure was one way in which he planned to do this. However, much to his chagrin, when he inspected the cars on

Bentley's own stand and that of coachbuilders Freestone & Webb, he found that there was no reference to him on the front casings of their blowers, and nor was he or his supercharger mentioned in Bentley's catalogue. Before the day was out, Amherst had instructed a firm of lawyers, Kenneth Brown Baker Baker, to write to Bentley Motors, demanding that it withdraw both cars and the catalogues.

The firm were the lawyers of his new brother-in-law, Desmond Fitz-Gerald, and intriguingly Fitz-Gerald had arranged for Amherst to see them over two weeks earlier. His diary entry for 1 October reads, 'Arranged with Mirkle of Kenneth Browns to see Amhurst [sic] re infringement of the patents of his supercharger.'[20] That for 7 October records, 'In the morning took Amhurst [sic] to Mirkle of Kenneth Browns re his supercharger rights, satisfactory discussion.'[21] If Amherst's visit to the Motor Show was the earliest he knew about Bentley's failure to acknowledge him or his supercharger, then Bentley Motors was not the only party about whom he was taking legal advice.

Amherst's reaction to Bentley's slight, for that was how he perceived it, is typical of the man. How could anyone not do what he said he would do? What injustice! Bentley moved quickly to put things right, reprinting its brochure so that the last line (printed at an angle to the rest of the text), read 'The supercharger is the "Amherst Villiers Mark IV",'[22] and running up a small plate on which to fit the requisite wording to the front of the supercharger. This offended Amherst still further, for he felt that the tiny plate in no way matched the embossed lettering he had designed for the blower's front casing, and which had appeared on the Birkin cars raced over the previous months. But Amherst was losing his objectivity here; Bentley may have contractually agreed to have the words 'AMHERST VILLIERS SUPERCHARGER MARK IV' written on the front of the supercharger, but they had not agreed to the casting of that wording, and nor had they raced the Blowers fitted with the embossed lettering – Birkin had. Amherst even complained about the lack of publicity that he received in initial road tests of the production Blower, to which WO responded personally that Bentley Motors could hardly be held responsible for what the motoring press did not write.

All in all, the case of Amherst Villiers *v.* Bentley Motors Limited was an unfortunate affair, even making the Law Reports of *The Times* on two days.[23] There is little reason to believe that Bentley's omissions were anything other than mere oversights, caused by the haste with which they were preparing for the Motor Show. Even if something more sinister was afoot, surely a telegram or a personal call would have been preferable to taking out an injunction. By appointing a lawyer to win back a lost opportunity to generate publicity for his business, Amherst put his name in the press in a less than positive light, and caused his judgement to be questioned. This is not the last time this would happen; he was missing the presence of a commercially adept partner such as Raymond Mays.

At least the new motor racing season started positively for the Blower Bentley. At the first Brooklands meeting of 1930, held in March, Birkin drove the new single-seater to a win in a 4-lap handicap race. Then, over the Easter weekend, he won another handicap and raised the Brooklands lap record to 135.33mph (217.26kmh). The record had been the subject of a wager Birkin had made with Barnato, and after breaking it, Birkin promptly flew to Le Touquet to dine with the Bentley chairman and collect his winnings.

Then on 21 and 22 June came the Le Mans 24-Hours race at which the legend of the Blower Bentley was born. Only two of Birkin's three road cars could be made ready in time, and they complemented three works Speed Six cars entered by Bentley. In a thin field of only 17 cars, the chief competition would come from Rudolf Caracciola and Christian Werner in a 7-litre supercharged Mercedes Benz. The 'Bentley Boys' were concerned that the Germans would use the superior speed of their car to either pull away early on and manage their lead for the duration of the race, or simply trail the Bentleys and pick them off near the end.

The complex arrangement of the supercharger on the Mercedes was thought by the Bentley teams to be a weak link. It was clutch-operated and was meant to be used only in short bursts. At a lunch attended by both Bentley and Mercedes personnel a few days before the race, it emerged that the Germans were genuinely concerned about their blower, and the Birkin and Bentley camps agreed to pool their resources in a bid to break the Mercedes.

Birkin volunteered to be the hare who would seek to push Caracciola into excessive use of his supercharger: 'The policy of wearing down was one after my own heart . . . I saw a glorious race ahead of me; my path was to be cleared, my car and my own strength strained to their limits, and with luck the great Mercedes would break up.'[24]

There may have been another, more pragmatic reason for Birkin's dramatic gesture. Leslie Pennel, an early recruit to Bentley Motors, told Nagle, 'I remember well Sammy Davis saying, "It was jolly sporty of Birkin possibly to sacrifice his car like that," but Davis did emphasise that Birkin didn't expect his "blower" to last the full race in any case – that was pretty common knowledge too.'[25]

From the start, Caracciola shot into the lead, while Birkin made his way through from the back of the pack, catching the Mercedes down the Mulsanne Straight on lap 3. As he drew nearer the German, he heard a noise from the rear of his own car, and glanced back to catch sight of the crumpled mudguard indicative of a thrown tyre tread, but still he pressed on at over 125mph (201kmh). Caracciola, sticking to the middle of the track, did not even know he was there, so Birkin took to the grass to overtake him. In *Full Throttle* he recalled, 'The car rocked, but got by just in time for me to change down and go round the corner. Caracciola said that this was one of the greatest shocks of his life, to see a car, whose imminence he had not dreamt of, come tearing past him at that speed on the outmost edge of the road, with a bare patch in its left rear tyre.'[26]

The tyre held together long enough for Birkin to set the fastest lap of the race next time round, but then it gave up and shredded itself to pieces, forcing him to head for the pits at under 40mph (64kmh), and allowing Caracciola to retake the lead. For the Englishman, 'It had been a thrilling interlude, of the kind so dear to my heart, combining a competition between two wonderful cars with a policy devised for the benefit of a team.'[27]

Birkin suffered three more tyre failures in the early hours of the race, and the second Blower of Benjafield and Ramponi was similarly affected, so it was the works Bentley team that did indeed benefit from the policy of hounding the Mercedes, when it was finally forced into retirement during the early hours of the morning. Babe Barnato and Glen Kidson ran out winners, Barnato taking his 'hat-trick' win from his third start and completing what remains the only 100 per cent winning record in the entire history of Le Mans. Sadly, neither Blower made it through to the end. They ran third and fourth behind the two surviving Speed Six works Bentleys well into the Sunday, but the Birkin/Chassagne car retired after 20 hours when a connecting rod broke, and the sister car of Benjafield and Ramponi stopped an hour later with a damaged piston.

After the race, Bentley Motors withdrew from motor racing, as the Great Depression began to bite into the company's finances. This left Birkin's team as the only representatives of 'the Flying B' on the circuits of Europe, but there was no improvement in results. The amount of oil thrown out by all three Blowers at July's Irish Grand Prix left Paget so disillusioned that she concluded it was time to drop motor racing and focus solely on horse racing. She was still bank-rolling Birkin in September, however, when he had what he later described as 'the last of all the big races in which I ever had any success with the old green Bentleys, and the most enjoyable'.[28]

The unlikely occasion was the French Grand Prix, held that year at Pau, in the south-west of the country. The race was run over 245 miles (394km) to Formule Libre rules and attracted 22 entries, including no fewer than 16 Bugattis, and a short-wheelbase Blower shorn of headlights, mudguards and other road-going accoutrements. Even modified in this way, Birkin's car was bound to lose out to the nimble Bugattis round the corners, but a 5mph advantage on top speed could be exploited down the circuit's long straight, and the Blower's 50-gallon fuel tank would enable it to run non-stop, whereas it was thought likely the Bugattis would need to refuel.

Long-time Birkin co-driver Jean Chassagne had local knowledge of Birkin's competition, as is revealed in a fascinating letter, written by the Englishman's secretary Bill Lambert to Paget some two weeks before the race:

Chassagne is of the opinion that your car stands a very good chance in this race as he is personally acquainted with all the Bugattis entered, and he does not think that they are likely to last the course, particularly if they are pressed. Your car will be completely stripped, and will carry no weight, and you, therefore, can look forward to seeing some very fast times.[29]

Birkin ran sixth in the early stages, but had climbed to fourth by the time he exited a corner and was confronted by a sight he would never forget: 'On the right hand of the road was a wrecked Bugatti, and lying across the middle, face downwards and arms stretched rigid by his side, was the driver, with a pool of blood oozing from beneath his chin.'[30] Birkin made for a gap on the left so tight that afterwards he found blood stains on his right-hand wheels, but squeezed through. He was visited in his hotel the following day by the man's grateful wife. Her husband, the French driver 'Sabipa', was recovering in hospital, and confirmed that he had been conscious throughout the episode, he had heard the hiss of the Bentley's wheels as they passed, and he doubted that Birkin had missed him by more than a couple of inches.

In the closing stages, when Juan Zanelli pulled into the pits for fuel, Birkin was promoted to second place and started to hunt down the leader, Philippe Etancelin. Under threat from the Bentley, the Frenchman felt obliged to forego his fuel stop and, hampered by a defective clutch, press on to the finish. He was still a little over three minutes ahead of Birkin when he crossed the line after some two and three-quarter hours of racing, but he was down to his last litre of fuel, and only one of six retaining bolts held his Bugatti's clutch plates together.

Birkin and the Blower Bentley had narrowly missed out on a famous win. Another of his road cars proved equally competitive a fortnight later at the Brooklands 500. The handicap handed out to the most powerful cars meant that they started almost precisely 100 minutes after the smallest cars such as the 750cc Austin Seven of Sammy Davis, but the Blower driven by Dudley Benjafield and Eddie Hall averaged more than 112mph (180kmh), and had closed the gap to Davis to just seven minutes by the conclusion of the 500 miles.

These two consecutive second places were not enough to prevent Paget withdrawing her patronage and selling the road cars. Though she would spend far more on horse racing and gambling, she felt she had seen too little return on the £32,000 (almost £1.5 million, or US$2 million in modern-day terms) she had expended on Birkin's team. She continued to support him when it came to the single-seater Blower, but regardless of what was done to it – swapping Amherst's blower for a vane-type Powerplus supercharger, for example, and fitting a vast pair of downdraft SU carburettors to increase the fuel flow – Birkin endured a miserable 1931 with the car. Indeed, during one of several attempts that year to regain the Brooklands lap record from Kaye Don, it caught fire. Even his one notable racing success of the year, his win with Earl Howe in an Alfa Romeo at Le Mans, was tempered by the telegram he received from Mussolini, congratulating him on his win 'for Italy'.

Birkin's finances were suffering, too. A new business venture at Welwyn with a partner named Mike Couper lost money, though it did enable him to arrange for a fifth Blower Bentley to be built up from spares and sold to a friend.

For the 1932 season, the single-seater was reunited with Amherst's supercharger, its engine bored out from 4,398cc to 4,442cc and larger pistons fitted. In this configuration Birkin was able to win back the Brooklands lap record, raising it to 137.96mph (222.02kmh) during practice for the Easter meeting. The car's swan song came that August, when Birkin went head-to-head with John Cobb's Delage in a 100 Sovereigns Match race, run over three laps of Brooklands. Setting off from the Railway Straight, Cobb exploited his car's superior acceleration to eke out a lead of some 500yd (450m), and Birkin needed all three laps to wind the Delage back in. He recalled that on the final lap, 'as we came off the Members' Banking I felt the Bentley, as it were, hang above it for an instant and then shoot ahead. We won by 25 yards or one-fifth of a second, covering the final lap at 137.3mph. It was a thrilling race, and the long, red single-seater never went better.'[31]

By 1933 Birkin's partnership with Couper had collapsed, the Welwyn works shut, and his wealth was all but exhausted. Fellow 'Bentley Boy' Bernard Rubin bought him a Maserati 8C, with which he entered the Tripoli Grand Prix in Libya that May. A bodged pit stop restricted him to third place, and at some point during the meeting he burned his forearms on the Maserati's exhaust. Less than seven weeks later, the last of the four Birkin siblings was dead, aged just 36.

Some motoring magazines of the time stated that the cause of his death was septicaemia, brought on by the burns, but since he did not fall ill until three weeks after the race, it appears that a return of the malaria he had first suffered in Palestine in 1918 was at least partly to blame. His death made comments in the final chapter of *Full Throttle* particularly poignant. After noting that 'disaster is as likely to meet us crossing a street as tearing round a track', he made it clear which fate he would rather meet: 'It is wrong that those who have met life with courage should at the end be worn down by lingering illness.'[32]

Captain Henry Birkin was buried back in Blakeney, his feet pointing out to sea as he wished, beneath a gravestone which read: 'A Racing Motorist of International Fame.' His 137.96mph Brooklands lap record, set in the single-seater Blower Bentley over a year earlier, would stand for another 14 months.

Dorothy Paget enjoyed longer-term success in the world of horse racing, twice becoming leading National Hunt owner, but it cost her a good deal more than Tim Birkin had – over £3 million, and that is without taking her massive gambling into account. She grew ever larger, to some 20st (127kg), and ever more obsessive, naming each of her all-female staff after a colour, hiring an entire railway carriage when travelling by train, and buying pairs of tickets for the theatre or Wimbledon, one for her handbag. Her weight and 100-cigarettes-a-day habit may well have been factors in the heart attack that killed her in 1960.

What are we to make of the enigma that is the Blower Bentley? It never won a race of any consequence, devoured its tyres and suffered perennial overheating and lubrication problems, yet today it makes wealthy men go weak at the knees and write seven-figure cheques for the privilege of owning one. Malcolm Barber is chief executive of the auctioneers Bonhams & Butterfields. He has brought his gavel down on more than one Blower, and knew Amherst in his final years. He is clear about what makes the car so special:

It's an icon in British motor racing history. WO had a background as a railway engineer, and yet he took on the Germans with all their Daimler-Benz backing. He needed some wealthy entrepreneurs and some guys with family money to pull it off, and it was at their request that Amherst came in, but the Blower is just so representative of that great British sprit of the time, the British Racing Green. Rare doesn't always mean good, but the Blower really is special. It's like James Hunt and Lord Hesketh, they carried on the same tradition in the '70s.[33]

Birkin's performance in the opening laps at Le Mans certainly marked the beginning of the Blower legend. The *Daily Express* lauded his 'Drive or Burst Decoy to the Germans',[34] and the treatment of the race in the British motoring press was just as melodramatic: in *The Motor*, the description of Birkin overtaking Caracciola concluded with, 'What a car, and *what* a driver!'[35] It seemed to matter little that Birkin carried the fight to Caracciola for less than an hour, and that it was Barnato and Kidson's duel with the Mercedes, which did not begin in earnest until after almost five hours of racing, and continued all the way to the German car's retirement some eight hours later, which really determined the outcome of the race.

A curious tale from the Second World War relates how strong the Blower's aura remained 14 years later. The Airborne Forces Experimental Establishment (AFEE) was based for a time at the

Yorkshire airfield of Sherburn-in-Elmet, and in 1943 was investigating ways of supporting the planned invasion of occupied France. One concern was the expense of sending Jeeps into a war zone by Horsa glider. The Horsa would almost certainly be written off, and extracting the Jeeps from a crash-landed aircraft may not be easy. An AFEE boffin named Raoul Hafner, who had already built an early helicopter, hit upon the idea of a 'flying Jeep'. Fitted with a tail fuselage and central pylon supporting a rotor like that of a helicopter, the Jeep would be towed across the English Channel and then dropped over France, floating down like a sycamore seed. Upon landing, the fuselage and rotor would be jettisoned and the pilot would become a driver and his co-pilot a machine-gunner as they drove into battle.

The first test took place at Sherburn on 16 November 1943, but the truck towing the 'flying Jeep' was too slow to get it airborne, and the man in charge of the experiments, Squadron Leader Ian Little, went to London to purchase the fastest car possible. He thought first of the Napier Railton, the car with which John Cobb set the all-time outright lap record of 143.44mph (230.84kmh) at Brooklands in October 1935. When this proved impossible, he returned to Sherburn with what he perceived to be the next-best thing – a Blower Bentley. Thus it was that on 27 November 1943 a 4½-litre Bentley with Amherst Villiers supercharger went into war service, towing a 'flying Jeep' into the air for the first time.

The following June, D-Day rendered the extraordinary 'flying Jeep' obsolete and the experiments were abandoned, but Squadron Leader Little and his men enjoyed the Blower, using it fairly roughly as an off-duty runabout on trips to country pubs and on hill-climbs. Bentley author Michael Hay learned about the car's involvement in the experiments from a letter sent to WO by a man who participated in them, and believes it was probably the car which Birkin drove to second place in the 1930 French Grand Prix, and which today is owned by fashion icon Ralph Lauren.

Into the 1950s, the Blower Bentley retained its mythological status. Motor racing historian Doug Nye thinks alliteration played its part:

'As a kid, I had a Matchbox model of YU3250 and used to play with it on a track marked out with straw bales I'd cut from bits of balsa wood. I loved the sound of "Birkin's Blower Bentleys". That's what I thought all Bentleys were called!'[36]

In the 1960s, Amherst played his own part in enhancing the legend of the Blower Bentley – and doing his own profile no harm in the process – when he acquired one of the production cars and lovingly restored it while working for the Douglas Corporation and living in California. He won the Bentley Class at the 1966 Pebble Beach *Concours d'Elégance* with the car and subsequently sold it to Le Mans winner and 1961 World Champion, the late Phil Hill.

There can be no better way of understanding the magic of the Blower Bentley than considering the sport Hill, surely America's finest racing driver of the late 1950s and early 1960s, had with Amherst's old car during the summer of 1979. That year the Monterey Historic Automobile Race Meeting was celebrating the Bentley marque, and Hill drove the Blower down to Carmel from his home in Santa Monica to compete in – and win – one of the races. The next day he let his friend Dan Gurney, another Le Mans winner, and the Grand Prix rival whom the incomparable Jim Clark most respected, drive the Blower the 250 miles back to Santa Monica. Gurney recalls the drive as though it were yesterday:

I'd heard of the Blower Bentley at Le Mans, and I love old cars like that. My mouth was watering. At first she seemed to be struggling, like she was starved of fuel. We had a few old wrenches and whatnot with us, so we took apart the carburettor and checked the fuel lines. Eventually we found that some debris had come loose in the fuel tank, so we cleaned the lines and the filter. After that, she ran like a champ and we truly got under way. She had tall gears and she loped along at 100 without straining at all. I was driving an open roadster with the windshield down, and I could have been in 1930 or '31. If ever there was a 'King of the Road' kind of feeling, it was in that car. It was easy, effortless, it just cantered along. It was capable of sustaining high speed motoring for a very long time. I knew she could do 130, so it was duck soup to do 100. If you had a gap to the next car which you needed to close, you could gas it at 100 and it would accelerate.

Cruising up the Pacific Coast Road at about 100, we came across a whole flock of Panteras, about nine or ten of them. I picked them off one at a time. I'm sure they couldn't believe such an old car could blow them away. Well, we started to get hungry so we pulled into a restaurant. Gradually we were joined by the Pantera drivers and we had a talk with them. After about half an hour, the last of them showed up, and he was obviously angry. He'd been given a speeding ticket by the police. They asked him if he'd seen a big old green roadster going way too fast. They'd been trying to follow us for half an hour![37]

For the last 20 years and more, Amherst's old Blower has been owned by Yorkshireman John Bentley, and he has driven more than 100,000 miles in it. His classic car stable also includes a 1914 Grand Prix Opel, Alfa Romeo 8C, Type 57 Bugatti and Ferrari 250GT SWB, and the last word on what is so special about the Blower Bentley should go to him: 'I'd have to take you up the road in it to tell you. Unless you wind a Blower up, it's heavy and numb, but at 90 or 100 it becomes a different car. It's fast, it handles well. If I could keep only one of them, it would be my Blower.'[38]

That is why at a Gooding & Co auction at Pebble Beach in August 2007 a 1931 Blower Bentley went for a record auction price of US$4.51 million (the Sterling equivalent that day was £2.28 million), and why, some years earlier, Ralph Lauren paid substantially more in a private transaction to acquire the Blower that may well have pulled the 'flying Jeep' into the air.

The fact remains that, as a racing car, the Blower Bentley had an indifferent career. To establish the reason for this, one need look no further than the compromising way in which it was born. Bentley Motors knew nothing about supercharging, their founder wanted nothing to do with the project, and they refused to race the Blower at all. The team that did race it was under-financed except during the

1930 season, when Dorothy Paget supported it. Amherst Villiers, the man who, in 1928, probably knew more about the supercharging of a racing car than anyone else in England, was kept at arm's length, and his specific advice regarding lubrication went ignored. As he himself said, it all went off half-cocked, and it is only too easy to understand why the results on the race track were so disappointing.

The irony is that, at the time, Amherst's reputation probably suffered by being involved with such a high-profile failure, and by bringing the High Court injunction against Bentley during the 1929 London Motor Show. He would have been better off if he had insisted at the outset on a closer, longer-term involvement with the project – either that, or he should never have got involved with the Blower at all, and simply brought forward his *Villiers Supercharge* developments. But, as the years rolled by and the Blower Bentley came to hold a place in the affection of car enthusiasts the world over, quite out of keeping with its racing record, so Amherst's reputation grew.

Besides, if Amherst Villiers had not supercharged the Blower Bentley, what would James Bond have driven?

Chapter 10

THE BUSINESSMAN

Through the latter years of the 1920s, and for most of the 1930s, Amherst was a director of several companies, variously called Amherst Villiers Superchargers Limited, Amherst Villiers Airmotors and Villiers Hay Development Limited. The general perception of those who knew him in later life is that he was not a good businessman, and did not manage his money well. Yet he displayed a range of business skills that would impress most entrepreneurs of today.

He was, for example, able to recruit staff of the highest calibre. Two of his employees at Amherst Villiers Superchargers Limited, whose initials are to be found on the supercharger drawings for the Blower Bentley, were Eric Richter and Tom Murray Jamieson. Richter qualified as a surveyor, but Amherst spotted a rare engineering talent in him, as his subsequent endeavours reveal. He was engaged on engine work for Raymond Mays at ERA before the Second World War and on Rolls-Royce aero engines during it, and subsequently played a key part in the development of the V16 BRM engine; the engine that won for Vanwall the inaugural World Constructors' Championship in 1958; and the extraordinary gas turbine engine that powered the Rover-BRM Le Mans car of the mid-1960s.

Murray Jamieson was a graduate of Battersea Polytechnic and one of Amherst's earliest employees, working on the supercharging of Jack Kruse's Phantom in 1927. After contributing to both the Blower Bentley and *Villiers Supercharge*, by 1932 Amherst had made him a director of the company. That Amherst was able to retain and promote such a talent over five years says something about his skills as a man manager. In due course Jamieson's work on Amherst's supercharged Austin Ulster, and his impressive test-driving of it, led Sir Herbert Austin to agree a deal with Amherst and employ Jamieson to develop a car which could win back the speed records which Austin were losing to MG. It is claimed that one of Jamieson's Austin designs, almost 30 years before Colin Chapman's Lotus 25, was a mid-engine monocoque, but this proved too outlandish for Sir Herbert, and Jamieson left Austin to join Mays at ERA.

In May 1938 Jamieson suffered fatal injuries spectating at Brooklands, when the burning Delage of Joseph Paul burst through the railings and into the crowd. Plans for a supercharged ERA Grand Prix racer and a 4-litre passenger car were scrapped soon afterwards. How different the course of British motor racing in general, and that of BRM in particular, might have been had he lived.

Amherst's choice of suppliers could prove just as inspiring. A Yorkshire-based gear manufacturer named David Brown & Sons made his superchargers, and he became great friends with a young member of the Brown family, also called David, who had steadily worked his way up from shop floor apprentice and would become managing director in 1932. Brown's involvement with Amherst's superchargers made him so enthusiastic about motor racing that he took up the sport. His 1930 appearance at Shelsley Walsh in a TT Vauxhall fitted with a Villiers blower was one of his last as a driver, for his father's stroke obliged him to focus on business, but after the war Brown found a way of dovetailing his two great interests. In 1947 he responded to an advertisement in *The Times* about a failed car company, and became the proud owner of Aston Martin. Twelve years later Brown finally achieved his great ambition when Roy Salvadori and Caroll Shelby won Le Mans at the wheel of an Aston Martin.

Amherst also displayed a keen awareness of the power of marketing and branding. Mays may never have paid him for his work on the Brescia Bugattis, the AC and the old TT Vauxhall, and Amherst may not have made a great deal of money from his involvement with

Bentley, but when the car known variously as the *Vauxhall Villiers* and the *Villiers Supercharge* won at Southport and Shelsley, and when Birkin broke the lap records at Brooklands and Le Mans in the Blower, so his 'brand value' as 'Mr Supercharger' grew.

Similarly, one of the first steps he took to announce his arrival in the field of aeronautic engineering was to purchase from the Air Ministry a Gloster IV biplane of the type flown in the 1927 Schneider Trophy. By removing the floats and fitting an undercarriage, Amherst planned to make an attempt on the world landplane (as opposed to seaplane) speed record. What better way to point to his prowess in automotive and aeronautic design than by referring to world speed records on land with *Bluebird* and in the air with the Gloster?

The brochure Amherst produced for the 1929 London Motor Show to coincide with the launch of the production Blower Bentley also reveals a sound understanding of marketing. With sections on Service, Science, Simplicity, Strength, Silence, Reliability, Effectiveness, Research, Efficiency, Flexibility, Perfection, Acceleration, Stiffness, Balance, Rigidity, Durability, Speed, Power, Regularity, Smoothness, Control, Experimental, Versatility and Supremacy, it would put much modern promotional material to shame.

Amherst could exploit his artist's eye in the pursuit of marketing opportunities, too, as witnessed by the advertisement he placed in the 1931 Schneider Trophy race programme. He commissioned artist Adrian Hill to produce an outstanding piece of art deco, a seaplane picked out in red silhouette against a royal blue sky, lifting off from a grey and white sea, its peaks pointing at the aircraft. Fanning off the nose of the plane are a series of waves representing speed and turbulence, while white streaks emanating from its floats represent the craft wrenching itself free from the water. Framed along the bottom by Amherst's name in capitals, and in the top left-hand corner by the logo of his aero engine company, it is a most striking image and makes one want to buy whatever it is that Amherst Villiers is selling.

A further factor boosting Amherst's potential as a businessman was his ability to diversify. As his supercharging brochure puts it, his 'Design Department . . . is ready to place its experience at the disposal of all engineers interested in Forced Induction for Automobile, Marine and Aircraft application.'[1] Marine application may refer to Tim Birkin's speedboat, and while Amherst would bookend the 1930s with yet more fascinating automotive projects, he would devote most of the decade to aircraft work. An interesting article in May 1932, entitled *Leading Men in the British Motor Industry*, was reprinted together with Amherst's supercharging brochure from the 1929 Motor Show by writer Eoin Young. It concludes:

Amherst Villiers, the British engineer who championed the cause of supercharging, can number speed records at Brooklands, Le Mans, the beaches at Pendine and Daytona, and British hill-climbs, among the fruits of his design labours. He is now actively engaged in the design of aero engines and plans to specialise in this field.[2]

Quite what drove Amherst in this direction is not clear. He had, of course, loved aircraft since childhood: he had made that old Curtiss Ox engine work at Oundle; he had enjoyed his brief apprenticeship at Farnborough as consolation for being too young to fly with the RFC; and he owned his own aircraft. Registered G-ABKH, the aircraft was a Martynside twin-seater biplane, based on the F4 model, but known as the AV1 because of the many modifications Amherst arranged to be made to its airframe and 300hp Hispano-Suiza engine. Finished in an engaging colour scheme of two-tone blue and called *Blue Print* (a reference to *Bluebird*, perhaps?), it was based at Heston, the aerodrome west of London.

Yet for all Amherst's love of aircraft, by 1932 he had been on the front line of British motor racing endeavour for nine years. Why leave that behind? And why break the enduringly successful partnership with Raymond Mays? One factor may have been the tragedy which befell Amherst's family in June 1930. His younger brother George had obtained his aviator's licence a year earlier and had recently joined 600 Squadron of the Auxiliary Air Force, based at Hendon. One early Saturday evening he decided to fly a Blackburn Bluebird, G-AASU, on the short trip to Heston. On take-off he climbed too quickly, too steeply, and at a height of only 100ft fought to avoid a stall. He turned left through 180 degrees in an attempt to complete a rapid circuit and make an emergency landing, but as he turned left again, the plane plummeted to the ground and he was killed. A full military funeral was held at Salisbury Cathedral four days later. He was just 18 years old.

In later life, Amherst rarely talked about the accident with friends, and never to journalists, but there is some indication that his sister Veronica held him responsible. She was unimpressed when, on a visit to his California home in 1964, she learned he was restoring his Bentley, and told friends of his that 'it was messing about with engines that got George killed'.[3] Perhaps in the early 1930s Amherst felt that by improving the performance of aero engines fewer young men might suffer George's fate.

Another factor in Amherst's switch to aero engines may have been that his hopes for his automotive supercharging business proved over-ambitious. As the new decade dawned, his plan had been to produce a range of superchargers for enthusiasts to buy off the shelf to fit to engines of all sizes. His profile on the British car scene, boosted by the launch of the production Blowers and by Mays's success with the *Villiers Supercharge*, had never been higher. It was quite natural for him to want to exploit this, and Mays tried to support him in his endeavours by persuading Lagonda to fit one of Amherst's blowers to its 2-litre saloon. In *Split Seconds* Mays writes, 'A great deal of work was done in this direction, but as Amherst was so busy on experimental work the Lagonda developments were much delayed. On this account, and in view of the rather high cost of the Villiers supercharger, when Lagonda did produce a blown edition of their 2-litre it was fitted with a Centric blower.'[4]

Mays records that this model was 'quite successful',[5] but it took two full years for the 50 production Blower Bentleys to be sold, in spite of the media frenzy over Birkin's heroics at Le Mans. The next remark in *Split Seconds* is key: 'Somehow or other supercharged road cars never seemed to catch the public imagination, and it was only the odd few super enthusiasts who purchased them.'[6]

One can point to today's Mini Cooper S, and say that Amherst was a man ahead of his time. One can argue that the disciplines of market research were only beginning to evolve at this time, but the harsh truth is that he had not done his homework. The demand was simply not there, and it appears that he got his pricing wrong, too.

Amherst dusted himself down and turned his attention to the Austin Seven. Back in 1925 Sir Herbert Austin's son-in-law Arthur Waite had begun experimenting with supercharging. Initial tests with a Berk blower proved unsuccessful, but a switch to the Roots-type design adopted by Amherst that same year enabled the Seven to break a number of Class H (501cc–750cc) speed records. The emergence of the Supersports Austin Seven, known as the Ulster after its gallant performance in the Ards TT race of 1929, enabled the Seven to push its Class H records still higher. However, much to Austin's chagrin, it was MG who was the first to break the 100mph barrier for Class H cars. Enter Amherst Villiers.

Amherst purchased an Ulster and, with Jamieson, set about fitting it with one of their superchargers and revising the bodywork. Mays did some initial tests in the car at Brooklands in May 1931, but it was the sight of Jamieson himself – no mean test driver by this time – lapping Brooklands very rapidly indeed in it 12 months later that brought Amherst's developments to the attention of Sir Herbert. An Austin mechanic, Stan Yeal, had been watching Jamieson from the paddock and was still more impressed once he had been given a ride in the car.

Amherst duly met with Sir Herbert and encouraged him to fit his superchargers as standard to the Ulster. Works driver Charles Goodacre was given the task of testing Amherst's blower, and though he could not distinguish any great advantage over the French Cozette supercharger, further tests with a methanol-based fuel were so impressive that Sir Herbert bought the car, the supercharger and Murray Jamieson from Amherst.

It was a significant decision, made by one of the giants of the British car industry, and a considerable gesture to Amherst as he took his leave of motor sport for the best part of three decades. His acolyte of the previous five years produced a low-line speedster that exceeded 120mph (193kmh), but Jamieson found it hard to stomach the political atmosphere at Austin and moved on to ERA.

Incidentally, Goodacre was one of those who retrospectively linked Amherst's work on Jack Kruse's Roll-Royce Phantom with his supercharging of the Ulster, and claimed that the little engine driving the supercharger on the running board of the Rolls was from an Austin Seven. This claim has surfaced from time to time, and incensed Amherst whenever it was made to his face. For the record, the engine which drove the blower of the world's first supercharged Rolls-Royce was designed by Amherst, not Austin.

It was in May 1930, two years before Sir Herbert Austin's head-hunting of Tom Murray Jamieson, that Amherst announced his arrival on the British aircraft scene by purchasing N224, the first of three Gloster IV biplanes designed for the 1927 Schneider Trophy race. The other planes entered that year were all monoplanes, but Gloster believed that the biplane's superior rigidity, shorter wingspan and greater wing area outweighed any advantage created by the monoplane's lower drag. Flight Lieutenant Sidney Webster's victory in the single-wing Supermarine S.5 suggested otherwise, and the 1927 event was the last time a biplane contested the Schneider Trophy.

Amherst's interest in acquiring N224 lay in stripping it of its floats and fitting it with a revised chassis and undercarriage for an assault on what was known as the world landplane (as opposed to seaplane) speed record. This must have seemed a highly attainable goal. The landplane record had stood since December 1924, when the Frenchman, Adjutant Bonnet, had recorded an average speed of 278.5mph (448.2kmh), and was a good deal lower than the overall air speed record set five years later by Squadron Leader Augustus Orlebar, in a Supermarine S.6 seaplane, at 357.7mph (575.7kmh). The plane itself seemed up to the job; as part of the research programme for the 1927 Schneider Trophy, a quarter-scale model had been tested in landplane configuration in the wind tunnel at Teddington's National Physical Laboratory.

Amherst's choice of pilot for the attempt was sound, too. Richard 'Batchy' Atcherley had been, like Amherst and Raymond Mays, a pupil at Oundle, and like Peter Berthon, a cadet at RAF Cranwell. Unlike Berthon, he went on to be Cranwell's Commandant, and to climb to the rank of Air Marshal. In 1929, he had been a member of the RAF High Speed Flight that contested the Schneider Trophy. Blinded by the slipstream at 300mph (483kmh) when he lost his goggles, he had turned inside a pylon marking one of the corners on the circuit and was disqualified. He had soon bounced back by winning the King's Cup, a two-day, cross-country air race from Croydon, south of London, to Glasgow and back. He was clearly made of the right stuff.

Atcherley had fond memories of his first experience of flying at speeds in excess of 300mph, recalling that it was as stimulating as his first solo flight. At the time, the fastest service aircraft were capable only of half that speed and a seaplane racer's take-off, stall and landing speeds were all higher, too. Therein lay Amherst's problem. There was a reason why high-speed air races had become the preserve of seaplanes. The sea provided an indefinitely long 'runway' for take-off, and an effective brake upon landing. On dry land there seemed no runway long enough to permit a plane as fast as the Gloster IV to take off and land.

Five years later, in an article about Amherst's aero engine in *The Aeroplane*, it was effectively admitted that the answer to the problem would have been flaps, the extensions from the trailing edge of a wing which increase lift, thereby reducing landing speed and the distance required to make a safe landing. They had first been seen on a British aircraft, the SE4 biplane, in 1914, but had yet to gain widespread adoption. Thus, states the article, 'no aerodrome was big enough to cope with the estimated landing run, so the idea had to lie dormant'.[7]

Amherst's mind certainly did not lie dormant. He sold the Gloster IV to the same man who had bought his Martynside, Charles Field, and promptly bought a Gloster VI. This was the last of the Gloster seaplanes, and the only monoplane in the series. Like the IV, it was powered by the Napier Lion engine, which Amherst had also used in Malcolm Campbell's *Bluebird*, and its wings were particularly distinctive, tapering at their roots in an attempt to improve control at low speeds. Two planes, N249 and N250, were built for the 1929 Schneider Trophy, though both were scratched from the race when fuel feed problems were identified.

However, the VI appeared to better suit Amherst's ambitions. For a start, the pilot's view was better – even if there had been a runway long enough for the IV, it is doubtful that Atcherley could have seen it from the cockpit – and it appears that the newer plane's take-off was shorter and easier than that of its contemporary rival, the Supermarine S.6, so the task of locating a suitable runway may have been made easier. The VI had sufficient speed to meet Amherst's objective. N249 was used just after the 1929 Schneider Trophy to raise the overall speed record to 336.3mph (541.2kmh) and though Orlebar swiftly pushed this past 350mph (563kmh), Amherst understood that the Gloster's run had been at 70 per cent power. With the drag-inducing floats removed and the throttle wide open, surely the landplane record could be beaten.

The Americans had produced both land and seaplane versions of their racers up until 1927, and another Schneider Trophy entry, the Bernard HV120 seaplane, was converted in a bid to retain the landplane record for France, so it was not just Amherst in search of a suitable location. There were probably military airfields in Britain with runways long enough to accommodate the Gloster VI on wheels, but some members of the RAF hierarchy were less than enamoured with the role of their high speed flight in the Schneider Trophy. Atcherley, with the odd crash and court martial on his record, was not universally popular with his seniors either, and it may be that the project was not considered appropriate for a military airfield. In the end Amherst was forced to change course, and decided to take his Gloster VI racing.

The Schneider Trophy had been a competition between nations rather than individuals, and had in any event been won outright by Britain in 1931. Amherst needed to get the Gloster out to the US, where it could compete in the major competitions organised by two Californian brothers, Cliff and Phil Henderson. In June 1932 Phil Henderson was particularly keen to bring Amherst and the Gloster VI over to the US. He and his brother were attempting to revive the Curtiss Marine Trophy, a race that had been run three times during the 1920s for US Navy pilots flying seaplanes. Henderson's plan was to make the revived race the feature event of a series of races planned to take place in New Orleans the following February. He advised Amherst, 'We would very much like to have you bring the Gloster VI to this country for the New Orleans Race. While I am not in a position at the present time to say just what financial assistance we could give you, I am quite positive that we will be able to make an offer to stand a part of the expense involved.'[8]

In London a month later Amherst lunched with a retired US Navy officer named Ellmer Langworthy. He was the London representative of 'A Century of Progress', the international exhibition which the city of Chicago was arranging for the following year as part of its centennial celebrations. Amherst proposed that the event should include a race for seaplanes off the shore of Lake Michigan – and also proposed that the organisers should contribute towards the cost of his participation.

Langworthy fully supported Amherst on this, writing, 'There is no question but that a race in Chicago similar to the Schneider Trophy race would be a great attraction.'[9] He reported back to his colleagues in Chicago and the proposal was taken up by the head of the exhibition's Applied Science & Industry Division, a Mr Parker van Zandt. He was sympathetic, having witnessed at first hand the 1929 Schneider Trophy race and remembered 'the large amount of publicity and interest which it aroused'.[10] However, van Zandt concluded that, since the exhibition was to be located along the open shore of Lake

Michigan, 'where the water conditions might prove extremely dangerous to these high speed racing planes',[11] it was not possible to host a seaplane race on the lake.

Van Zandt recommended that Amherst remained in touch with the Henderson brothers, but in the end the hoped-for revival of the Curtiss Marine Trophy never went ahead, and though the Hendersons did indeed organise an air race event at Chicago in September 1933, it was held at Curtiss-Reynolds Airport, not on Lake Michigan, and did not include a seaplane race. Amherst was forced to drop his ambitions for the Gloster and move on.

He was able to find consolation in a particularly attractive form. Langworthy's letter to Amherst had concluded, 'I would ask you to kindly convey my respects to Madame DeLisle when you next see the charming lady.'[12] Amherst did indeed see the charming lady again. In fact, two weeks later, he married her! Born Marietta Nungovich in Cairo in about 1893, she was the daughter of George Nungovich, who had risen from railway station porter to own many of the best hotels in the city. This was her second marriage; her first husband, George Strakosch, had died, leaving her with a son. She had been a singer in the 1920s, known professionally as Maya de Lisle, and Maya is how Amherst addressed her. She was a slim, dark-haired beauty, and the tall, handsome Amherst and petite Maya made a most striking couple.

The wedding took place at Princes Row Registry Office on 30 July 1932, and the following May *The Times* recorded that Amherst's mother Elaine presented Maya to Queen Mary at General Court 'on her wedding'.[13] A month later Sasha Stone, the Russian-born fashion photographer who had taken the couple's pre-nuptial photographs, visited their home on Farm Street, just west of Berkeley Square in London's Mayfair, to capture what Maya, a gifted interior designer, had done to it.

The entrance hall was particularly impressive, with the walls decorated in linen fold panelling, a statue of the Madonna in a Gothic alcove, and a carved wooden staircase leading upstairs. Stone's photograph of an elaborately marbled bathroom also survives, but if he did take any pictures of Amherst's studio, then sadly these do not.

Even by his standards, Amherst's summer of 1932 was a busy one: in June he supported Raymond Mays in the *Villiers Supercharge* at Shelsley Walsh; in July he married Maya; he tried to persuade Chicago to host a seaplane race on Lake Michigan; he finally got round to obtaining his pilot's 'A licence' (Royal Aero Club aviator's certificate number 10592), in a 60G Gipsy Moth at the London Aeroplane Club; and in August he was at an international conference in London, proposing radical plans 'for a stratospheric plane which will carry 30 men propelled by a 2,000hp engine'.[14]

But the aeronautic project of which he was most proud was on an altogether smaller scale, and involved a new company. On 22 March 1934, *Flight* magazine recorded, 'VILLIERS HAY DEVELOPMENT LTD, 48 Albermarle Street, W.1. Capital £7,000 in £1 shares. Aeroplane engineers and builders, type testers of engines and aeroplanes, etc. Directors: Charles A Villiers, 22 Farm Street, W.1; Lt-Col Thomas W Hay, Fulmer Place, Fulmer, Bucks.'[15]

Hay was a 52-year-old stockbroker and a keen pilot, the son of the late Lord John Hay, former Admiral of the Fleet. It is not known how or when he and Amherst met, though they were good friends by August 1930, when they sailed from Liverpool to Boston, on Amherst's first trip to America, to stay in Newport, Rhode Island. Since Amherst was exclusively involved in any publicity concerning the company, it seems that Hay's involvement in it may have been restricted to the provision of capital.

The objective of Villiers Hay Development Ltd was to exploit the burgeoning interest in civil aviation. Once the preserve of wealthy individuals who could withstand the cold, danger and heavy maintenance overheads involved in flying biplanes, a new breed of relatively inexpensive, reliable monoplanes was emerging, with enclosed cockpits inside which two enthusiasts could actually talk while flying, rather than yelling down a speaking tube.

Foremost among the movement was Willard Whitney Straight, who had won Shelsley Walsh in September 1933, beating Raymond Mays in his last appearance in the *Villiers Supercharge*. Over the following couple of seasons, Straight had enjoyed a successful and profitable career as a driver/entrant and was invited to join Germany's Auto Union team for the 1935 season, declining on the grounds that he thought he might kill himself. The following winter he embarked on a change in career and devised a plan to establish flying clubs near major towns. To help bring civil aviation to the masses, he also worked with Frederick Miles, designer of a successful light plane called the Falcon, on a monoplane with a roomy, enclosed cabin providing side-by-side seating. This was the Miles Whitney Straight M11, and its vacuum-operated flaps enabled it to take off and land at just 50mph. Priced at £985 (the modern-day equivalent would be just under £48,000, or almost US$65,000), it was the ideal plane for the budding pilot of the 1930s.

It was also the ideal test bed for the Maya, the four-cylinder in-line, air-cooled aero engine designed by Amherst in 1936. He purchased G-AERC, the second of the production M11s, and fitted his engine in it. The Maya was less than 23in (58cm) tall and only 16in (41cm) wide. Shorn of its starter and spinner, it was also less than 44in (112cm) long and, like many aero engines of the time, it was 'inverted', with the cylinders pointing down, so that the propeller shaft could sit at the top of the unit and give the pilot an unimpeded view over the nose of the plane. All in all, it was a tidy design and sat snugly in the very nose of the aircraft, leaving plenty of room for ancillaries.

Amherst paid particular attention to cooling. A slot in the cowling diverted air down channels between the widely splayed valves, and the cylinders were lined with deep, fine-pitched fins, which he felt would also reduce the likelihood of carbon deposits building up. Even after extended flying at full throttle, engine temperature stayed below 220°C.

Initially designed to deliver 120hp at 2,300rpm, and peak at 130hp at a maximum 2,600 rpm, the Maya weighed only 275lb (125kg), and *The Aeroplane* considered this power-to-weight ratio to be 'the best figure that we have seen for a motor of this class'.[16] In the M11B, as Amherst's plane was designated, this enabled a cruising speed of almost 140mph (225kmh) to be maintained. Indeed, it has been claimed that the plane enjoyed a higher top speed and rate of climb than the standard M11A, which was fitted with a de Havilland Gipsy Major engine.

In later life Amherst was not infrequently frustrated at the way UK manufacturers baulked at the cost of a new engine design. He believed that what made it so expensive was the development programme necessitated by the fact that UK engineering companies employed so few people experienced in engine design. By way of contrast, Amherst designed the Maya engine in his offices on Albemarle Street, and built it up in the basement below from components supplied by a wide range of subcontractors. This was precisely the same approach he had adopted on the little engine and supercharger he designed and built for Jack Kruse's Rolls-Royce Phantom. He traced the only problem he encountered when he first ran the Maya to a faulty carburettor, and then fitted it in the M11B. Throughout the time he flew the plane, all he changed were the spark plugs – KLG of course. 'Where's the development programme in that?' he would ask as an old man.[17]

Commentators of the time were complimentary about the engine. On 23 April 1936 *Flight* devoted a page and half to 'A NEW BRITISH "FOUR"', and a year later, a journalist named Peter Masefield enthused in *The Aeroplane* over a test flight in the M11B:

In all positions of the throttle and in all attitudes the Maya ran sweetly without vibration or roughness and one felt the very hearty push behind when it was suddenly opened up. The motor is quiet enough, too, and one could always talk comfortably with voices only slightly raised . . . Mr Villiers has very definite plans for extending the number and range of his motors both in the four and supercharged six-cylinder fields and possibly with an even larger type.[18]

Indeed, during the following winter, when plans were announced for the C-W Swan, a twin-engine monoplane designed to carry eight passengers, *Flight* noted that 'this machine has been planned to take two Villiers-Hay Mayas of either the present standard type or a new design offering 170hp.'[19] Into the spring of 1937 the same magazine wrote that the Maya 'which seems destined to make quite a name for itself is outstanding for its compactness'.[20] In October of that year, patent specifications were drawn up in the names of Amherst and Villiers Hay Development Ltd for 'cylinder heads and valve gear of multi-cylinder air-cooled internal-combustion engines'.[21]

Yet, in spite of the apparent progress, the C-W Swan passenger aircraft never left the drawing board, the Maya never went into production, and Amherst's plans for other aero engines were never realised. In January 1938 the Maya was taken out of G-AERC and, like its 49 sister aircraft, fitted with a Gipsy Major.

In hindsight there were two reasons for the ultimate failure of the Maya. First, in spite of the undisputed quality of his design and the positive press comment, Amherst faced very stiff competition. *Flight* regularly published reviews of light aircraft engines, and the issue of 23 April 1936 itemises no fewer than 14 alternatives to the Maya. Primary among these was De Havilland's Gipsy Major, *Flight* noting that 'neatly-cowled noses bearing inverted Gipsy engines are every day [sic] sights at all British aerodromes patronised by private owners.'[22] Quite apart from the ubiquitous Tiger Moth, the engine was fitted in at least ten other types of aircraft, and Villiers Hay could not possibly enjoy the economies of scale this gave De Havilland. Other household names such as Armstrong Siddeley and Napier (albeit at the luxury end of the market) had similar benefits, and there was also a host of smaller manufacturers trying to grasp a share of the market. Unlike Amherst's supercharging business earlier in the decade, demand was not the problem, at least initially. The issue was the very ready supply of legitimate alternatives to the Maya.

Second, throughout 1938 the threat from Hitler's Germany grew, and though the Munich agreement of September would buy Britain a further 12 months of peace, much of that time would be spent in gearing up for war. Soon, thousands of young men would indeed be flying small fleet monoplanes, but they would not be flying for pleasure; they would be fighting for their lives and for their countries. The environment in which small-scale aero engine manufacturers could have prospered was about to vanish.

His aero engine plans dashed, Amherst returned briefly to the automotive world, and chose as his focus an American saloon car, the Graham-Paige. This offered the discerning motorist more performance than most American road cars. Many were supercharged, and an old 5½-litre model driven by G. L. Baker would win the final race on the card at the Brooklands meeting of 7 August 1939 – the last ever race at the circuit. Two Paige-based specials from earlier in the decade – a supercharged, 8-cylinder, two door saloon and the turbocharged, 3½-litre Lammas-Graham tourer – had failed to impress the British market, but Amherst felt that the striking 'Spirit of Motion' model of 1939, also known as the 'Shark Nose', offered better raw material.

He engaged with Coachcraft, a West London-based coachbuilding firm, on a pair of cars to be called Villiers-Grahams. Car historian John Dyson has identified that the first, chassis number 501333, was the only sedanca coupé to be built on a 'Spirit of Motion' chassis, and was delivered to Amherst for his personal use on 13 August, precisely three weeks before Britain declared war on Germany. The second, chassis number 5000883, carried a drop-head coupé body and was delivered to Paige distributor Jack Olding in November, on its way to a female customer of Amherst's whose identity is no longer known. Nor is it known if these cars were delivered with standard blowers or whether Amherst fitted them with superchargers of his own design. In his 1974 Car and Sports Car World articles, Eoin Young wrote that the delivery of the first car just before the outbreak of war occurred 'in haunting Villiers fashion',[23] presumably after being told this by the fatalistic Amherst.

The brief Villiers-Graham project illustrates why Amherst – for all his enormous energy, his extraordinary talents as an engineer, and his great potential as a businessman – failed to achieve any lasting success during the 1930s. He seems to have lacked the acumen to understand that, as Europe slid precipitously towards war, it was not the time to start developing a luxury car business. Whether it was over-estimating the demand for automotive superchargers in the early years of the decade, or under-estimating the competition for small aero engines a few years later, Amherst tended to focus too much on the project itself, and too little on its chances of success. In earlier years Raymond Mays had generally taken care of business matters; Thomas Hay appears not to have fulfilled this role to the same extent at Villiers Hay Development. This absence of a proactive business partner restricted Amherst's potential.

It seems there was no one, for example, to point out to him the fatal flaw in the brochure he produced to coincide with the launch of the production Blowers at the 1929 Motor Show. Excellent marketing document though it was, its effectiveness was negated by the fact that he produced only 50 copies, one for the owner of each of the production cars. These individuals, surely, were already convinced of Amherst's supercharging capabilities. It was to the rest of Britain's sporting motorists he should have been appealing.

Amherst had failed to realise his potential as a businessman, and by the time the war was over he had returned to a position he had only briefly experienced once before, with Armstrong Whitworth in the early 1920s. He was an employee – and he was in North America.

Chapter 11

WAR

One man who did not believe that the Munich Agreement of 1938 would bring lasting peace was Gerard d'Erlanger. A member of a renowned European banking family and a chartered accountant by profession, d'Erlanger was also an enthusiastic pilot and a director of a prominent airline which would merge during the war with Imperial Airways to form BOAC, the forerunner of British Airways.

D'Erlanger proposed that in the event of war the many civilian pilots above the RAF's then upper age limit of 25, and those who could not pass its stringent medical tests, should be used to fly important passengers, medical supplies and mail to their destinations. Initial reactions from the Air Ministry were indifferent and it was only upon the declaration of war that the scheme was rushed through, with one significant enhancement. Though transporting passengers and supplies would form part of the new service, of far greater importance was the task from which it relieved regular RAF pilots: it would take responsibility for the delivery of military aircraft from factories and maintenance plants to operational airfields.

The Air Transport Auxiliary (ATA) was established at White Waltham, near Maidenhead in Berkshire, with D'Erlanger as its commandant. Its motto was *Aetheris avidi* ('Eager for the air'). As the holder of an 'A' pilot's licence with many hours' flying experience, Amherst was an early volunteer. He joined as a First Officer (with only Flight Captain and Captain above this), wearing the two thick bars of his rank on his single-breasted, dark blue uniform with pride.

The ATA's nickname was 'Ancient and Tattered Airmen', which was true neither of Amherst, a tall and handsome man in his late 30s, nor of the women who joined from January 1940, among them the famous pre-war aviatrix Amy Johnson and Wolf Barnato's daughter Diana. More than 1,200 men and women flew in excess of 300,000 flights for the ATA, in almost 150 different types of plane. They performed a vital job, relieving the RAF of so much work, and their part in the Battle of Britain, in particular, cannot be understated. When peace returned and the ATA was disbanded in 1945, Lord Beaverbrook, Minister of Aircraft Production, commented, 'Without the ATA the days and nights of the Battle of Britain would have been conducted under conditions quite different from the actual events . . . They were soldiers fighting in the struggle just as completely as if they had been engaged on the battlefront.'[1]

The ATA pilot's life was far from easy. Today, Wing Commander Eric Viles is chairman of the ATA Association, but in February 1944 he lied about his age – he was just 15 – to join the ATA as a cadet. He explains, 'You turned up at a ferry pool and were given a chit to take an aircraft to a given destination. You may never have seen the plane before, or know how to get into it, never mind fly it. But you simply read the take-off speed of the thing and got on with it.'[2] In particular, no training in instrument flying was given, which, given the vagaries of the British weather, made the job particularly hazardous. Of the 173 ATA pilots who were killed while flying, most were lost to bad weather, including Amy Johnson, who ditched in the Thames Estuary in thick fog, and whose body was never recovered. It is not that life was cheap; indeed, ATA pilots were repeatedly told to save themselves rather than their plane – 'when in doubt, bale out' – but there was a war on, attitudes to risk were different than they are today and compromises were required. Winston Churchill was surprised that the accident rate was not higher, telling d'Erlanger, 'That this formidable task should have been performed with so low an accident record resounds greatly to the credit of both your pilots and ground staff.'[3]

The ingenious ways in which ATA pilots overcame the challenges they faced were one reason for the impressive accident record. In her entertaining autobiography, *Spreading My Wings*, Diana Barnato revealed that she once flew in an Avro Anson piloted by Captain Douglas 'Poppa' Fairweather, from Belfast to White Waltham.[4] The entire journey was made in thick cloud, yet Fairweather, who was not wearing a watch, knew exactly when to descend out of the cloud over White Waltham – he chain-smoked precisely 23 cigarettes for seven minutes each.

Amherst applied his ingenuity to the challenges of navigation. He liked to equip himself with a large-scale map for his overall journey, and a smaller-scale one of his destination, and then reconcile the distances displayed on each by stretching a lady's stocking over them. Quite who owned the stocking is not clear, since he and Maya grew apart as the war progressed and would eventually divorce. Amherst and his family would, however, remain on friendly terms with her.

His first ATA flight was at the controls of a Fairey Battle, a single-engine light bomber. As a First Officer, Amherst was able to operate any plane the ATA was asked to fly. He flew no fewer than 25 different types of aircraft, from old biplanes such as the Fairey Swordfish and Avro Tutor, to twin-engine legends such as the Mosquito and Beaufighter, and from medium bombers like the Hampden and Wellington, to the most famous of the single-seater fighters, the Spitfire, Hurricane and Mustang. He even put four hours in on the Supermarine Walrus flying boat.

The biggest scare of his ATA days came in the cockpit of a Hurricane. On take-off and retraction of the undercarriage, a Hurricane pilot had to apply his wheel brakes so as to stop the wheels from revolving inside the wings during the flight. Naturally, when lowering the undercarriage prior to landing, the pilot had to take the wheel brakes off, but on this occasion Amherst neglected to, and the nose-heavy Hurricane flipped over on landing, injuring his back.

A happier experience came when he accompanied a Vickers pilot out of Brooklands on a flight to Little Rissington in Gloucestershire. Some 48 years later, Amherst wrote about it in a letter to the man who had praised the Maya engine in *The Aeroplane*. By then, after a highly successful career with British European Airways, Bristol

Aircraft, the British Airports Authority and British Caledonian, Amherst's correspondent was known as Sir Peter Masefield and, as the first chairman of the Brooklands Museum Trust, he was busy overseeing the renovation of the old Brooklands clubhouse, a key moment in the creation of the wonderful museum we know today.

Amherst explained to Masefield how, in September 1942, he was given the task of flying a one-off, pressurised, high-altitude Wellington out of Brooklands. He recalled how a barrage balloon had to be lowered to permit his departure, and how the Vickers pilot with him deliberately took off on only one engine, to demonstrate the great torque of the Rolls-Royce Merlin engine!

In fact, as Amherst flew to Little Rissington in the Wellington, his time with the ATA was drawing to a conclusion. Though his skills as a pilot had enabled him to play his part in the war effort, he felt that he could make a bigger contribution as a design engineer, and discussions with the London office of a company named Canadian Car and Foundry (CCF) presented him with the opportunity he was seeking.

The company, with headquarters in Montreal, had been formed in 1909 by the merger of three businesses engaged in the manufacture of passenger railway carriages and freight cars. Two of the businesses were located in Montreal, and the third had been based in the town of Amherst, Nova Scotia. This may be why, once he had embarked upon a life in North America, which, apart from brief interruptions in Europe, would last more for than two decades, Amherst was generally known as Charles and not infrequently addressed by colleagues as Charlie, or even Chuck.

In 1939 CCF had begun a production run of some 1,400 Hurricane fighters and as this was to draw to a close in 1943, the company began to seek alternative ways of utilising a workforce that had become as skilled in manufacturing military aircraft as railway carriages. It is not known how Amherst first came into contact with CCF, but in the autumn of 1942 its London office, at 28 St James's Square, concluded that he was the man to help take it into a new era and invited him out to Montreal.

On 31 October 1942 Amherst made the last recorded flight of his ATA career, at the controls of an old Armstrong Whitworth Whitley bomber, flying out of White Waltham on a journey that lasted some 3 hours 40 minutes. Eight days later, he was on board the *Queen Elizabeth* as she slipped away from her mooring at Gourock on the River Clyde, bound for New York.

The entry in his brother-in-law Desmond Fitz-Gerald's diary that day gives a clue to the danger that lay ahead of Amherst: 'Great news, British are routing the Germans & Italian forces in Africa & huge landings of US troops are taking place in French North Africa.'[5] The invasion of North Africa had involved 500 merchant ships, protected by 350 warships – at the time, Churchill called it 'the largest amphibious operation ever conceived'[6] – but that meant there were 350 fewer Navy vessels to protect the North Atlantic.

At the same time, the U-boat threat had never been greater. Indeed, while Amherst was at sea, Field Marshal Jan Smuts, the South African member of the Imperial War Cabinet, gave an impassioned speech on the subject in London: 'Germany is making an unheard-of concentration of materials, manpower and engineering resources for the building and operation of her U-boats. They roam the seas in numbers, over distances, and for endurance periods that were formally thought impossible.'[7]

In spite of the inherent dangers, the British and American governments had agreed earlier in the year to operate the *Queen Elizabeth* as a troop-carrying ferry ship. Plans were already being developed for the allied invasion of Europe, and vast numbers of US troops needed to be brought over to Britain. The ship could cross the Atlantic in half the time of a normal convoy vessel, and carry more troops. This was the logic that overruled fears that a regular ferry service would be vulnerable to U-boat attack.

In a bid to throw submarines off her trail, the *Queen Elizabeth* followed a zig-zag path in all but the worst of sea conditions – but then bad weather was no help to a U-boat captain either, since torpedo aiming was harder and his conning tower might be spotted in the trough between waves. There was another circumstance in which the *Queen Elizabeth* would stop zig-zagging – if a submarine was sighted. Then, the objective became presenting as small a target as possible to the submarine, and sailing at full speed either towards or away from it.

The day after leaving Gourock, the ship carrying Amherst and his 7,300 fellow passengers and crew was forced to take such evasive action. She was some 200 miles north-west of Northern Ireland when one of her gun crews spotted a U-boat periscope. Kapitänleutnant Kessler, commander of *U-704*, had the great vessel in his sights and fired four torpedoes. Two minutes later, he heard an explosion, and was sufficiently confident that he had scored a direct hit that he sent a signal to this effect to U-Boat Command Headquarters in Berlin.

Two days later, the story hit the German press. It was claimed that 'a German submarine scored a torpedo hit on a British battleship of the Queen Elizabeth class. A heavy explosion was observed aboard the battleship.'[8] On 13 November the *New York Times* picked up on the claims, noting that the Germans had changed their story:

> *The German High Command announced yesterday that the British passenger liner Queen Elizabeth had been torpedoed and damaged in the North Atlantic, according to a German broadcast recorded by the Associated Press in New York. The Germans, on the previous day, had reported that it was a battleship of the Queen Elizabeth class that was damaged but yesterday the High Command corrected its report to make it the 85,000-ton passenger vessel, the largest in the world.[9]*

Had this claim been true, it would have spelt catastrophe for the Allied war effort, and, of course, for Amherst and all aboard the ship. Mercifully, the explosion heard by Kessler was presumably the self-destructing device on one of his torpedoes. On the very same day that New Yorkers read of the loss of the *Queen Elizabeth*, she arrived safely in their midst. Security aboard the ship had clearly been well-maintained, for rumours of the U-boat sighting had not spread and many of the passengers were amazed to learn the 'news' when they disembarked. Amherst appears not to have been one of them. He would have loved to regale friends and family with this story, but he appears not to have and must have pressed on for Montreal without learning of his narrow escape.

Amherst moved into the Hotel Windsor near the city's railway station. He soon discovered that food rationing was as severe in Canada as it was in Britain, and that the winters were a good deal worse. Business trips to New York and Washington kept his spirits up, and he reported in a letter to his mother Elaine that 'New York is crazy about Winston.'[10] One of his first tasks was a report into a large two-stroke engine, the Harper, but he soon became involved in a much bigger project.

CCF was looking ahead, not just to the end of its Hurricane contract, but to peace and to the demand for transatlantic passenger flight, and it gave Amherst a brief to design a long-range military transport plane that could also form the basis for a passenger aircraft. More than 60 years before the Airbus A380, he came up with a double-decker airliner, with not four engines, but six.

The V-1000, as the project became known, had a tubby, largely circular fuselage, 136ft (41.5m) in length. The wings were particularly distinctive, elliptical in plan and slightly dihedral in section. They were enormous, with an overall wingspan of 220ft (67m), and supported the six Pratt & Whitney Wasp engines, each driving a pair of contra-rotating propellers. The cantilever tail plane had a more pronounced angle from the horizontal, causing the tops of the fins to lean towards each other.

The man who knew all about the pilot's visibility challenges in the Gloster IV seaplane gave the crew of the V-1000 an excellent view, by providing them with a largely transparent nose. A report on the plane, and on a series of parallel projects being undertaken at CCF, noted that the crew also had 'an auxiliary rest quarters immediately aft'.[11] The passenger compartment was laid out on two floors, connected by staircases towards the front and rear, and took full account of what was envisaged to be a 'trans-ocean night express service', with 'deluxe reclining chairs or sleeping berths convertible in flight'.[12]

Motor racing historian Doug Nye recalls seeing a drawing shown to him by Amherst, portraying the interior of the plane in full military transport mode, and capable of holding six Jeeps side by side. A hybrid version was said to be capable of transporting 160 passengers and 4½ tons of freight over 3,000 miles, or 80 passengers and 6 tons of freight over 4,500 miles. The full passenger variant was planned to carry 135 passengers and their baggage over a similar distance.

Amherst's V-1000 was designed to cruise at a speed of 220mph (354kmh), and a height of 25,000ft (7,600m). This would, the report states, have involved using the Pratt & Whitney Wasps at some 45 per cent of their take-off power. Top speed was calculated, at 75 per cent of take-off power, to be 300mph (483kmh).

CCF's parallel projects were led by a Texan some five years Amherst's senior, Vincent Burnelli, who had joined the company as a consulting engineer a year before Amherst. For some considerable time, he had pursued an interest in generating lift from the fuselage itself. In its purest form, this involved giving the fuselage an aerofoil section and blending it into a 'continuous wing', in pursuit of greater lift.

In comparison with such a design philosophy, Amherst's approach to the V-1000, ambitious though it was, could be argued to be 'conventional' and it was unlikely that the two men could have been expected to work well together. No record remains of what Burnelli thought of his English colleague, but in his 1983 interview with Mike McCarthy, Amherst made his views about Burnelli quite clear: he was a 'blatherskite', which the *Oxford English Dictionary* describes as 'a blustering kind of fellow', but which, to quote McCarthy, 'in Villiers' dictionary means someone who won't change his mind and has to have his own way.'[13]

Regardless of the rivalry between the two men, CCF tested a model of the V-1000 in the National Research Council's wind tunnel in Ottawa, but the project was not pursued by the company. In old age Amherst claimed that this was because the Canadian Government did not understand the commercial benefits of developing a transatlantic airliner. In hindsight it can be argued that the creation of

Newfoundland and Labrador as Canada's tenth province in 1949, and the development of Newfoundland's Gander Airport as an intermediary stop in the early years of commercial transatlantic fight, would not have benefited from an airliner capable of carrying 135 passengers over 4,500 miles, but these are unlikely to have been criteria in a decision taken years earlier.

Whatever the reason for the ultimate failure of Amherst's V-1000 aircraft to enter production, the project had enabled him to demonstrate that his design skills were now every bit as capable as his development skills. As victory in Europe finally arrived in May 1945, and in the Pacific in September, he considered his options.

The pre-war life he had known in England was gone forever. He and Maya were divorced. The man who had taken their pre-wedding photographs and the images of their beautiful home, Sasha Stone, had died in a French internment camp. So too had Jack Kruse, the man who had commissioned Amherst to create the first supercharged Rolls-Royce. Wimborne House, scene of so many wonderful family occasions, was about to become the headquarters of an insurance company. Brooklands would never host another motor race.

There was little call for Amherst Villiers to go home. He would try his luck in America.

Chapter 12

ROCKETRY

Amherst got lucky straight away. He was visiting New York's St Patrick's Cathedral one day when he met a softly spoken, raven-haired young woman with a radiant smile. Juanita Lorraine Brown had been born in Minnesota in August 1918, and was known as Nita. Amherst fell in love with her and, after a whirlwind romance, they married. In June 1946 their daughter Janie was born. The baby's christening was held at the city's St John's Cathedral, and one of her godmothers brought further good fortune to Amherst.

Amy Guest was the eldest child of steel magnate Harry Phipps and wife of Amherst's maternal uncle Freddy Guest, one-time private secretary to Winston Churchill, and Britain's Secretary of State for Air in the early 1920s. At some point in their marriage Freddy and Amy concluded that they were best off on opposite sides of the Atlantic, and Amy raised their three children as American citizens at Roslyn Manor, a Long Island mansion.

Freddy's great love of flying rubbed off on other members of his family – his daughter Diana competed with him in the 1931 King's Cup air race, and his son Winston would found Guest Airlines, a Mexican-based transatlantic and pan-American airline. Amy was no exception; in the late 1920s she had hoped to become the first woman to fly the Atlantic, and though her children persuaded her not to make the trip herself, she played a key part in the selection of the woman who set the record, Amelia Earhart, and provided the plane, a Fokker F7 tri-motor, in which the feat was accomplished.

By 1946, Amherst had devoted much of the previous 15 years to aircraft and aero engine design, so Amy Guest could not help but have a natural soft spot for her English nephew and his young family, and she invited them to move into a cottage on the Roslyn Manor estate. It was an idyllic home for Amherst as he sought to establish himself in early post-war America.

The first project of his American years was not actually connected with wings, but involved a return to wheels, albeit only three. He had gone to work for Emile Mathis, the Frenchman 20 years his senior, who had risen from Strasbourg-based car dealer and co-manufacturer of some of Ettore Bugatti's earliest automotive designs, to become, by the 1920s, France's fourth-largest car builder. A joint venture with Ford had proved less successful and during the Second World War he had moved to the United States to run a factory on Long Island manufacturing anti-aircraft munitions.

On the return of peace, Mathis wanted to interest the American market in a small, three-wheel car. It was this project which briefly involved Amherst, who recalled with Mike MacCarthy during their 1983 interview that the Frenchman could be difficult:

'I think his wife beat him on the head with a champagne bottle or something. One minute he'd be charming, the next he'd blow up like an inflated frog! But I liked him.' Mathis wanted to make a three-wheeler in the States, but Villiers wasn't keen on the idea: 'I told him, look, drive down to Washington and you'll see lots of cars overturned. If they've got four wheels nobody says anything – but if they've only got three the accident will be blamed on that fact. You're beaten from the start.'[1]

Shortly afterwards, Mathis decided to return to France and set about reviving his Alsace factories. Amherst was forced to look elsewhere for work in a difficult economy. Fortunately, his Aunt Amy was able to provide further help. She took Amherst on an enjoyable visit to Mexico City and then used her contacts with another Long Island-based business, Grumman, to provide him with his first rocket-based project, working for the company's 'Pilotless Small Aircraft Group'.

Grumman was bidding for a government contract for a ship-to-ship missile with a range of 500 miles. Amherst found that the consensus at Grumman was in favour of a ramjet for propelling the missile, but he proposed that a rocket should also be considered. More than 20 years earlier, when he first began researching superchargers, he went to someone with ten years' experience in the field, Auguste Rateau, before testing his first Roots-type blower. Now, in order to develop his knowledge of rocketry, he turned to a unique source of information. He was able to ask for, and obtain, the V-2 designs captured from the Germans.

He told McCarthy, 'It was very exciting – there were cases and tea-chests full of blue prints. In among them I found a design for a winged rocket which could glide onto its target: this, to me, was the way to go.'[2]

It is an intriguing thought. In war-time London, suspicions on a street hit several times by V-2s would run high against neighbours on an unscathed street, the inference being that a spy must live in their midst. In the end, government statisticians were obliged to plot the landing site of every V-2 rocket and reached the conclusion that the pattern was entirely random. Only after the war did it emerge that this was not correct. The V-2 was found to have a rudimentary guidance system, a gyropilot controlling exhaust vanes and rudders. However, as Brian Macfie and Philip Nufrio wrote in their *Applied Statistics for Public Policy*, this gave it 'a circular error probability (CEP; the diameter of a circle within which half the missiles would land) of 11 miles.'[3]

Grumman's objective was to hit a ship at 500 miles, and while this had indeed been the range of the V-2, its guidance system could not provide anything like the required accuracy. In a sense, the method of propulsion was a side issue; the missile could not be successful unless a means of providing pin-point accuracy over that range could be established. However, Amherst chose not to stay with the company to work on this. In McCarthy's words, 'Grumman didn't want it (his V-2-

based gliding wing rocket proposal), so Villiers packed up and left.'[4] The episode is revealing. Amherst had quite correctly identified the significance of the V-2 programme – its co-director Wernher von Braun would play a central role in the American space programme, and his Saturn V rocket would take man to the moon – but he had also demonstrated an inability to lose a reasoned argument and remain within the team. It was to become a familiar pattern in the years ahead.

Amherst was able to apply the knowledge gained at Grumman to good effect. He was elected president of the American Rocket Society (ARS) for 1948. This, the forerunner of today's American Institute of Aeronautics and Astronautics, had been founded by a group of science fiction writers in 1930 as the American Interplanetary Society, to discuss the prospects for space exploration. By the time of Amherst's election, the ARS had more than 800 members, the great bulk of whom were scientists or engineers, and were headquartered in permanent offices on New York's West 29th Street. It was now 'an incorporated organization devoted to the encouragement of scientific research and engineering development of jet-propulsion devices and their application to problems of transportation and communication. At the present time it is also concerned with the military uses of rocket power.'[5]

The ARS published a quality journal: volume 73, dated March 1948, will have been of particular interest to Amherst. Not only did it give the news of his election, but it also carried an article entitled 'Trends on Guided Missiles', by a Lieutenant Colonel in the Ordnance Department of the US Army, who objectively weighed the pros and cons of rocket propulsion and ramjets, and also reported on the continuing challenges of gyroscopic guidance: 'There is no control after launching and the accuracy depends on the precision of the gyro. Present accuracy is approximately four per cent of range.'[6] At a range of 500 miles, this meant that accuracy was still no better than 20 miles, and that the target ship remained in little danger.

The following article, *Navy Plans Rocket Tests*, must have particularly pleased Amherst. Vice-Admiral Forest P. Sherman, deputy chief of naval operations, who had watched the recent 'firing of a V-2 from the deck of the USS *Midway*, said that the Navy obtained "a great deal of valuable information" from this initial test . . . He disagreed emphatically with unidentified Army ordnance experts, who have been quoted as saying that guided missiles, such as the V-2, cannot be fired accurately at sea because of the pitch and roll of ships.'[7] Directly or indirectly, Amherst had his admirers.

His last task as president of the ARS came on 2 December 1948, at the Society's Third Annual Convention, held at New York's Hotel Pennsylvania. He presided over lunch and invited the guest speaker K. F. Mundt, chief engineer at Aerojet Engineering, to talk on 'The Muroc Facility', better known today as Edwards Air Force Base. In old age, Amherst would look back with pride on his presidency of the American Rocket Society, and his subsequent fellowship of the American Institute of Aeronautics and Astronautics – into which the ARS and the Institute of Aerospace Science merged in 1963 – and even took to using the designation 'FAIAA' after his name.

As 1948 ended and his term drew to a close, he seized the opportunity to take Nita and Janie over to England on holiday. His mother Elaine had been widowed a second time during 1942, and had recently decided to move back to London. Her new home, on Holland Street in Kensington, was within walking distance of Kensington Palace Gardens and Hyde Park, and has been the London home of Amherst's family ever since.

Amherst's tour took in not only London, but also a visit to his sister Veronica and her ailing husband Desmond Fitz-Gerald at Glin Castle in Ireland. Fitz-Gerald had been suffering from tuberculosis for some time, and spells in an Arizona desert and a Swiss sanatorium had done little to alter the course of his illness, which was entering its final stages. Amherst's month-long stay at Glin was a stressful one; he was so sensitive to his brother-in-law passing the disease on to his little girl that Fitz-Gerald was effectively confined to his quarters.

Fitz-Gerald died some three months later and in 1954 Veronica married a wealthy Canadian industrialist and banker, Ray Milner.

Elaine subsequently referred to the wedding as the moment when 'that wonderful Ray (of light) came along with his love (and dollars) and illuminated the whole scene – bless him'.[8] Veronica's son, also called Desmond, who inherited Glin Castle as the 29th Knight of Glin on the death of his father, puts its more frankly: 'He saved the lot of us!'[9] Amherst would himself, on occasion, be the beneficiary of Milner dollars – and his smart, hand-me-down tweed jackets – but in 1950 a new opportunity emerged for him.

Amherst took a role with the Eclipse-Pioneer division of Bendix Aviation, based in Teterboro, New Jersey, and the family moved first to nearby Hackensack and then a few miles further west to Paterson. Eclipse had enjoyed a successful war, producing some 70 types of aircraft instrumentation and engine components in October 1943 alone, and winning 20 'E' awards from the US Army and Navy for engineering excellence. The company had endured a downturn in the early post-war years, but when Amherst joined – the 1951 ARS Roster of Members gives his position as design engineer – its fortunes were on the rise again, partly because of the success of its autopilots for civil airliners such as Douglas's DC-6, and partly because the onset of the Korean War meant that demand for military components had increased again.

In April 1951 Nita gave birth to a son, Charles. The christening was arranged to take place at St Thomas's Church on New York's Fifth Avenue in early August, and Amherst wrote to a second cousin of his, enquiring if he would consent to be godfather in proxy to the boy. In the letter, he explained that his correspondent may not remember him from visits half a century earlier to Canford, but that he would perhaps recall his father as the man who had been Liberal MP in Brighton. Now, Amherst continued, he planned to call his son Charles Churchill Villiers, in commemoration of the union between the two men's families. A reference to Amherst's great talisman Amy Guest sending her love may have done the trick, for his second cousin broke off from his heavy workload – he was Leader of His Majesty's Opposition, after all – not only to give his consent, but to choose a present for his new godson. Thus it was that Winston Churchill became godfather to Amherst's young son, and sent the boy a signed copy of *My Early Life* as a present, specially bound in red leather.

In his letter to Churchill, Amherst wrote that he was designing rockets for Bendix, and family correspondence indicates he was working on military rather than civilian projects. Beyond that, there remains little record of what aspects of rocketry Amherst was working on, though during his seven-year tenure the Teterboro site was primarily engaged in air data computers, which provided more accurate calculations of air speed and temperature; vertical scale indicators, which offered pilots thermometer-style gauges, which were easier to read in confined cockpits than traditional clock-style instruments; and dead reckoning computers, which deduced current location by tracking direction, time, speed and distance from start point.

Into the second half of his career with Eclipse, Amherst left design work altogether and became the company's liaison engineer, supporting its overseas licensees in countries including Australia, Japan and Spain on technical questions arising from their Eclipse licences.

Clearly happy with his prospects at the company, and mindful of their growing family, Amherst and Nita spent the spring of 1954 house-hunting, and found what they were looking for on Saddle River Road, Ridgewood, some 13 miles north of Teterboro. It was, Amherst explained in a letter to Veronica, a modern ranch house in a new development, in a smart area with good schools. The house – which had three bedrooms, two bathrooms, a basement playroom and a two-car garage – occupied a plot 125 x 135ft (38m x 41m), which he thought an ideal size as any larger would mean that too much of his time would have to be devoted to lawn mowing! This, and a similar comment made by his mother Elaine in a letter to Veronica from around the same time, are more indicative of Amherst's aversion to lawn-mowing than any sign that, at the age of 53, with a full-time job and two children under the age of eight, the enormous stamina he had exploited in getting so many racing cars to the start line more than 20 years earlier was diminishing. While Amherst sorted out the release of monies from his trust fund, his new brother-in-law, Ray Milner, helped him complete the purchase of the house with a bridging loan, and the family moved into their new home that summer.

But in August 1955, as the torrential rains caused by Hurricane Connie lashed New Jersey, Amherst felt ostracised by Eclipse and became keen to leave. The director of engineering who had given him the liaison engineering role left to take up another appointment within Bendix, and a Mr Isaacs, formerly director of sales, became general manager. He concluded that a new, de-centralised strategy was required, and he made other divisions responsible for many of Eclipse's products. This meant there was no need for an engineer to liaise with overseas licensees, and Isaacs proposed that Amherst should return to project engineering.

Most people familiar with corporate life would find Isaacs's position reasonable enough; a company's strategy has to change to meet altered economic circumstances, and while Amherst's role may have become redundant, he was being offered a future in a highly reputable company which respected his skills. But he had such an acute sense of trust, that he reacted strongly whenever he felt that trust had been breached. In an interview 30 years later, Brian Palmer asked him what he thought of working for American companies. He replied, 'In America they have these organisation charts and they are always changing who's in charge of this, that or the other until you don't know where you are – and it's all too high pressure altogether.'[10]

Nonetheless, Amherst's return to project engineering certainly resulted in a fascinating assignment. In the search for greater stability, and more accurate measurement of distance during flight, he was given the task of producing Eclipse's first Rate Integrating Gyro, or RIG. Bill Ficken, the young man who took over the project a year later when Amherst finally left Eclipse in the summer of 1956, recalls that the Englishman

had largely completed the design on paper, and had released his drawings to the model shop for them to develop half a dozen prototypes. It was a fully floated, neutrally buoyant, single degree of freedom gyro, about 2 inches diameter by 3 inches long. There were few glitches in his design; overall, he left a good design that went together and tested quite well. The following year, the focus at Bendix shifted to Air Bearing Gyros when we were awarded a big Pershing contract, but work continued on the Villiers Gyro, as I called it, and those efforts eventually led to Bendix being awarded major Navy contracts for Polaris and Poseidon, and work for the USAF and NASA too.[11]

Ficken believes that even if Amherst applied for patents on the 'Villiers Gyro', they would probably have been assigned to Bendix, and that the Englishman showed little interest in the project when he rang him on several occasions to discuss it with him. It seems likely, therefore, that Amherst never knew about the legacy he left behind at Eclipse, and it is unfortunate that responsibility for such a critical project did not enable him to overcome his reservations about working for a company which he perceived had not honoured its promises.

Yet within months, when Amherst and his family arrived in England for a holiday that autumn, he was already lining up a return to rocketry, with the Livermore Laboratory, the establishment founded by the University of California in 1952 to support research into and development of nuclear weapons science and technology. In spite of Amherst having taken US citizenship, the process of gaining security clearance was a complex one, and involved, recorded Elaine, 'the names, dates, ages of all relations for many generations, [and] the exact dates of his every movement and journey for the last 20 years. They are leaving no chance of a hidden communist or association with any of the hundreds of societies at all suspect in the USA.'[12]

Sadly, no trace of these security clearance forms can now be found, and little evidence exists of Amherst's brief time at Livermore. What is known is that the university confirmed in late October 1956 that Amherst could commence work there independent of security clearance, and that he, Nita and the children sailed from Southampton on the *Île de France* on 2 November, docking in New York five days later. The Livermore telephone directory for that winter indicates that Amherst worked in Building 141, which housed Project Rover. This had begun the previous year, and focused on the development of a nuclear reactor engine to power intercontinental missiles and rockets for space exploration.

During 1957 Project Rover was relocated to Los Alamos, New Mexico, home of the Manhattan Project, which had developed the atomic bombs dropped on Hiroshima and Nagasaki. It is not certain that this move was the reason for the shortness of Amherst's employment at Livermore, but the relocation would surely have been a closely guarded secret and one can imagine his reaction if the news was given to him only after his arrival in California.

He was soon back in gainful employment, with the electronics division of Hamilton Standard, a part of United Aircraft Corporation located in East Hartford, Connecticut. This operation, which would later become part of Hamilton Standard's Missiles and Space Systems Department, was a space project management and systems integration business, developing system requirements for customer projects and managing the construction of airframes, ground support units, and propulsion and guidance systems.

Throughout 1957 signs that the Soviet Union was preparing the launch of a satellite went unheeded in the West, even when advice began to be broadcast to amateur radio hams about the frequencies on which they would be able to monitor its orbits. On 4 October Sputnik 1 was launched, and on 3 November Sputnik 2 carried Laika the dog into orbit. America's humiliation was complete four days later, when the Moscow parade marking the 40th anniversary of the Soviet revolution featured a medium-range ballistic missile, the SS-3 Shyster. The Soviets could put satellites into orbit at will, and demonstrably had the means to fire nuclear warheads on America. Explorer 1 was America's response, going into orbit on 31 January 1958. The Cold War had just got colder, and the space race had begun.

Amherst explained his reaction to Sputnik to Mike McCarthy in 1983: 'I went to Hamilton Standard's Electronics Division, which was actually their missiles and space department, and said "look, the Russians have put up one ton, in five years they'll put up ten tons, let's jump way ahead and put up 100 tons!" This led on to Project Arcturus, the intention being to put up 100 tons, using liquid nitrogen as fuel.'[13]

Amherst's enthusiasm for his new role was evident in family correspondence. In March 1958, Elaine, now suffering from advanced osteoporosis and in the final months of her life, told Veronica, 'Nita writes that Amherst's project is a Space Ship!!! What next? She says it is like a new toy to him. I suppose he is taken with it, even without the contract and salary which you wished for him and which apparently he could not get.'[14]

While the work at East Hartford remained fascinating – another project in which he was involved was a ten-man lunar base – Amherst felt unable to commit to moving the family to Connecticut, preferring for them to maintain a base in New York and for him to commute the 120 miles or so back and forth each weekend. There were two reasons for this. First, Elaine, the last-surviving of the first Baron Wimborne's nine children, died in July at the age of 87, and bequeathed to Amherst her Holland Street property, now divided into a smaller home and two rent-generating flats. Since he and Nita therefore expected to move to London in the mid-term, there was little point uprooting the family any more than was necessary. Second, Amherst shared Veronica's disappointment about his earnings, but as he explained to her in a letter written in October, he had high hopes for a substantial increase in pay, and he felt he may have more chance of achieving the type of salary being offered to engineers joining the business if he declined to demonstrate the type of commitment that moving the family to Connecticut might imply.

His hopes of a pay rise rested on a brochure describing his satellites and lunar vehicles, which he was waiting to be published. If it did go into print, no copy survives, but somehow or other Amherst's work with Hamilton Standard's Missiles and Space Systems Division came to the attention of Boeing, who invited him to come out to Seattle, Washington, to join its Lunar Systems Group as technical manager.

At a sad time for the family – his elder sister Barbara's husband died in November – Amherst drew comfort from the location, as Seattle put him near to Veronica and her husband Ray Milner's beautiful home at Qualicum on Vancouver Island. Veronica devoted much time to developing one of the great woodland gardens there, and over the years Amherst would enjoy his visits, admiring its vast Douglas firs, humming birds and eagles. Before her death in 1998, Veronica assured the future of Qualicum by selling it to Malpasina University-College, whose horticultural faculty keep the gardens in their splendour for the public to enjoy to this day.

Amherst's time at Boeing was less happy. As he told McCarthy, 'a new fellow came on the scene with his own pet project and took all my men – they do things like that in America! – and I retired because I didn't think they were paying enough attention to the Moon.'[15]

Thus did Amherst's first, two-decade-long stay in North America draw to a close. Manifestly challenged by life as an employee, he had nonetheless made his contribution, like thousands of others, to America's space programme, and would rejoin it three years later. But in March 1960, as he, Nita and the children boarded the SS *United States* in New York, bound for Southampton, they understood they were sailing to a new life in England.

Chapter 13

PAINTING

Painting was in Amherst's blood. It came to him from both sides of his family: his paternal great aunt, Amelie Amherst, sister of the first Baron Amherst, was a particularly gifted water-colourist, and the walls of Glin Castle are adorned with her work. Amherst's mother Elaine's watercolour landscapes display great skill, too, and her sketch in a visitor's book at Canford House of her husband Ernest singing to the accompaniment of a violinist, against a background of ferns and classical columns, demonstrates a confident hand.

The earliest known example of Amherst displaying his artistic capabilities in adulthood is a simple watercolour from 1923, depicting Raymond Mays roaring up a hill-climb in *Cordon Rouge*. There is no mistaking the distinctive radiator and high bonnet line of the Brescia, or indeed Mays's high hair line, as the car swings right, but Amherst is not using the precision he brought later to his portraits. He is creating an impression – of the speed of the car, leaving a cloud of dust in its wake and raising its inside front wheel, the exuberance of Mays in the cockpit, and the sheer joy of a sporting event in the country.

More than 50 years later, a hill-climb and *Concours d'Elégance* meeting were held at Prescott, home to the Bugatti Owners' Club, and since its opening in 1938, one of England's most prestigious hill-climb venues. When the UK importers of Cordon Rouge champagne agreed to sponsor the event, it was only fitting that Amherst's depiction of Mays in *Cordon Rouge* should be used for the poster, and the painting came to the attention of a wider audience.

Other than this watercolour, Amherst's motor racing and aeronautic associates in pre-Second World War England would have had little awareness of his skills as an artist. They would have been familiar with two significantly different ways in which he committed images to paper. One was the type of engineering drawing he produced for his designs, which were by their very nature utterly precise. The other was the type of quick sketch he would draw to make a point or explain the purpose of something.

An excellent example of the latter is the sketch Amherst gave to *Bugantics*, the magazine of the Bugatti Owners' Club, to illustrate how the 'rat traps' on *Cordon Rouge* improved lubrication at the higher engine speeds he had generated.

Interestingly, after Amherst's death, when Sir Peter Masefield began work on his *Times* obituary, another friend, John Millar, gave him a note Amherst had sent, complimenting Millar on a letter he had written to a newspaper about the engineering capabilities of Ettore Bugatti. Amherst had, by way of example, drawn a rough sketch of the Brescia's 4-valve cam tappet arrangement. It probably took him all of 30 seconds to draw, and was simply labelled '1, 2, 3' to illustrate various aspects of the design. Brilliant in its simplicity of argument, it makes one wish Amherst had written and illustrated a performance engineering textbook, but at the bottom of the note Sir Peter scrawled 'Don't believe he was a painter'.[1]

If Masefield had not seen Amherst's portraits, it would have been a reasonable enough assumption, but his observation helps to counter the criticism that is sometimes made of them. It is said that in their almost photographic likeness to their subjects, his portraits demonstrate the precise eye and hand of an engineer at work, and lack artistic merit. This is grossly unfair. Those rough sketches, knocked off quickly to demonstrate an engineering point, and the impressionistic watercolour of Mays in *Cordon Rouge*, are but two points on what will be seen was a broad spectrum of expression. That Amherst eventually chose to adopt a naturalistic form for his portrait work tells us more about his personal tastes and influences as an artist, rather than any restriction imposed on him by his background as an engineer.

Primary among his influences was one of the mid-20th century's most well-known portrait painters, Pietro Annigoni. Born in Milan in 1910, he had forged a highly successful career painting naturalistic portraits of high profile subjects using the techniques of the Italian masters. His portrait of Queen Elizabeth, which was exhibited in London's Royal Academy in 1955, was painted so early in a new Elizabethan era of hope after years of post-war austerity, that it etched itself in the consciousness of Britain. Amherst's mother Elaine was particularly taken with it, mentioning it in no fewer than three letters to Veronica and hanging a copy of it on her wall. Amherst was more than 3,500 miles away at the time, but Annigoni was equally famous in the US, and would go on to paint both presidents Kennedy and Johnson. It is likely that, when Amherst finally decided to pursue a naturalistic form of portraiture as a career, using classical methods for preparing his oils, he was also showing the influence of Annigoni.

The Bugatti watercolour apart, Amherst's artistic ambitions lay so deeply submerged beneath his automotive, aeronautic and rocketry work that it was not until his late 50s that frustration with employment in large US corporations led him to take up art professionally. Even Nita, profoundly shocked at this turn of events, had not seen it coming. Living on New York's East 81st Street, just three blocks from the Metropolitan Museum of Art, was an advantage. Enamoured by 16th-century Renaissance artists, Amherst gained permission to go to the museum and undertake a copy of Titian's *Venus and the Lute Player*. This depicts a fully clothed lutenist sitting at the feet of a reclining, naked Venus, who turns away from him to be crowned by Cupid. It is not only a celebration of love and music; it is also, says the museum, 'thought to address the Neo-Platonic debate of seeing versus hearing as the primary means for perceiving beauty'.[2]

This ambitious undertaking, at the outset of his new career, was a way for Amherst to practise life painting and to experiment with his favoured medium, oil. But he was quite pragmatic in the way he set about making a living as a painter. He concluded that there was money to be made from portrait commissions, and he chose his 6-year-old son Charles as the subject for the portrait he would use to demonstrate his prowess.

For a month, most afternoons after school, Charles would sit for Amherst, and the result was an impressively bold debut. A bright-eyed, alert little boy with dark blonde hair, dressed in white shirt and striped pullover, stares confidently at the viewer. On a narrow stage in the foreground, a little mouse in trousers and tailcoat stands in the bottom left-hand corner with 'arms' outstretched, as though he were introducing Charles. In the opposite corner, the artist has signed with his surname, but does not date his work, while along the top of the canvas, the words CHARLES CHURCHILL VILLIERS are printed in capitals. In all of Amherst's most important portraits, he would formally name his subject. The reason for this is not certain, but the name Churchill cannot have hurt Amherst's prospects of finding commissions. Indeed, he sent Winston Churchill a photograph of the portrait, noting that he and Nita had enjoyed the exhibition at the Metropolitan of the great man's own art – said to be the only activity he undertook in silence.

The letter caught up with Churchill – now retired from politics – on one of his frequent stays on the south coast of France. He was at the villa in Roquebrune-Cap-Martin, a few miles east of Monte Carlo, owned by his sometime overseas press and literary agent, Emery Reeves. Churchill replied, 'Dear Amherst, Thank you for your thought in sending me a photograph of the portrait you have painted of your son Charles. It gave me much pleasure to see this. I hope that your son will like the photograph I enclose, which I have signed for him . . .[3]'

Once the portrait of Charles was finished and framed, Amherst took it to a socialite art and antique dealer named Lois Shaw. She had run a gallery on Park Avenue since the 1930s, but in November 1940 she began a 'match-making' service, introducing clients and portraitists. She founded Portraits Inc two years later, and was so taken with the painting of Charles that she not only added Amherst to her roster of artists, but also used it for Portraits Inc advertisements in *The New Yorker* magazine.

No records survive of Amherst's work commissioned through Portraits Inc. Friends from his time in California in the 1960s recall him describing a trip to paint a family in Montreal, and a letter from his mother to his sister Veronica in August 1957 notes with pride, 'It is wonderful Amherst getting this order to paint two little boys in California – a good price and all expenses paid . . . Everyone here who sees the photo I have of little Charles thinks it "masterly".'[4] Across North America today, men and women in their 60s who own portraits of themselves as children may not know that the courteous Englishman who painted them was, at the time, in between engagements in the US space programme.

On holiday in England the previous winter, before his brief stint at the Livermore Laboratories, Amherst had taken the opportunity to paint his beautiful niece, Rachel Severne. She was Veronica's younger daughter and a professional model who worked on assignments across Europe. She did not sit for him in person, as he explained in a letter to her mother: instead, in typically experimental fashion, he used a slide projector to display a coloured image of Rachel into a cardboard box facing him, enabling him to study her features in great detail, and at the same time use his paints in daylight.

Elaine hosted a cocktail party at Holland Street before Amherst and his family headed back to America. His portrait of Rachel was exhibited and she was delighted when he presented her with it. Elaine told Veronica: 'All agreed it was lovely . . . It is done in the medium of the old Masters and is certainly different to the usual modern paintings. Even Anthony (who fancies himself a bit) was impressed.'[5] Elaine was referring to Anthony Devas, a gifted portrait painter who had enjoyed much success before and during the war, and whose work is still displayed today in many British galleries. He had exhibited in every Royal Academy Summer Exhibition since 1939, but had endured years of ill-health and would die, aged only 47, in 1958. For such a highly respected artist to be impressed by the picture of Rachel, at such an early stage in Amherst's life as a portrait painter, speaks volumes.

Back in the US, Amherst's painting commissions were obliged to fall in behind his work at United Aircraft and Boeing, and the second phase of his life as a painter only began once he and his family had settled in England in 1960. Once based in London, the opportunity to formally study under Pietro Annigoni at his studio in Florence was too exciting to ignore, and in December 1960 Amherst was able to fulfil his ambition. He was entering his seventh decade, and was about to enjoy an astonishing period of creativity. A single paragraph in a letter he wrote to Veronica on 1 December captures the breadth of what he was about to undertake. In it, he explained that he had accepted a role as consultant to the Owen Racing Organisation, owner of the BRM Grand Prix team, but that first he was going to Florence, to study the mixed oil tempera medium of the old masters under Annigoni.

The following week, Amherst checked into the Pensione Pitto Palace on Via Barbadori, a short walk from the Ponte Vecchio. His initial impressions of Florence, where it appears he celebrated his 60th birthday without his family, were positive, though he was disappointed by the continual rain.

Amherst was grateful to find that the maestro had set him up in a corner of the studio where the light was particularly good, and set to work with a student, preparing his colours with tempera powders and learning how to use a special pallet fitted with 15 deep cup sections. Preparation of the colours began with mixing nine eggs with a specified weight of a tree resin called copal. From his research to date, Amherst preferred another resin called dammar, but wisely chose to keep this observation to himself. Then each colour was weighed and mixed to a paste with white wine, and added to the emulsion. The use of wine, rather than water, was key, as this meant the egg emulsion would stay fresh for weeks rather than days.

Three weeks rushed by and then Amherst made the return trip to London, to celebrate Christmas with Nita and the children, now aged 14 and 9. He kept Veronica updated of progress with letters each side of Christmas, telling her he thought Annigoni could not have been more kind to him personally, and that he was impressed by the exacting yet generous approach the artist adopted with his students.

There was little time over Christmas for rest, for Amherst had to complete the portrait of a Mrs Morton he had begun before his trip to Florence. He also sent precise instructions to Veronica and her husband Ray Milner on the types of photograph he wanted of each of them so that he could start on their portraits – large enough for eye and mouth expressions to be clear, and perhaps Ray should be portrayed in his chancellor's robes from the University of King's College, Nova Scotia. Amherst was keen that his portraits of Veronica and Milner should be displayed out in Qualicum, as he hoped this might lead to commissions from the good and the great of Canada. By the middle of January he was back in Florence for a second, longer stint, to complete his course under Annigoni.

Into the summer of 1961 Amherst remained busy on engine development work with BRM, and on his portrait of Veronica. To Annigoni's instructions on the preparation of paint and emulsion he added elements from a book he admired, *The Secret Formulas and Techniques of the Masters*, written in 1948 by Jacques Maroger. Maroger had been technical director of the laboratory at the Louvre, and went on to found a school of painters in Maryland, Baltimore, which focused on realism as opposed to abstract. The meticulous mixing and cooking of linseed oil and lead oxide powder litharge, which Amherst learned from Maroger's writing, strikes a chord with the way he would tune the carburettors on *Cordon Rouge*, leaning the mixture back until no exhaust smoke could be seen against the light road surface. In this case, he would place a card behind the saucepan so that he could easily spot the first signs of smoke, at which point the cooking process was complete.

As his confidence as an artist grew, so Amherst felt able to approach an employee of the BRM team on whose Grand Prix engine he was working, and propose that he should paint his portrait. It was to be one of Amherst's best-known paintings. Graham Hill had been born in the London suburb of Hampstead in February 1929, and educated at Hendon Technical College. After an apprenticeship with Smiths Instruments and three years' National Service in the Royal Navy, three laps of Brands Hatch at the wheel of a 500cc Cooper in 1953 were enough to persuade him that he wanted to be a racing driver. He spent several years hawking his services as a mechanic in return for drives, and by 1957 had become a works driver with Lotus. His Grand Prix debut came at Monaco in 1958. Famously, he would win the race five times, but on this occasion he retired from fourth place when a rear wheel came off. It was representative of a poor, unreliable pair of seasons with Lotus, which delivered but a single point-scoring finish. For 1960 Hill switched to the BRM team, which is where he met Amherst the following year.

The sittings took place in Amherst's studio at Holland Street. Hill wore his pale blue Dunlop racing overalls, though the Dunlop logo on his left breast was hidden beneath a dark blue rally jacket. He sat on a stool sufficiently high for Amherst to work at eye level to his subject. A photograph of a late sitting reveals Hill's likeness to have a swarthy chin and slightly flat forehead, but the completed portrait is a fine painting, the handsome racing driver gazing out in assured fashion to the left of the viewer. By the end of the following year, Graham Hill had become world champion, and this, together with the fact that some of the detailed design work on the engine that had driven him to the title had been undertaken by the man who had painted him, can only have raised Amherst's profile.

In May 1962, while Hill was beginning his championship year in style with victory in the Dutch Grand Prix, Amherst carried out his most famous artistic commission of all. The painting of his long-term friend, the James Bond novelist Ian Fleming, is described fully in Chapter 15. It was another confident step forward for Amherst, and a future as a London-based society painter seemed assured, especially when the Fleming portrait was used as the frontispiece for a limited edition, pre-release version of *On Her Majesty's Secret Service*.

The disadvantage to Amherst of having such a breadth of capability was that the demands on his time were enormous, and when Douglas Corporation invited him to California to work on various projects connected with Mars, and when much of his spare time out there was spent restoring the Blower Bentley that Fleming had helped him procure, there was little time for portraiture and the momentum was lost.

When, in the late 1960s, he finally returned to painting in a serious way, it was because his beloved Nita had died and, just as it is said that Churchill needed to lay 200 bricks a day or write 2,000 words a day to keep the 'black dog' of depression off his shoulder at fallow points in his career, so Amherst found solace in art, and set about reviving his career as a portraitist. In 1969, his painting of Charles as a young boy was displayed at a Royal Society of Portrait Painters' exhibition in London, and this portrait, together with those of Hill and Fleming, appeared in a Chelsea Artists' exhibition of the same year.

One of Amherst's bolt-holes during those difficult times was Palma, in Mallorca. He became friendly with the Franciscan monks living in a monastery behind the cathedral and through them received commissions for a portrait of Cardinal Francis Spellman, Archbishop of New York, and a local church restorer.

The Franciscan connection also led Amherst, at the age of 70, to take on his most ambitious art project. On an earlier trip to Italy, he had been impressed to learn about Saint Clare, a wealthy Italian woman born in 1194, who had followed Saint Francis of Assisi into a life of poverty and founded the 'Poor Clare' order of nuns in a convent called San Damiano. In 1240 Saracen mercenaries attacked the convent and it is said that St Clare forced them to flee by appearing at an upstairs window with a communion host, thereby saving Assisi.

Amherst had considered undertaking a painting to be called *The*

Miracle of Santa Clara for some time, and discussions with the Franciscan clerics at the monastery in Palma prompted him into action. They permitted him to use a room in the monastery as a studio – the most apt of surroundings – and he set to work on a vast canvas some 8 x 10ft (2.4 x 3m).

Over the next ten years, Amherst worked intermittently on *The Miracle of Santa Clara*, in Palma and in London, and even for a time at Lord Montagu of Beaulieu's Hampshire home, Palace House. The work involved him in taking classes in painting horses and the study of 13th-century Saracen armour. Saint Clare's face turned out to be not unlike that of actress Elizabeth Taylor in her prime, and Amherst conceded that this might not have been entirely coincidental. As recently as 2004, the huge painting still dominated his old studio in Holland Street.

It appears that Amherst was most struck with Elizabeth Taylor. Once, when he was staying at Glin Castle while his nephew Desmond Fitz-Gerald was working in the US, he decided that some of the knight's ancestors, depicted in portraits around the castle, were not attractive enough. He felt that, by touching them up a little, he could keep his hand in at painting and bring some glamour to the place. One lady ended up, like Saint Clare, looking very like Ms Taylor. When Fitz-Gerald returned from the US, he was appalled at what Amherst had done, and had to spend a considerable sum of money having the paintings restored to their former state.

As with *The Miracle of Santa Clara*, there was a strong religious focus to the last of Amherst's well-known portraits. In October 1978, Cardinal Karol Wojtyła was elected the first non-Italian Pope in centuries, and took the name John Paul II. As he went about his many missions – it is claimed he was the most-travelled world leader ever – Amherst came to admire him deeply, and decided to paint his portrait. There was no question of a sitting. He simply worked with photographs, on a canvas of some 72 x 50in (183 x 127 cm), and chose to depict the Pope standing in front of Bernini's famous dove window, above the altar in St Peter's Basilica.

The painting was not yet complete when plans were announced for Pope John Paul's tour of Britain in May 1982. Amherst contacted the Apostolic Nunciature, effectively the Vatican's embassy in Britain, overlooking Wimbledon Common in south-west London. The Pope was due to spend two nights there during his tour and Amherst asked if his painting could be displayed in the building. The outcome was better than even he had anticipated. Not only was the portrait put on view at Parkside, but Amherst was granted an audience with the Pope.

The completed portrait is considered by some familiar with Amherst's work to be his finest. The Pope's craggy features, the definition and colouring of his mitre, vestments and crucifix, and the light streaming through Bernini's window, are all caught to great effect. Perhaps in a deliberate link between painter and subject, Amherst, whom readers will recall had lost part of a finger in the accident with a wheel-jack over 50 years earlier, portrayed the Pope with a finger in plaster, a legacy of an assassination attempt. The Villiers trademark is present, too, the subject's name spelled out in capitals across the top of the canvas, but on this occasion in Latin.

Like Amherst, a devout Anglican who was so in awe of a Pope that he painted a portrait of him, a man with similarly open mind and artistic talent was Archbishop Bruno Heim, Apostolic Pro-Nuncio to Britain at the time. The Vatican's ambassador in Britain, Heim once took the counsel of the Archbishop of Canterbury, spiritual leader of the Anglican Church, before advising Rome on the appointment of the next Catholic Archbishop of Westminster. He was also an expert in heraldry, personally designing the coats of arms of four popes, and publishing three books on the subject. Amherst was, therefore, justifiably proud of Heim's opinion of his portrait of Pope John Paul II. In November 1984, Heim wrote, 'I should consider this most painstaking and carefully executed work to be worthy of exhibition in any place that would intend to honour the Pope in this way.'[6]

In 2003 Janie Villiers lent her father's portraits of Ian Fleming and Graham Hill to London's National Portrait Gallery, and the paintings spent the next five years on view in what was then known as the Twentieth Century Room. The subjects of the paintings, the creator of James Bond and the only driver to win the 'triple crown' of Formula One World Championship, Indy 500 and Le Mans, fitted in well among scores of other British heroes, but Amherst the artist was there on merit, too. Pietro Annigoni's second portrait of Queen Elizabeth, painted in 1969, hung not far away. More than 40 years after Amherst had studied in the Italian's Florentine studio, the works of pupil and mentor were on display in one of the world's most prestigious galleries.

Chapter 14

BRM

By 1961, Amherst's old friend Raymond Mays had experienced a wide range of success and failure since the pair had gone their separate ways. ERA's maiden season in 1934 saw wins at Brooklands and the new road racing circuit at Donington, another FTD for Mays at Shelsley Walsh, and the sale of the first customer car. The following year saw the Siamese Prince Chula acquire an ERA as a 21st birthday present for his cousin 'Bira' to drive with success for the newly formed White House Stable team, while both Mays and one of Britain's finest pre-war drivers, Richard Seaman, recorded wins for ERA on the Continent.

After further success in 1936 and 1937, plans were developed for a full-scale ERA Grand Prix car and a road car, but both foundered in the wake of Tom Murray Jamieson's tragic death at Brooklands in May 1938. Mays himself resigned as a director of the company in 1939, having fallen out with backer Humphrey Cook, upon whose generosity he had leaned too heavily. Nevertheless, he went on winning in a privately entered ERA, 'R4D', right up to the outbreak of war, most notably another FTD and course record at Shelsley in June, victory in the Campbell Trophy at Brooklands in August, and a new lap record, which would never be bettered, on the Campbell 'road circuit' there the following day.

Mays spent the war years taking 'R4D' to various speaking engagements and charity events, and dreaming of creating a British Grand Prix team when peace returned. To that end, in the spring of 1945 he wrote to the captains of British industry, seeking support for his aspirations. Among early backers was Britain's largest family-owned industrial enterprise, Rubery Owen, which was managed by Alfred Owen, another Oundle old boy, some nine years Mays's junior.

The British Motor Racing Research Trust (BMRRT) was set up in April 1947 to raise funds for the project, and over 100 companies joined a cumbersome operation which employed little project or financial management. In December it was announced that the car would be known as the British Racing Motor, or BRM. Two years would pass before it was so much as shown to the press, and even then it was very far from ready, as evidenced by its inauspicious debut eight months later, when transmission failure meant the car never left the starting grid.

In 1952 Rubery Owen acquired BRM from the BMRRT, but there was no great change in the team's fortunes. It was not until 1959 that a BRM finally won a World Championship Grand Prix, when Swedish driver Jo Bonnier triumphed at Zandvoort in Holland. By then, former trustee Tony Vandervell's own team Vanwall had already won nine Grands Prix, and been crowned World Constructors' Champions for 1958. The Constructors' Trophy was presented to Vandervell during a meeting in October of the International Sporting Committee of the Fédération Internationale de l'Automobile. Another item on the meeting's agenda was the announcement of the new 1,500cc Grand Prix formula, to take effect from 1961.

BRM had 18 months to design and develop a 1½-litre engine for the new formula, but in common with the other British teams, they were not in favour of the rule changes and chose to argue about them rather than focus on a new engine. Meanwhile, the 1960 season unfolded with the usual BRM signs of promise and failure. Graham Hill's heroic drive from last place to first in the British Grand Prix ended when brake failure caused him to spin just five laps from the finish, while at Zandvoort, scene of so many important moments in the team's history, Dan Gurney's car also suffered brake failure and somersaulted off the track, killing a teenage spectator who had been standing in a prohibited area. It was the prompt for all three BRM drivers – Hill, Gurney and Bonnier – to demand changes, and it was from this point that Mays and his long-term chief engineer Peter Berthon began to lose influence over the team, and Tony Rudd, who had joined from Rolls-Royce in the early days, assumed greater responsibility for design and team management.

Thirteen years after BRM's formation, the team had only ever designed two engines, the original, overly complex V16 and the four-cylinder, 2½-litre engine of the 1950s, which was arguably too simple. The essential architecture of the former had been laid out in a pre-war article in *The Motor*, while the latter had begun life as a freelance project. Berthon's formal engineering training was restricted to his unfinished cadetship at RAF Cranwell, and the definitive BRM expert, motor racing historian Doug Nye, notes that 'while quite gifted forensically in identifying the causes of mechanical failure, PB did not necessarily possess an equal grasp of how to avoid them'.[1]

Even though the FIA rejected the British teams' protest against the new formula in May 1960, by the end of July, with the first Grand Prix of the new formula less than 10 months away, BRM had still not begun work on a 1,500cc engine. One option being considered by Berthon was to convert the current 2½-litre unit to 1,500cc specification. This, he advised Owen in a letter, 'would not be the correct long-term answer . . . [but] . . . would give us an engine that would be competitive for possibly a couple of years and would utilise the bulk of the components that we have on hand here at Bourne.'[2] Another option was to buy a customer engine from Porsche or Coventry Climax. In the end a V8 design was settled upon, and Berthon and his principal design draughtsman Aubrey Woods began work on the BRM P56 engine in earnest in August. Tony Rudd first saw the layout drawings upon his return to Bourne from the final Grand Prix of 1960, at Riverside in California, in late November.

It was a week later that Amherst wrote in a letter to his sister Veronica that he was to join BRM as a consultant because they wanted to do better. BRM would not do better in 1961. Forced by the delays to use a hybrid chassis and customer Coventry Climax engines, they were no match for the all-conquering, shark-nose Ferraris, and the best they could muster was a third place at the US Grand Prix in which Innes Ireland gave Team Lotus its debut win.

Sir Alfred Owen – he was knighted during 1961 – demanded an immediate change in fortunes for 1962. The team had only won a single Grand Prix in ten years of trying. Now, unless there were at least two wins in 1962 *and* business success in the form of sales of the new engine to customer teams, then the Owen Racing Organisation would pull the plug on BRM. Fortunately, with Amherst's input, the P56 more than delivered on Owen's ultimatum.

That Amherst came, at the age of 60, to be back in front-line British motor sport the best part of three decades after having left it owes much to his enduring friendship with Raymond Mays. Though hardly directly relevant to motor racing, if anything the experience Amherst had gained in designing missiles, rockets and satellites had only increased the awe in which Mays held him. The pair had stayed in contact over the years, and had seen each other regularly since Amherst had come back to England during 1960. Even though Mays was gradually losing influence at BRM, he still retained the trust of Sir Alfred and persuaded him that Amherst could offer valuable objective support as a design consultant.

Alec Osborn was part of the drawing office team that worked on the design of the P56 engine. He had joined Rubery Owen as a student apprentice at the tender age of 16 and had been pleasantly surprised to learn that the division to which he had been sent ran a Grand Prix team. After a long and varied career with BRM, Osborn went on to spend 32 years with Perkins Engines, rising to chief engineer, with responsibility for engine design and development. He was awarded an MBE in 2005 and became the 121st president of the Institution of Mechanical Engineers the following year. His opinions on the hiring of Amherst therefore carry some weight: 'I can see why Sir Alfred agreed to hire Amherst. Quality external consultancy provides a useful discipline. Amherst brought judgement value. He brought the seal of approval of a quite famous name. We didn't see him out and about in the office very much, but he spent a lot of time with PB, and made some comments to Aubrey Woods.'[3]

It appears from family correspondence that Amherst did not begin work with BRM in earnest until the spring of 1961, once he had finished his time with Annigoni in Florence and had freed himself of his painting commitments, and by then the essential architecture of the engine had been mapped out by Berthon and Woods. Where possible, the pair also tried to use components from the V16 1½-litre engine. What Amherst provided, assisted by a draughtsman working with him in Kensington, was an able sounding board and an additional resource when it came to the detailed design of new internals. After a regrettably long gestation the P56 engine ran on a test bed in July 1961, ten months to the day from a clean sheet of paper, Woods would later tell Nye. On 20 July, Amherst wrote to Veronica that he had been busy up at Bourne with the new engine, that it was now running, and that he hoped it would be in a car in time for September's Italian Grand prix, at Monza.

By the middle of August the engine was indeed sitting in the back of the neat little car designed for it, the P578, and testing was able to start in earnest at Monza the following month, though only either side of the Italian Grand Prix, rather than during the race meeting itself. The Italian press liked what they saw, labelling the car 'Little Miss Elegance'. The old V16 connecting rods failed during the tests – a consequence, in part, of the P56 drawings being in metric, and the V16 drawings in imperial – and were replaced, and fuel injection problems identified, most of which were eliminated over the winter.

A pair of wins in non-championship races during the spring of 1962 gave the team cause for optimism and on 20 May, when the Dutch Grand Prix heralded the start of the World Championship season, Graham Hill drove his V8-powered BRM to victory by almost half a minute. For Raymond Mays, sitting quietly in a corner of the pits for the last few laps, it was a moment of intense pride and gratification and, unlike Jo Bonnier's solitary win in the same event three years earlier, it signalled the start of a glorious campaign.

In the Monaco Grand Prix two weeks later Hill took the lead after seven laps and held it until an oil leak caused his engine to seize just 13 miles from the finish, close enough for him to be classified sixth and earn a single championship point. At Spa in late June, Hill consolidated his championship lead with a solid second place in the Belgian Grand Prix, but finished over 40 seconds behind the Lotus of his main rival for the title, Jim Clark.

July saw the pair to the forefront once more, at Rouen in the French Grand Prix. This time Hill seemed to be in the ascendancy, pulling out a 20-second lead over Clark until the BRM was hit and tapped into a spin by a back-marker. Clark's retirement handed the initiative back to Hill, but a fuel-injection problem slowed his car to a crawl and he limped home tenth, the only occasion he would finish outside the points all season. At Aintree for the British Grand Prix two weeks later, Clark won and Hill, suffering from tyre wear, could manage only fourth,

Hill's Championship lead over the Scot was down to a single point, but in August's German Grand Prix, run at the daunting Nürburgring in appallingly wet conditions, Hill won narrowly from John Surtees and Gurney, and it was the turn of Clark to trail home fourth. September's Italian Grand Prix went even better: Clark was the first to retire from the race and Hill and team-mate Ritchie Ginther finished first and second to record BRM's first ever 1–2.

At Watkins Glen in upstate New York the following month, Clark won the US Grand Prix, the penultimate round of the World Championship, but Hill finished second to set up a tense climax to the season. Under the prevailing rules, only the points scored by driver and team in their best five of the season's nine Grands Prix counted for Championship-ranking purposes. The only way Hill and BRM could add to their tally in the final race of the year, in South Africa, would be by winning. Finishing second to Clark in the less reliable Lotus would only increase their anguish, as drivers and teams would be level on points and Clark and Lotus would pip Hill and BRM to respective Drivers' and Constructors' Championships by means of having scored one more win.

For three-quarters of the South African Grand Prix, held on 29 December, it appeared that this was the cruel fate awaiting Graham Hill and his team, as Clark snatched the lead from the outset and opened up a half-minute lead over the Englishman. But then the Lotus was seen trailing oil smoke from the rear of its engine and, less than 50 miles from the final chequered flag of the season, Clark pulled into the pits and retired. A core plug in the oil gallery of his Climax engine had dropped out, permitting his precious lubricant to leak away. Hill cruised the remaining 20 laps to his fourth Grand Prix win of the year and the first of his two World Championships. BRM were World Constructors' Champions, too, and had delivered handsomely on Sir Alfred Owen's ultimatum. Even his requirement that the P56 should contribute to the team's coffers in terms of customer sales would be satisfied, since the majority of the 29 engines manufactured made their way into customer cars.

Back home in Kensington, Amherst was delighted with the news from South Africa, and busier than ever. His personal design for a new house, next door to the existing family home and incorporating a large upstairs studio, was nearing completion. Within a fortnight he would be bound for California to begin work with Douglas Corporation on a series of Mars projects. And now he found that he was the portraitist to motor racing's new World Champion, and that his detail work on the BRM engine had played a part in his friend's triumph.

In the book about BRM which Raymond Mays wrote with Peter Roberts in 1962, he gives a fascinatingly understated description of Amherst's time with the team: 'My old friend Amherst Villiers, who had been working on space vehicles in the United States, joined us as a consultant and brought the American approach, combined with his experience, to bear on many of our problems. Sometimes he approached from one direction, while we attacked the problem from another, but we generally met in the middle.'[4]

In the context of a small motor racing team employing fewer than

100 people, Amherst's 'American approach' brought with it some challenges. For much of the previous 15 years he had been a design engineer with vast corporations and had been encouraged to think 'outside the box' about projects that did not necessarily have a chance of short-term practical success. By way of example, his reaction to the Soviet launch of *Sputnik* – 'look, the Russians have put up one ton, in five years they'll put up ten tons, let's jump way ahead and put up 100 tons!'[5] – was laudable within a company of United Aircraft's size, but he did not have to concern himself with the fact that, at the time, the Americans did not possess a rocket powerful enough to put a 100-ton satellite into orbit.

At BRM the paramount requirement was to get the P56 engine designed, built and into the back of a racing car that could wrestle the advantage from Ferrari. Thus, Amherst's insistence on the evaluation of a twin-engine, four-wheel-drive design was not received with universal enthusiasm. His creativity, his intimate knowledge of the new formula's regulations, and his willingness to explore any loophole in them are to be admired, and today Alec Osborn has some sympathy with the basic principle: 'If you can manage the downside of a likely increase in un-sprung weight, all-wheel-drive, with the power source near each wheel as on an electric rail locomotive, has it merits'.[6] However, the idea of designing two further engines, when one seemed almost beyond BRM, mating them with pairs of clutches and transmissions, and synchronising them in a way workable for the driver, and all the while getting as near to the new formula's minimum weight limit of only 450kg (992lb), does seems fanciful.

Yet there was some method in Amherst's madness. Before the decade was out, most of Britain's Grand Prix teams would have given very serious consideration to four-wheel drive, as a way of generating more grip. As early as October 1963 Rubery Owen went into partnership with Harry Ferguson Research – constructors of the Ferguson P99 which, in the hands of Stirling Moss, won the 1961 Oulton Park Gold Cup, Formula One's only four-wheel-drive victory –

with the idea of producing such a car. The four-wheel-drive BRM got no further than the practice session of the 1964 British Grand Prix, where it was more than seven seconds off the pole position time. At least it gave the team advanced notice that when the Formula One engine capacity was raised to 3 litres from 1966, and the increased power meant grip was at even more of a premium, four-wheel drive would be a challenge. In 1969 Lotus, Tyrrell, McLaren and Cosworth all developed such cars, but none was successful, and the objective of greater grip came to be satisfied by aerodynamic rather than mechanical development. Yet Amherst had urged consideration of four-wheel drive, albeit in an overly-ambitious way, eight years earlier.

In spite of the challenges created by hiring Amherst as a consultant, BRM was happy to re-engage him when he returned to England from California in 1967. The new 3-litre Grand Prix formula had begun a year earlier, and once again the team had not been ready, opting for an overly complex H16 unit which would only ever win a single Grand Prix, and that in the back of Jim Clark's Lotus rather than in a BRM. Amherst worked with a team of draughtsmen in his new studio in Holland Street on a four-valve head for the H16, and on detailed design work for the V12 engine that replaced it.

By this time, Raymond Mays was little more than a figurehead, though he still retained the confidence and affection of Sir Alfred Owen at Rubery Owen, and Peter Berthon had long since left the team. Tony Rudd remained in charge of team management and design, but the husband of Owen's sister Jean, Louis Stanley, had grown in influence. Indeed, Amherst believed it was the presence of his sister Veronica and her wealthy husband Ray Milner at a social occasion in the autumn of 1966, also attended by Louis and Jean Stanley, which helped pave the way for his second stint with the team.

Rudd was less happy with Amherst's involvement, viewing the Owen/Mays/Villiers axis with suspicion, and it is true that Sir Alfred welcomed 'outside' advice. He and Mays had regular meetings away from Bourne, at the Welcome Hotel in Stratford, and it seems that Amherst attended some of these. Alec Osborn recalls Amherst was also in the design offices at Bourne more often during this period, and while he found him good company socially, he sometimes found his advice less than helpful, most notably when the design team felt obliged to ignore his opinion that the V12 crankshaft was not balanced properly. Long-term BRM gearbox engineer, the late Alec Stokes, told Doug Nye that Amherst 'was always on transmit, never on receive'.[7]

In terms of both Grand Prix wins and customer sales, the V12 achieved more than the H16, but after a brief flare of success in the early 1970s, BRM began a long and painful decline, finally disappearing from the Grand Prix scene during 1977. When Sir Alfred Owen died two years earlier, one obituary recorded that the timing was kind, as BRM was returning to the joke it had been when Rubery Owen first acquired it. Peter Berthon died, aged 65, in January 1971, apparently drowning after suffering a heart attack while swimming in the Indian Ocean off Durban. Raymond Mays passed away in January 1980, aged 80, leaving Amherst, his friend for more than 60 years, two large silver trophies won over half a century earlier at Shelsley Walsh.

Amherst may never have been one of the central figures at BRM, and his importance to the team lies less in the detailed drawings which he and his draughtsmen provided to the V8 or V12 projects, and more in his overall influence. As Doug Nye explains,

'I think he exercised considerable influence over what happened at Bourne. He may not have been universally welcomed. Indeed, he irritated many people. But when they finally got their heads down and committed to the P56, that engine was through the drawing office and into the car like a dose of salts, and that was stoked in part by Villiers' input. A consultant can influence a project without having every one of his ideas adopted. He was a motivating factor, a catalyst. And goodness me, in 1961 the people at BRM did need a catalyst.'[8]

The bequest of those Shelsley Walsh trophies hints at another contribution Amherst made to Britain's first post-war Grand Prix team. Mays was acknowledging that without the 'unfair advantage' his friend had given him with *Quicksilver*, *Cordon Rouge*, *Cordon Bleu* and the *Villiers Supercharge*, he may never have attained the standing that made so many captains of industry fund his vision of a British Racing Motor. Without Amherst, there may never have been a BRM at all.

Chapter 15

'BOND DROVE IT HARD AND WELL'

Apart from the four Birkin cars, the one built out of spares, and the 50 production models, there was a 56th 'original' Blower Bentley and, albeit fictional, it is by some considerable way the most famous of them all. It made its debut appearance in a novel first published in 1953, but barely got a mention in the follow-up book a year later. In the next in the series, the car played a starring role, but was damaged beyond repair and went 'to its grave in a Maidstone garage'.[1] The three works, which to date have sold more than nine million copies between them, in 25 languages, and spawned movies watched by many millions more, are *Casino Royale*, *Live and Let Die* and *Moonraker*, and the owner of the Bentley was James Bond.

We first learn about his Blower in the fifth chapter of *Casino Royale*, the first of Ian Fleming's James Bond novels:

Bond's car was his only personal hobby. One of the last of the 4½ litre Bentleys with the supercharger by Amherst Villiers, he had bought it almost new in 1933 and had kept it in careful storage through the war. It was still serviced every year and, in London, a former Bentley mechanic who worked in a garage near Bond's Chelsea flat, tended it with jealous care. Bond drove it hard and well and with an almost sensual pleasure. It was a battleship-grey convertible coupé, which really did convert, and it was capable of touring at ninety with thirty miles an hour in reserve.[2]

In December 1964, five months after Fleming died, *Playboy* published an interview with him. In it, he was asked why Bond drove a Blower.

The reply was illuminating: 'I probably chose the supercharged Bentley because Amherst Villiers was and is a great friend of mine and I knew something about it from my friendship with him. I put Bond in a Bentley simply because I like him to use dashing, interesting things.'[3]

Amherst and Fleming first met at an Oxford ball, some time around 1927. Amherst was chaperoning his sister Veronica, and was much taken with the fun-loving man some seven years his junior. The two became great friends, as relaxed in each other's company on incident-packed trips to Paris as at the lavish parties and concerts thrown by Fleming's mother and grandmother.

Ian Lancaster Fleming was born on 28 May 1908, on Green Street, just off London's Park Lane, a few minutes' walk from where Amherst himself had been born. His grandfather Robert's meteoric career took him from Dundee bookkeeper to the helm of his eponymous bank, where he came to specialise in the types of American railway securities in which the trustees of Ernest and Elaine Villiers's marriage settlement had invested. Robert's son Valentine was a model student at Eton and Oxford, went to work in the family bank and was elected Conservative MP for Henley in the January 1910 general election at which Ernest had stood down. In May 1917 a promising business and political career was abruptly cut short by a German shell. Ian Fleming was not yet nine, but the pattern of his life for the next two decades was swiftly established, heavily influenced by an over-bearing mother who required him to maintain the apparently impossibly high standards of his dead father.

At Eton Fleming achieved the unheard-of feat of becoming Victor Ludorum – champion of the games – two years in succession, but he left the school early to attend officer training at Sandhurst. This, too, came to a premature end, but was followed by a seminal period at a finishing school for young gentlemen in Austria. It was while driving with friends in the Alps, stuck behind a lorry loaded with heavy machinery, that he first imagined the scenario which would lead to the destruction of Bond's Blower Bentley in *Moonraker*.

When employment finally beckoned in the autumn of 1931, Fleming joined Reuters, where his first overseas assignment was to cover the following summer's Alpine motor trials, as navigator to Donald Healey in a 4½-litre Invicta. On the final day's run from Grenoble to San Remo some smaller cars began to challenge the leaders, and *Autocar* reported that the driver of one was confronted 'by Fleming, Healy's navigator, with "What on earth are you doing amongst the grown-ups?"'[4]

Further maternal pressure caused Fleming to resign from Reuters in order to try his hand at the family business of banking. When this failed, he joined the leading stock-broking firm Rowe and Pitman, but he felt unfulfilled in this profession, too. Fortunately he was about to be offered a role in which he could truly excel.

In February 1939 Admiral John Godfrey – on whom Fleming would later model Bond's boss, 'M' – was appointed director of Naval Intelligence (NID). He was advised to find a first-rate personal assistant, someone like the Old Etonian stockbroker Claud Serocold, who had supported Admiral 'Blinker' Hall at the NID during the First World War. Sir Montagu Norman, governor of the Bank of England and a friend of the Fleming family, knew Ian to have just such a background, and introduced him to Godfrey. Just as war broke Fleming was appointed to Section 17 of NID and given the rank of Commander. He celebrated by arranging for the tips of the 400 Morland Special cigarettes he consumed each week to be marked, like the cuffs of his new uniform, with three gold bands.

War was to be the making of Ian Fleming. In June 1940 he went to France to support British intelligence interests as the Germans overran the country, and ended up supervising the evacuation of refugees from the Bordeaux coast. The following year he coordinated NID personnel in Spain, Gibraltar and North Africa to set up *Operation Golden Eye*, the plan by which Allied communications could be maintained in Spain and sabotage undertaken in the event of German invasion. In August 1942 he observed from a naval ship the controversial Dieppe raid, which was an early test for the intelligence assault unit he had proposed to steal enemy documents and codes before they could be destroyed by retreating forces. Attendance at a joint Anglo-American naval conference in Jamaica meant that, long before the war was over, Fleming had ambitions of living on the island and writing for a living.

When peace came Fleming accepted a highly attractive offer from his friend, the newspaper proprietor Lord Kemsley. He became foreign manager of Kemsley Newspapers (including *The Sunday Times*), directing the organisation's coverage abroad, on a substantial remuneration package and two months' guaranteed holiday. Shortly afterwards he acquired some land on the north coast of Jamaica and built a home, naming it 'Goldeneye' – though his friend Noel Coward, complaining about the absence of glass in the property's windows, called it 'Golden Ear Nose and Throat'.

In March 1952 Fleming married his long-term mistress Ann Charteris, who was pregnant with their son Caspar. In the weeks preceding the wedding, he finally sat down and wrote the thriller he had long wanted to – some 62,000 words about the man whom he would come to describe as a 'blunt instrument of the government',[5] and whom he named after the author of a work that he referred to frequently at Goldeneye, *Field Guide to the Birds of the West Indies*.

The following October Amherst and his family made a trip home from New York, and he and Nita arranged to meet with Fleming to celebrate Caspar's birth. Over dinner Fleming explained about the manuscript he had written, that it was due to be published the following spring under the title *Casino Royale*, and that Amherst should read it because its hero James Bond drove a 4½-litre Bentley supercharged by him. Fleming well knew that Amherst did not read novels, and as Bond's profile grew with the publication of each ensuing adventure, so this became a running joke between the pair. In 1964, when *You Only Live Twice* was published, Fleming inscribed the copy he gave to his friend, 'To Amherst. Read it, damn you!'

Fleming took particular care with his description of Bond's Bentley. Examination of a late *Casino Royale* manuscript reveals that, having originally typed 1933 as the year in which Bond bought the car, the author amended this by hand to 1932, but finally went with the later date in the book. Similarly, the manuscript shows that he deleted the words 'by Bentley' when describing that the car was still serviced every year.[6]

The last of the production Blowers were sold new in September 1931 and so Bond could have bought his Bentley 'almost new' in either 1932 or 1933. This tweaking may have had less to do with accuracy and more with the way Fleming used words – 1933 simply sounded better. When, for example, on the recommendation of Bond fan and gun expert Geoffrey Boothroyd, Fleming switched 007's weapon of choice to a Walter PPK, drawn from a Berns-Martin triple draw holster, he ignored the fact that this was the wrong holster for the gun. According to Fleming collector Brad Frank, 'He twisted it for his own purposes. That's why he's so readable – he's focused on the sound.'[7]

Sound is an important element of Fleming's writing. Just as his report to the NID about the Dieppe raid is littered with separate descriptions of the noise of 4in naval guns, machine-guns and the aircraft overhead, so it is clear he was familiar with the sound of a Blower Bentley, 'the loitering drum-beat of the two-inch exhaust . . . echoing down the tree-lined boulevard',[8] in *Casino Royale* being followed almost word-for-word in *Live and Let Die*, as Bond drives slowly through a foggy London for a meeting with 'M'.

There is no question that Fleming was an expert in the art of describing a car chase. When Bond's romantic interest Vesper Lynd is kidnapped and driven away, he leaps into his Blower and races after her, 'his new Marchal headlights boring a safe white tunnel, nearly half a mile long, between the walls of the night'.[9]

A few paragraphs on, Amherst gets another name-check, and this too was the subject of a late change before publication: 'On straight sections the Amherst Villiers supercharger dug spurs into the Bentley's twenty-five horses and the engine sent a high-pitched scream of pain into the night. Then the revolutions mounted until he was past 110 and on to the 120 mph mark on the speedometer.'[10] Fleming deleted 'thirty' from his manuscript and inserted 'twenty-five'[11] by hand, but either seems a long way wide of the mark – Bentley historian Michael Hay understands the production Blowers gave about 175bhp at 9½lbs' boost – and whether this is another example of Fleming preferring the sound of a word, or simply getting it wrong, is not known.

The former Bentley mechanic back in Chelsea would have winced had he known what was about to happen to the car he tended with jealous care: Bond races round a corner to encounter a spiked tyre trap,

the heavy car whirled across the road in a tearing dry skid, slammed the left bank with a crash that knocked Bond out of the driving seat on to the floor, and then, facing back up the road, it reared slowly up, its front wheels spinning and its great headlights searching the sky. For a split second, resting on the petrol tank, it seemed to paw at the heavens like a giant praying-mantis. Then slowly it toppled over backwards and fell with a splintering crash of coach-work and glass.[12]

This was one of many departures *Casino Royale* made from the run-of-the-mill thrillers of the 1950s. Our fallible hero does not win the car chase, he requires the help of a Russian assassin to save him from torture, and Vesper turns out to be a double agent, her suicide prompting the book's famous final line, 'The bitch is dead now.'[13] But Vesper was not all bad; while Bond recovered in hospital from the effects of torture, at least she 'kept an eye on the repairs to the Bentley which had been towed down to coach-builders in Rouen'.[14]

The action in *Live and Let Die* takes place in New York, Florida and Jamaica, and Bond's Blower is restricted to that single, foggy drive along the King's Road, up Sloane Street and into Hyde Park. But in *Moonraker*, first published in April 1955, the car has centre stage and participates in arguably English literature's greatest car chase.

The story concerns Sir Hugo Drax, millionaire industrialist and the man behind the Moonraker super atomic missile being developed to protect Britain from nuclear attack. In an early chapter Bond rigs a bridge deal – the 'Duke of Cumberland hand' – to inflict a heavy defeat on Drax in order to make him realise that he has been rumbled as a card cheat. When two Moonraker plant workers die the same night, Bond is sent there to investigate. Later, when Bond parks his Blower next to Drax's Mercedes 300S, Fleming displays a detailed knowledge of motor racing history as he describes the kind of reverie that many men fall into when they see a certain type of car.

Bond's daydream ranges from the Blitzen Benz's land speed record, via Lang, Seaman and von Brauchitsch, to 'the harsh scream of Caracciola's great white beast of a car as it howled past the grandstands at Le Mans'.[15] It ends abruptly when Drax interrupts him: 'He gestured towards the Bentley. "They used to be good in the old days," he added with a touch of patronage.'[16] At that moment we realise what Bond is really up against: Drax cheats at bridge, he is about to turn a nuclear missile on London . . . and he is rude about our hero's car.

Fortunately, when Drax and his henchman Krebs bundle Bond's romantic interest, Gala Brand, into the back of the Mercedes in central London the following evening and drive away with her, Bond's skill behind the wheel of the Blower makes up for any deficiency in performance from his 20-year-old car: 'He just had to play on his brakes and gears and hope for the best.'[17] He crosses Clapham Common at 80mph, and his week-old racing Michelins scream as he leaves the South Circular Road for the A20. At the next traffic lights Bond screws down the windscreen, pulls on his racing goggles and resumes his chase of the Mercedes, 'the shrill scream of his supercharger riding with him for company'.[18]

It is only at Maidstone that Krebs realises that Bond is following them, and informs Drax, who muses, 'So that old museum-piece of his can still move.'[19] Bond is doing 95mph as he passes Leeds Castle and, remarkably, is overtaken by a third car: 'Alfa Romeo supercharged straight-eight, he thought to himself. Must be nearly as old as mine. 'Thirty-two or '33 probably. And only half my c.c. Targo Florio in 1931 and did well everywhere after that.'[20]

Moments later Drax nerfs the Alfa off the road into fiery oblivion, and as he and Bond take to the long hill beyond the Charing-fork, the Bentley is not far from meeting its own fate. Recalling the truck he had seen carrying machinery in the Alps more than 20 years earlier, Fleming's device is a heavy eight-wheeler carrying 20 giant rolls of newsprint.

To be sure of his facts at this critical point, Fleming had written to newsprint manufacturers Bowaters, introducing himself charmingly as 'a spare-time writer of thrillers'.[21] He accepted the guidance of Mr John B. Reed of Bowaters' advertising department, and changed the make of truck from Foden to AEG. However, other aspects of Reed's advice – that the rolls of newsprint would be covered, and that the firm would not deliver to its East Kent customers at night – were not permitted to stand in the way of Fleming's narrative.

On Drax's instructions, Krebs clambers on board the truck and cuts the ropes securing its load. Not even a driver of Bond's skill can avoid 20 rolls of newsprint tumbling down a one-in-ten slope to meet him. He will, of course, live to fight another day, but his trusty Blower Bentley has met its end, and is replaced in the closing chapter with a 1953 Mark VI Bentley with open touring body.

As to how James Bond first came by his Blower, opinions differ. John Pearson, a colleague of the writer on *The Sunday Times* and author of *The Life of Ian Fleming* (1966), wrote the 'authorised biography' of James Bond himself ten years later. This was based on the fascinating premise that Bond was a highly successful, real-life MI6 agent, and that the Fleming novels were written to dupe the Russians into believing there was no point trying to assassinate a fictional character. In the book, Pearson reveals that the Blower was bought for Bond by his lover, Marthe de Brandt, the owner of a Parisian brothel. When he is told, erroneously, that she is betraying British and French secrets to the Germans, Bond kills her by deliberately driving the Blower off the road at speed.

Conversely, Charlie Higson, writer of the recent *Young Bond* novels, explains in *Double or Die* that James and an Eton friend discovered the car in poor condition and resting on blocks in a yard in the village of Upton, on the outskirts of Slough. Later Bond is able to acquire the Blower with his share of some roulette winnings. In the closing pages Higson describes a scene 'twelve years later, at the close of the Second World War',[22] when Bond drives the Blower to Bletchley Park, where the German's Enigma code was deciphered. Even over the course of Fleming's 14 Bond books, it was a challenge to preserve strict chronological consistency, but with those few words, Higson remains true to 1933 as the date of Bond's purchase of the Blower. Unfortunately, he is less of a car expert than Fleming was, describing the Bentley crashing in a race at 'Brook*field*', and that it was Bond who 'made some modifications to the car and added an Amherst Villiers supercharger'[23] – unlikely, given that the car was already a Blower when it was discovered in Upton.

Incidentally, the cinematic James Bond never drove a Blower Bentley. In the second movie, *From Russia With Love*, released in 1963, Sean Connery's Bond is seen receiving a call from Miss Moneypenny on one of the world's earliest – and largest – car phones. It is fitted to the dashboard of a Bentley which automotive historian Tom Clarke has identified as an overdrive 4¼-litre model, built no earlier than 1936. In the following movie, *Goldfinger*, 'Q' decides that the Bentley has had its day, and provides Bond with the incomparable Aston Martin DB5, complete with ejector seat, machine guns, tyre shredders and bullet-proof shield.

In the bizarre 1967 version of *Casino Royale*, numerous members of the ensemble cast play James, or in the case of Woody Allen, Jimmy Bond. One, David Niven, drives a Bentley which appears to have a Villiers supercharger fitted to it, but in reality the car began life as a 3-litre, was much hacked about, and by the time of the movie may well have had a 4½-litre engine, but the 'supercharger' appears to have been a dummy.

In 1962 the first Bond movie, *Dr No*, was released, and the tenth book in the canon, *The Spy Who Loved Me*, was published. Fleming, who had suffered a severe heart attack the previous April, was becoming famous in his own right – President Kennedy had named *From Russia With Love* one of his ten favourite books – and his Bond earnings were climbing exponentially. He and his wife Ann finally moved into Sevenhampton Place, the large country house near Swindon in Wiltshire, which had been renovated for them over the previous four years, and he decided that one of its walls should be adorned with his portrait.

Amherst was back in England at this time, enjoying a purple patch of automotive and artistic creativity between lengthy stints working on the American space programme. Fleming was a frequent visitor to the Villiers' family home in Kensington, and enjoyed his lengthy conversations about cars, guns and gadgets with Amherst and his young son Charles. He was well aware that Amherst had spent the winter of 1960/61 enjoying an extended visit to Florence to study under Annigoni, and he had also seen Amherst's recently completed portrait of Graham Hill. So, in spite of all his artistic connections, Ian Fleming chose Amherst Villiers to paint his portrait.

It was arranged that he would sit for the painting in the studio Amherst had created at his Holland Street home. This caused Nita some concern; neither she nor Amherst was a great lunch-eater, and she was also aware of their friend's poor health. She checked with Fleming's long-term personal assistant, Beryl Griffie-Williams, and she advised that, regardless of doctors' orders, he would like scrambled eggs and sausages. Thus, on each of some 20 visits, Amherst, Nita and the creator of James Bond sat down to a lunch of sausage and egg, washed down with a bottle of red wine. Then the serious work would begin, with Fleming sitting for Amherst and chatting with Nita, although there were occasions when the conversation made it impossible to be serious and Amherst would have to banish his wife from the room.

For the sessions, which took up much of May 1962, Fleming wore a favourite, light blue, short-sleeved shirt and black bow tie, and turned 60 degrees away from the artist, so that Amherst could catch something of his unique profile, set off by the nose he had smashed against the head of Henry Douglas-Home, brother of the future British prime minister, in an Eton football match. He crossed his arms and Amherst faithfully detailed the Rolex Explorer on his left wrist.

Beyond Fleming's right elbow, Amherst portrayed a simple table or shelf, on which sat hardback copies of *From Russia with Love*, *Live and Let Die*, *Casino Royale* and *Thunderball*, without their dust jackets. Whether it was Fleming or Amherst who chose these four titles is not known, but the canvas would have had to have been much wider were the other six Bond books published up to that time to have been included. As with most of Amherst's portraits, the writer's name was picked out against the dark background in uppercase letters.

Towards the end of the sittings, Amherst became concerned that the expression around Fleming's mouth was too serious. He was in favour of changing it, but his subject and his wife persuaded him otherwise, and Fleming was so satisfied with the end result that he not only paid his friend the agreed £500, but decided to use the portrait as the frontispiece to a signed, leather-bound, limited-edition release of the following year's *On Her Majesty's Secret Service*.

Fleming's publishers, Jonathan Cape, also liked Amherst's portrait of their star writer, and used it in posters publicising the launch of the new novel in April 1963. By then Amherst was already living in California, having commenced employment with Douglas. Nita had stayed behind – in appalling weather – to make their Kensington home ready for tenants, and the lavish *OHMSS* launch party was one of her last nights out in London before leaving to join her husband.

Two years earlier, while Ian Fleming recuperated after his heart attack, a friend visiting him in hospital gave him a copy of Beatrix Potter's *Squirrel Nutkin*, and suggested he should write a children's book of his own, based on the bedtime stories he told his son Caspar. These concerned a magical car which could fly and sail, and Fleming was soon at work on what would become *Chitty-Chitty-Bang-Bang*, famously telling Cape director Michael Howard, 'So you will see that there is never a moment, even on the edge of the tomb, when I am not slaving for you.'[24]

ABOVE: *The tiny plate bearing Amherst's name which Bentley placed on the nose of his supercharger, after Amherst had placed an injunction on them.* (Author's collection)

ABOVE: *The legend of the Blower Bentley may have been born at Le Mans in 1930, but in truth Birkin spent more time changing tyres than harrying Rudolf Caracciola's Mercedes.* (Clare Hay)

BELOW: *The 137.96mph (222.02kmh) Brooklands lap record established by Birkin in the single-seater Blower in 1932 stood for 14 months after his untimely death.* (National Motor Museum, Beaulieu)

RIGHT: *The brochure Amherst published in 1929 to coincide with the launch of the production Blower Bentley.* (Eoin Young)

BELOW LEFT: *Amherst and Maya Nungovich pose for fashion photographer Sasha Stone shortly before their wedding in July 1932.* (Getty Images)

BELOW RIGHT: *Maya in the reception hall of the Farm Street home she shared with Amherst in Mayfair. She designed the linen fold panelling and carved wooden staircase behind her.* (Getty Images)

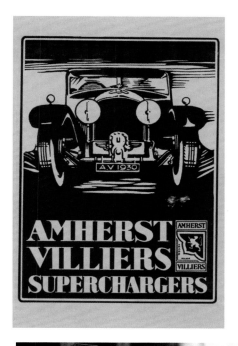

ABOVE: *The inverted, four-cylinder, in-line aero engine designed by Amherst, which he named after Maya.* (Flight)

BELOW: *The Miles Whitney Straight M11B, test bed for Amherst's engine.* (The A. J. Jackson Collection at Brooklands Museum, http://www.ajjcollection.co.uk)

ABOVE: *The striking illustration Amherst commissioned from Adrian Hill for his advertisement in the 1931 Schneider Trophy programme.* (Science and Society Picture Library)

ABOVE: *This wind tunnel model of the Gloster IV, fitted with wheels rather than floats, demonstrates not only that Amherst's plans to use the aircraft for a world landplane speed record attempt were sound. It also shows the neat contours of the W-12 Napier Lion engine, which he exploited in the design of* Bluebird. (HMSO)

BELOW: *The six-engine, double-decker, transatlantic airliner designed by Amherst during the Second World War.* (Bombardier)

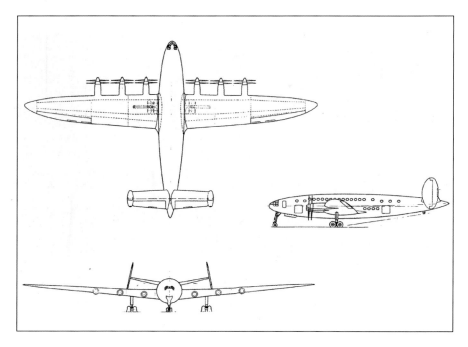

RIGHT: *Amherst at the time he joined United Aircraft's Missiles & Space Systems Division in early 1958. The natty tweed jacket may be one of brother-in-law Ray Milner's hand-me-downs.* (American Institute of Aeronautics and Astronautics)

BELOW: *Graham Hill posing alongside Amherst's unfinished portrait, 1961.* (LAT Photographic Digital Archive)

RIGHT: *Ian Fleming in his London study, March 1958. A week later, the sixth Bond novel,* Dr No, *was published.* (Getty Images)

OPPOSITE TOP: *The original* Chitty-Bang-Bang *[sic], with Count Louis Zbrowski aboard, in the Brooklands paddock, 1921.* (National Motor Museum, Beaulieu)

OPPOSITE BOTTOM: *That John Burningham's illustrations for* Chitty-Chitty-Bang-Bang *resembled a stretched SSK Mercedes with the circular radiator of a Delaunay-Bellville had much to do with the coloured technical drawing prepared by Amherst for Ian Fleming.* (Jonathan Cape, used by permission of The Random House Group Ltd)

RIGHT: *In the 2006 movie* Casino Royale, *Tobias Menzies played M's assistant, Villiers. Screenplay co-writer Robert Wade confirmed that the character's name was a deliberate nod to Amherst.* (Casino Royale © 2006 Danjaq, LLC, United Artists Corporation, Columbia Pictures Industries, Inc. All rights reserved)

LEFT: *The BRM P56 engine, which Amherst consulted on, drove Graham Hill and BRM to the 1962 Drivers' and Constructors' World Championships.* (LAT Photographic Digital Archive)

BELOW: *Graham Hill winning the 1962 Dutch Grand Prix at Zandvoort, the first of four victories he achieved on his way to the World Championship.* (LAT Photographic Digital Archive)

ABOVE: *In January 1963 Amherst poses with son Charles and his newly acquired Blower Bentley, just before moving to California to work on Mars projects with the Douglas Corporation.* (W.O. Bentley Memorial Foundation)

Below: The newly fitted-out garage at Amherst's Pacific Palisades home, 1963. Note the Bentley's supercharger lying beneath the bench. (Bruce Pounds)

ABOVE LEFT: *Amherst clearly enjoying restoring his Blower Bentley.* (Bruce Pounds)

ABOVE RIGHT: *Amherst with the counter-balanced crankshaft he designed after finding that Bentley had not fitted his original design to the car.* (Bruce Pounds)

BELOW: *Amherst with the fully restored Blower, outside the family home, 1966.* (Bruce Pounds)

ABOVE: *Amherst and his second wife Nita at the 1966 Pebble Beach Concours d'Elégance, when his Blower won Best in Class.* (Piers and Eleanor Carlson)

BELOW: *Two of America's finest racing drivers, Phil Hill (left) and Dan Gurney, out-paced the Californian chapter of the De Tomaso Pantera owners' club in Amherst's old Blower – and clearly enjoyed the experience, 1979.* (Dan and Evi Gurney)

LEFT: *Amherst at the helm of his friend John Millar's brigantine, the* Centurion, *in the Solent – note the missing finger tip on his right hand, lost when a jack collapsed on him in 1927.*
(Joanna Millar)

BELOW: *Reunited with the one Birkin Blower which never raced, chassis HR3977, in 1983. The front of the supercharger casing is an original Villiers casting, with the embossed lettering Amherst favoured, but which Bentley refused to adopt for the production cars*
(W.O. Bentley Memorial Foundation).

RIGHT: *On the third day of his High Court action against Rolls-Royce, in July 1991, Amherst and Judge Prosser were given a short trip in the car at the centre of the dispute. There was considerable public and newspaper interest in the case. That evening, Amherst fell heavily, breaking his hip. Five months later he died.* (Louis Hollingsbee)

BELOW: *The Phantom III is put up for sale after Amherst's daughter Janie finally wins the action against Rolls-Royce in 1996.* (Paul Woods)

ABOVE: *Portrait of the artist as an old man, 1990.* (LAT Photographic Digital Archive)

The central character of the story is Commander Caractacus Pott, Royal Navy (retired). His Navy rank has often led to the assumption that Fleming based the character on himself. Certainly Pott's favourite breakfast – 'he ate four fried eggs and bacon and drank a huge pot of coffee'[25] – would have appealed to Fleming, but there is an argument that the inventive Pott, his gentle wife Mimsie and their children, the black-haired Jeremy and blonde Jemima, were based at least in part on Amherst, Nita, Charles and Janie. This does not seem to have occurred to Amherst, even though, at Fleming's request, he did read his friend's original manuscript. But then, in his unique fashion, he would have been focused on the car, and not on the narrative or the characters.

Of course, Amherst was familiar with the real-life *Chitty-Bang-Bang* (note the single 'Chitty') from his days supporting Raymond Mays in *Quicksilver* at Brooklands; Count Louis Zbrowski's Mercedes had been put together by Amherst's nemesis on the Blower Bentley, Clive Gallop. It was one of those crude, chain-driven, aero engine specials, employing a 23-litre Maybach engine of the type originally used by Germany in her Gotha bombers during the First World War. The name of the real-life *Chitty* was not, as book, movie and stage show suggest, derived from the sound of its engine ticking over, but from a crude First World War song about the weekend passes, or chits, given to officers to enjoy a little relaxation in the bordellos of Paris.

Fleming was after something very different. Indeed, he was far from convinced for most of the project that he even wanted to call the car *Chitty*. On 8 May 1961 – less than four weeks after his heart attack – he had typed up a brief set of research notes about Zbrowski's car, clearly using Bill Boddy's *History of Brooklands Motor Course* as his source, but the working title of his book for children was soon established as *The Magical Car*. Even at unpaginated galley proof stage, not much more than six months before publication, this was still the title. But in another of his late changes, Fleming finally committed to *Chitty-Chitty-Bang-Bang*, and added a dedication to the 1921 racing car, relying on the notes he had made from Boddy's book almost three years earlier. 'The Bod', today still writing for *Motor Sport* in his 90s, was rather impressed when he learned this, saying, 'I had no idea I was so famous!'[26]

Fleming first briefed Amherst on *Chitty* in May 1962, shortly before work started on the portrait. Entrusting his friend with what was then the only copy of the manuscript, he believed Amherst was the ideal candidate to illustrate the book, and gave him precise instructions regarding the wraparound cover illustration, colour centre spread, a dashboard cluttered with knobs, and the engine bay. Amherst later described what emerged from their discussions as having the appearance of a low, green, rakish-looking SSK Mercedes, with the circular radiator of a Delaunay Bellville. Fleming collector Brad Frank is the proud owner not only of Amherst's initial sketches of the car, but also the coloured technical drawing he gave to Fleming. Sure enough, the front elevation of this later work shows off its distinctive radiator, while the side elevation looks for all the world as though Amherst has stretched the bonnet of an SSK to take not three exhaust stubs each side, but six.

In 1964, with Amherst in California and focused more on space craft than a flying car, and Fleming in failing health, Cape passed the drawing to a young author and artist, John Burningham, whose debut book, *Borka: the Adventures of a Goose with No Feathers*, they had published to prize-winning acclaim the year before. His illustrations in the three *Chitty* volumes, which remain much-loved by children of all ages to this day, follow Fleming's original instructions closely and bear a striking resemblance to Amherst's coloured drawing.

Equally, Fleming's narrative description of Chitty bears many hallmarks of a real-life Blower Bentley. She had raced in the early 1930s and was supercharged, and she had large Marchal headlights and an alliterative name – the Paragon Panther. But she was bigger, with a 12-cylinder, 8-litre engine, and she enjoyed other advantages over 007's Blower. In the 10 years or so since *Moonraker*, parts of the A20 down which Bond had chased Drax had become a motorway, the M20, and when this became choked with traffic around Canterbury one August Saturday, *Chitty* simply took to the skies. The Pott family were equally grateful to learn, when the tide threatened to engulf them and their car on the Goodwin Sands in the English Channel, that she could sail, too.

In the 1968 *Chitty-Chitty-Bang-Bang* movie, Chitty, of course, is neither green nor rakish looking, and resembles neither an SSK Mercedes nor a Delaunay Bellville. Production designer Ken Adam and the man who 'invented' Caractacus Pott's inventions, Rowland Emett, were responsible for its design. The car was built by Alan Mann Racing, which managed many of Ford's sports and touring car activities in the 1960s. They built up a bespoke chassis, into which they fitted the V6 engine and automatic transmission from a Mark IV Ford Zodiac.

To return to the book, *Chitty-Chitty-Bang-Bang* was published in three volumes, the first of them in October 1964. Ian Fleming did not live to see that day. He had died of heart failure the previous August, on the 12th birthday of the boy to whom he had first told the story of 'The Magical Car', his son Caspar. Fleming's final resting place is in the little churchyard in Sevenhampton, beneath a stone obelisk. The inscription on his plinth is a line from the Roman philosopher Lucretius, '*omnia perfunctus vitae praemia marces*' – 'Having done with all of life's pleasures, (now) you wither away'.

Amherst was more than 5,000 miles away when he heard the news, and found that he had therefore influenced the last of his friend's literary cars, just as he had the first. A year and a half later, both he and Nita sent letters reminiscing about the great man to a researcher working on Pearson's *The Life of Ian Fleming*. Nita's concluded that she and Amherst had both loved Fleming, and that the world would be the less without him.

In 2006 Fleming's first Bond thriller, *Casino Royale*, finally got the film treatment it deserved, more than 50 years after it had been published. Daniel Craig plays a darker, more fallible Bond, much nearer to his literary counterpart than his recent predecessors. An Aston Martin DBS takes the part of the Blower Bentley, and it is

Vesper's prone body in the road, rather than a tyre trap, which causes it to crash. Yet the movie is remarkably loyal to the novel, and the card game, car chase and torture scene from the book are all put in motion when Dame Judi Dench as 'M' tells Bond he must go to Montenegro to play Le Chiffre in a high-stakes card tournament because, 'According to Villiers, you're the best player in the Service.'[27]

Dench articulates a three-syllable Vill-i-ers rather than Amherst's two-syllable Vill-ers, but screenplay co-writer Robert Wade confirms that it was indeed a deliberate name-check to Amherst: 'It was just a reference for our own titillation, but we thought a few dyed-in-the-wool fans might spot it. We never imagined it coinciding with a book on the man who supercharged Bond.'[28]

Chapter 16

CALIFORNIA

In the winter of 1961, upon the completion of his first spell with BRM, Amherst once more planned for life as a Kensington-based society portrait painter. He also turned his hand to architecture, drawing up plans for an extensive studio residence to be built alongside the family home on Holland Street. Nita restored the splendid garden, which Elaine had nurtured over many years, while Janie endured foggy bus trips to the US Forces school in Teddington's Bushy Park, where, during the war, American troops had gathered in the run-up to D-Day and SHAEF (Supreme Headquarters Allied Expeditionary Force) had been established. The school closed the following summer, and it was decided that Janie should spend her last year of secondary education in the US, so she moved out to Pacific Palisades on the California coast, to live with Nita's sister Mary Jane.

At the same time, young Charles, now aged 11, started at yet another school. Forty-seven years after Amherst had left Windlesham House, his son was welcomed there by the fifth generation of Maldens. Yet, just a month later, news came which meant that Charles would be changing school, and crossing the Atlantic, again.

Amherst had been approached by the Missile and Space Systems Division of Santa Monica-based aerospace company Douglas Aircraft. The offer represented an opportunity for him to rejoin the US space programme at a time when the next objectives beyond landing a man on the moon were being defined. California would offer better weather than London, Janie was out there already, and Santa Monica was no more than ten minutes' drive from Pacific Palisades. Amherst and Nita concluded that they should sell their existing Holland Street home, complete and rent out the studio, and move back to the US. By Christmas Amherst, now 62 years old, had accepted the offer from Douglas and passed his medical, and young Charles had left Windlesham House after a single term.

Thus it was that in January 1963 Nita remained in Kensington, overseeing the completion of the studio and sale of the family home, while Amherst and his son set sail for America. Before they left they posed for photographers with the Blower Bentley – chassis number 3797, registration number GP42 – which Ian Fleming had helped Amherst to acquire, and which was to be shipped out to California on a cargo vessel via the Panama Canal. The *Motor Sport* of March 1963 published a picture of the pair in the car, and noted that Amherst was now 'with the Douglas Corporation in California, engaged on inter-planetary work . . . Mr Villiers intends to use the Bentley daily in the Los Angeles district but intends eventually to give it to his son, now 12 years old and a godson of Sir Winston Churchill – so one day it may return to England.'[1]

Amherst found a property to rent on Erskine Drive, just a few blocks from his sister-in-law, and bought a 1957 Studebaker to run around in. He began work with Douglas on 21 January 1963, studying some HLLVs (heavy lift launch vehicles) known as Post Nova. The Nova concept had been envisaged as early as 1959 as an expendable rocket to power a manned moon mission, but when the Saturn V rocket was chosen as the launch vehicle for Apollo in early 1962, Douglas was one of the companies to be asked by NASA to consider the types of vehicle which would be needed after the race for the moon had been won.

Whether the objective would be Mars, or a space station in earth or lunar orbit, or a moon base, the payload might be expected to be far heavier than Apollo, and would therefore require an immensely powerful set of rockets to haul it clear of the earth's gravity. Other criteria for Post Nova included: the potential for transporting both humans and cargo; vertical take-off; at least partial reusability of launch vehicle components; clustered tanks to reduce production and operational costs; and multi-sectional structures, again to reduce production costs. It will be seen that all these factors influenced the design of the space shuttle, the first operational flight of which lay almost 20 years away.

Back in Kensington, just as Elaine's move to Holland Street in 1947 had been held up by the appalling weather that winter, so the deep snows, burst pipes and power cuts of 1963's 'big freeze' delayed the sale of the house and completion of the studio. Nita was, nonetheless, impressed with what Amherst had achieved with the studio, telling her sister-in-law Veronica that no one but he could have accomplished so much with the available space. In the end, the Bentley beat Nita out to Pacific Palisades by a month, and she finally joined her family in April.

Nita found that Amherst had already made some good friends. Piers Carlson was working as a systems analyst with RAND Corporation, on Santa Monica's Olympic Boulevard, only a mile from Douglas, but it was not this that brought him into contact with Amherst. He and his wife Eleanor had bought a 3-litre Bentley a couple of years earlier before moving out to Malibu. Now, they read in the Bentley Drivers' Club magazine, their nearest fellow member would be the man who had supercharged the Blower Bentley.

Indeed, cars played an important part in how Amherst's social circle grew at this time. A few years earlier the Carlsons had spotted a 1933 Le Mans Aston Martin parked outside a motel. They stopped to introduce themselves to its owner, an Englishman named Bruce Pounds, who had moved out to the US to work for Panavision and now designed helicopter-mounted guns for Hughes Aircraft. The Aston, which Pounds says was responsible for many friendships and many girlfriends, also helped him with this career move; Hughes's head of ordnance, Ian Crundle, owned an old Bugatti, and came to know him through classic car circles.

Now Carlson told Pounds that he had met Amherst in Santa Monica. 'I thought he was bloody dead!' was Pounds's reply.[2] Amherst, of course, had the best part of 30 years still ahead of him, and was delighted to make the acquaintance of the Englishman. Not only was he great company – giving Amherst and Nita turns at riding pillion on the back of his Vincent Black Shadow on hair-raising rides around the Malibu Hills – but he had also done some restoration work on his brother's un-blown 4½-litre Bentley. Amherst was only too pleased to have such an experienced man to support him in the restoration of GP42.

Since Amherst was on the west coast of America, immersed in space exploration during the week and restoring his Blower at weekends, he was effectively shut off from whatever benefits may have accrued from his portrait of Ian Fleming featuring as the frontispiece to the pre-release, limited edition run of *On Her Majesty's Secret Service*, published in April. Even if Amherst was not in Kensington to accept painting commissions, he had left for California with an offer from Fleming's publishers, Jonathan Cape, to publish his autobiography. They were impressed by the breadth of his talent, and were keen to receive a manuscript from him, with the focus on space and speed.

The plan was for Nita to support him in writing it when she arrived from London. It would have made the most fantastic read, and been the ultimate sales document for Amherst's myriad talents, but he never made the time for it. He was far more interested in his current projects than describing his past – his willingness to talk to journalists would only begin after he had retired from Douglas and completed the restoration of the Blower – and the opportunity was lost.

Once settled in, Nita turned to the challenges of developing a garden as good as the one she had left behind in Kensington, though the combination of California's clay soil and baking sun – a heat wave would hit Los Angeles that autumn – made her realise why she found gardens in the region slightly impersonal. She began a horticultural course at the university and learned which roses were able to flourish locally. She was less happy with the results of her driving lessons; after several months, she felt no more confident that when she had started. The wife of one of Britain's greatest automotive engineers simply did not like driving. Eleanor Carlson remembers Nita with great affection: 'She was the most charming woman you could ever meet. She was so much fun, we just loved her.'[3]

At Douglas, Amherst became part of the team working on Project EMPIRE (Early Manned Planetary-Interplanetary Roundtrip Expeditions). Just months after the selection of the Saturn V as Apollo's launch vehicle, the decision had been taken to make Apollo a Lunar Orbital Rendezvous (LOR) mission. This involved a small lunar module, requiring relatively little propellant, separating from and then re-docking with a command module which stayed in lunar orbit while surface exploration of the moon was undertaken. This meant only a single Saturn V rocket was required for the mission.

The alternative method would have been direct ascent, in which Apollo would have flown from the surface of the Earth to the lunar surface and back, and would have required a massive launch vehicle, carrying much more fuel. In the wake of the Apollo LOR decision, NASA's Marshall Space Flight Center became concerned that the relatively straightforward, lightweight approach would have limited relevance to ongoing interplanetary exploration. There was a danger that, once the late President Kennedy's 'by-the-end-of-the-decade' target to land a man on the moon had been achieved, then the Saturn V would be redundant. Hence EMPIRE was an attempt to ensure that a manned mission to Mars, requiring a new generation of HLLV, immediately followed the successful conclusion to Apollo.

The difficulty with this objective is that Mars's orbit of the sun is more elliptical than the Earth's. The cycle between the points at which the distance between the two planets is at its minimum, and when a less powerful launch vehicle, carrying less fuel, could be employed, lasts some 15 years. Unfortunately for NASA, the next set of ideal launch windows would fall between 1969 and 1971, just as the Apollo project was scheduled to reach its apogee. Thus, while three companies – Lockheed, General Dynamics and Aeronutronic – were tasked with considering vehicle designs and landing options for a mission to Mars,

Amherst was part of the team at Douglas which was asked by NASA to establish the ideal launch window and journey profile.

The assignment was nicknamed UMPIRE (U stood for 'unfavourable'), and considered the relative merits of 'conjunction-class' and 'opposition-class' journeys. These respectively scheduled the halfway point of the expedition for when Mars moves behind the sun, or is opposite it, when viewed from the Earth. Douglas concluded that it was best to schedule a 'conjunction-class' mission, comprising two journeys of some six months each, interspersed by a long stay on Mars of some 500 days. This was thought better than an 'opposition-class' approach, because even though this would take some 400 days off the overall roundtrip, involving only a month on Mars, ten times the propellant would be needed to cope with the longer leg of the trip, necessitating a much bigger launch vehicle.

The 'conjunction-class' model also had its drawbacks. The orbiting mother ship would be exposed far longer to the risks of meteorites and radiation, and how were the crew to maintain morale while living and working on Mars for the best part of two years? In due course, President Nixon would conclude in favour of the space shuttle, and the plan to put man on Mars was put on hold.

Nevertheless, while at Douglas, Amherst designed his own heavy lift launch vehicle, clustering four Saturn V rockets together. Piers Carlson recalls seeing a drawing Amherst had made of the design, and querying what a small spike alongside the vehicle signified. Amherst replied it was a representation of the 555ft-tall Washington Memorial, drawn to scale. Piers concluded that, were Amherst's HLLV to take off, it would obliterate not only Cape Canaveral, but most of Florida too. His wife Eleanor recalls Amherst 'was quite disappointed when they rejected it'.[4] During the summer of 1965 he retired from Douglas, bidding the US space programme a final farewell.

* * * * *

The Blower Bentley which Amherst's great friend Ian Fleming had helped him procure was a couple of years older than James Bond's. It had originally been sold in July 1931 to a Mr C. J. L. Langlands of Epsom, Surrey. It had the classic four-seater, Le Mans Green, Vanden Plas body on a Le Mans chassis, with long bonnet, twin aero shields and – a special refinement for Langlands – a cigar lighter. He had taken the car out to the Riviera with him and how it survived the war is not clear – one tale describes it being hidden in time-honoured fashion in a barn, while another says it was commandeered by the Germans. Regardless, on 4 January 1963 Amherst paid Jack Barclay £1,000 (the modern equivalent is a little over £15,000, or US$20,000) to become the car's second legitimate owner, and he was delighted to have found it in such sound, original condition.

Amherst had just his own Erskine Drive garage and yard in which to work on the Blower and swiftly fitted out the garage with a workbench and every conceivable tool and piece of equipment. Even so, when Bruce Pounds looks now at the photographs he took during the restoration, he chuckles to himself and says, 'Talk about crude!'[5] Nevertheless, each weekend the pair worked on the car for most of their waking hours. Amherst was also joined on the project by Charles, who was proving mechanically adept himself.

When he first stripped the engine down, Amherst was surprised to find that the crankshaft had not been balanced, assuming that the counter-balanced shaft he had designed for the Birkin team cars had also made its way on to the production models. Regardless of the weight penalty of full balance weights, he believed they were to the overall benefit of the engine, since the stresses induced by a non-balanced crank were reduced, and bearings lasted longer because there would be less crank or block distortion. While complaining once more to his friends about 'Old Pussy Face', as he referred to W.O. Bentley, he drew up a new, counter-balanced crank and had it made, even posing with the finished item before fitting it.

Amherst and Pounds modified the supercharger itself, as Pounds explains: 'The top rotor had a hollow tube running through it, and oil got sucked straight through it into the engine, oiling up the plugs. So we created a brass frame with gauze on top, and a flap over that, effectively a clap valve. When pressure built up, the flap rose and the sucking stopped, preventing the plugs from oiling up.[6] Would that the Birkin team had been supported by such ingenuity.

Pounds laughs again when he recalls the many ways in which he supported the project. When Amherst learned Bruce was returning home on holiday, he asked him to collect new pistons from a specialist manufacturer deep in the English countryside. Pounds became frustrated when he could not find the company, and eventually called in at a cherry farm to ask for directions: 'They were only making the pistons right there on the farm – in a bloody cowshed! And then I had to bring the pistons through US Customs with them hidden in my trench coat!'[7]

Another Pounds story relates to what it was like to drive the car: 'As the driver, you sat up very high. Once, when I was about to overtake a modern sports car, I looked over my shoulder before pulling out, and when I turned back I wondered where the car had gone. Amherst became very agitated and was yelling that I was about to run it down. It had completely vanished. I couldn't see it.'[8]

The final stages of the restoration were completed on El Medio Drive, in a new home near Erskine Drive, which the family purchased in August 1965. They were fond of their new house, and Amherst was particularly taken with its large studio.

Eventually, after almost three years, the car's restoration was completed. Amherst's commitment to the project had been extraordinary. He made the body panels and mudguards himself, and even sourced, cut and fitted the fabric, too. Finally, he and young Charles, the boy he had promised the car to, were able to take it out on drives, cutting a dash around Pacific Palisades. The local newspaper, the *Evening Outlook*, published a photograph of them in the handsome old car, writing: 'Space scientist Charles Amherst Villiers, inventor-developer of the silent supercharger used in pre-war Bentley sports cars, shows his 15-year-old son Charles Churchill, how the famous 007 would handle his rare vehicle, which writer Ian Fleming labeled [sic] as Bond's preference in speedy automobiles.'[9]

When the car was finally finished, Amherst offered Pounds, by way of thanks, the engraved watch that Malcolm Campbell had given him for his camshaft work on the Itala almost 40 years earlier. Pounds would not hear of it, of course. It was reward enough to be on hand to see the Blower take first in class at the 16th *Concours d'Elégance* at Pebble Beach, and for Amherst to make him a very personal dedication on a marvellous photograph he gave him of the car: 'Dear Bruce, Thanks for all the grand work you put into the restoration of this car, Amherst Villiers.'

Interestingly, Amherst did not drive his restored Blower all that often, and nor would he sail more than a handful of times the sloop he restored in the late 1960s. For him, it was the doing that counted more than enjoying the end result. As he explained to Piers Carlson, 'I'm a project man. I like to do projects.'[10]

In May 1966, Amherst's old friend Graham Hill won the Indianapolis 500, arguably the world's most prestigious motor race, at his first attempt. It was the first Indy win by a rookie for 40 years, and his victory, his easy style with the press, and his campaign to have doors fitted to the drivers' toilets at the circuit, gave him an instant profile with the American public.

Amherst decided to exploit this with a little publicity of his own, and he arranged to meet with Wally Wilson, sports writer on the *Evening Outlook*. An article ensued, illustrated with a striking image of Hill posing while Amherst paints his portrait, only now the picture had been painted not in Kensington, but 'in the Pacific Palisades studio of racing enthusiast Charles Amherst Villiers'.[11] The accompanying article also describes the Blower Bentley as 'a winner at Le Mans in 1930',[12] and Amherst's car as 'one of but four such vehicles in the world'.[13] In later life, as contemporaries who could make their own interpretation of events involving Amherst passed away, so he became more able to make these kinds of exaggerated claims for himself or his family, especially in America, where there were still fewer people around capable of challenging his versions of events.

Does this tendency of Amherst to exaggerate matter? It is, after all, a natural inclination in many of us. It has been said that if one reads the diaries and memoirs of senior Conservative Party politicians serving at the time of Margaret Thatcher's resignation as British prime minister, it will seem as though each played a pivotal part in her departure, but one will search in vain in any of the other books for a description of it. Yet with Amherst this penchant went further. He was beginning to create his own legend and over time he would come to believe in it. When linked to his inability to maintain business relationships, this disconnection from reality would eventually come to harm him. Quite why he chose to behave in this way is mystifying. He came from an extraordinary family and led an extraordinary life, reaching a standard of excellence across a bewildering range of disciplines. Even told objectively, the story of Charles Amherst Villiers is astonishing; there was no need for him to embellish it.

Over and above the fact that Amherst considered himself a 'projects man' – if you like, more interested in the 'getting there' than the 'being there' – there was another reason why he did not drive the restored Blower much. In the early months of 1966 Nita fell ill. Her doctor could not detect what was wrong, but she felt there must be a reason why she had to keep letting her belt out. Eventually, it was discovered she had contracted cancer. In March she had both ovaries removed and embarked on a course of chemotherapy. Mercifully, she pulled through, but it was a grave shock to the family, and eventually she and Amherst concluded that it would be best for them to move back to Kensington. Amherst decided at that point to raise some cash, too, and sold the Blower to former world champion racing driver Phil Hill, who had a classic car dealership on Santa Monica's Washington Boulevard.

For young Charles in particular, it was a difficult time. In the autumn of 1965 a brief spell at a Canadian boarding school had ended when he underwent an abdominal operation himself. Shortly after he had returned to Pacific Palisades his mother had fallen ill, and now he found he would be leaving the US again, and that the car his father had told him would be his, and on which he had devoted many evenings and weekends, had been sold. The whole experience inflicted a wound in the relationship between father and son which never really healed.

Chapter 17

AFTER NITA

Just as the family had moved out to California in piecemeal fashion four years earlier, so they came back to Kensington gradually during the course of 1967. Amherst was first to leave Pacific Palisades, in order to return to consultancy work with BRM. Nita joined him in the Holland Street studio in mid-June and Janie, now 21, arrived with Charles, 16, once school term had finished. Amherst's children had the opportunity to experience the 'Summer of Love' in what could be argued were its two epicentres – Los Angeles and London.

Janie decided to try working in the landmark Biba boutique on nearby Kensington High Street as a way of meeting people her own age, and for young Charles yet another upheaval was made easier by the fact that he was joined by a schoolfriend, Andrew Gold. The son of Ernest Gold, who won an Oscar for his musical score to the movie *Exodus*, and Marni Nixon, 'ghost-singer' to Deborah Kerr in *The King and I*, Natalie Wood in *West Side Story*, and Audrey Hepburn in *My Fair Lady*, Andrew was steeped in music. Charles and he set themselves up as Villiers and Gold, hawking themselves round London's record companies. The precocious pair won a recording contract with Polydor, but their only single vanished without trace.

Gold went on to enjoy enormous success as a singer-songwriter in the 1970s, with hits such as *Lonely Boy*, *Never Let Her Slip Away* and *Thank You for Being a Friend*, which became the theme song for the comedy show *The Golden Girls*, yet he retains fond memories of his year in Kensington: 'I recall that Mr Villiers was quite a charming and eccentric man, full of creativity and very English. He was tall, thin, and distant yet warm, not at all stuck up. I loved him and Mrs Villiers. She was so sweet, soft-spoken and mild. Janie and Charlie were just wonderful to live with. I miss those days.'[1]

Amherst took Nita, her sister Mary Jane (over from California), and Janie on a continental touring holiday later that summer. After a brief stay in Paris, they drove on through Switzerland and over the Alps to Venice, which was still recovering from the floods of the previous November, and to Florence, where Pietro Annigoni welcomed his former pupil and family and showed them around his studio. Visits to Rome and Nice were further highlights of the trip, and then, after touring back up through France, Amherst returned to his BRM work, the upstairs studio set up as a drawing office where he was joined regularly by draughtsmen.

The routine of life in Kensington was shattered when, in March 1968, Nita was found to have cancer in her abdomen and a second operation was required. She remained optimistic; she devoured the books borrowed from the Harrods library on the subscription which her Canadian brother-in-law Ray Milner had arranged for her, and she was thankful she had stocked the Holland Street garden so well before moving out to California four years earlier. On her return from hospital, she took great pleasure from the cherry and laburnum trees and early lilacs, and from a pair of young thrushes which had hatched. But two alternative forms of chemotherapy caused her intolerable side effects, and radiotherapy was not able to prevent the spread of the disease. In August she suffered a complete blockage of her small intestine and on 17 September she died. She was just 50 years old.

Amherst's marriage to Nita had been a critical feature of his life for 22 years. Throughout his restless pursuit of a bewildering range of projects on both sides of the Atlantic, and throughout all his frustrations with corporate life, she had been there, not just for him, but as the fulcrum around which the entire family functioned. He loved his children dearly, but he was in his mid-40s when Janie was born and over 50 when Charles arrived, and his own upbringing, in an independently wealthy household of eight staff, hardly equipped him for fatherhood in a family environment which lacked the kind of capital he had experienced as a child. Nita had been the unifying factor in the family and with her gone Amherst was not only grief-stricken, he seemed quite unable to play any meaningful role as father to Janie or Charles.

Janie may have been an independent woman in her early 20s, and would shortly embark on a career in *cordon bleu* cookery, but she was unimpressed with the speed with which Amherst began to date girlfriends, while his relationship with his son, which had suffered over his unilateral sale of the Blower he had told the boy would be his, grew distant. Charles wanted to be in California, but did not enjoy living with his aunt and, aged just 18, took to living alone back on El Medio Drive. Amherst, meanwhile, took himself off to paint on the island of Mallorca, off Spain's Mediterranean coast.

A letter of Amherst's to his sister Veronica in December 1969 makes particularly poignant reading, and demonstrates just how difficult he found fatherhood at this time. He begins by asking if she and her husband Ray have been to California and if they have seen Janie and Charles, and concludes by asking his sister if she has any idea what should be done about his children.

Then a further blow befell the family, when Janie was struck down with the debilitating eye disorder which she has had to endure ever since. Amherst comforted her as best as he could and sought out expert medical opinion, but it was all he could do to look after himself and gradually, as a way of overcoming his grief and distracting himself from practical problems he found too challenging, he put in place a series of projects in which he could become absorbed.

Key to his survival plan was Mallorca. He could draw an income on Holland Street by letting it out, the island was sunnier and warmer in winter than London, and cheaper than California, and he could avoid what he perceived as swingeing UK taxes. On his occasional visits to London, he could stay with Veronica's daughter Rachel and her husband Michael Severne, on Kensington's Mulberry Walk. Their daughter, the late Amanda Severne, remembered his visits with affection:

He was a very gentle man, with a gentle outlook on life. He had a very enquiring mind, he would always take great interest in what you were doing, and why, and might suggest other ways of doing it. That must be why he was so good at design. He liked to believe the best of people, until shown otherwise, but he was a bit impractical on the business side. He might have been more successful – probably richer too – if he'd been more practical.[2]

On Amherst's first visit to Mallorca, he stayed in the Hotel Maricel, on the southern coast just to the west of Palma, but by March 1970 he had rented an apartment in Genova, then a hillside village overlooking the city. It had two bedrooms and a studio, and was the place where the general composition of his painting *The Miracle of Santa Clara* was formed (see Chapter 13). An early visitor there was Charles, who celebrated his 19th birthday in the company of his father and, during a five-week stay, worked on half a dozen highly original paintings of his own. He was finding his feet as a modern artist, at the outset of a career that has, thus far, led to 35 solo exhibitions.

Amherst found that one of his neighbours in Genova was the film actor George Sanders, the Oscar-winning star of *All About Eve*, whose rich vocal tones had more recently been put to excellent effect as the voice of the tiger Shere Khan in the Disney cartoon *The Jungle Book*. Born in St Petersburg in Russia in 1906 (his family emigrated to England during the Bolshevik Revolution 11 years later), Sanders had much in common with Amherst. He had ended up on Mallorca after the loss of his wife Benita to cancer, and he also possessed an astonishing array of skills. In addition to his acting, he was a fine singer, guitarist and pianist, a handy electrician, and he certainly knew his way around a car. Once he brought a convertible Cadillac over to England from New York and took it straight into his workshop to fit it with two large reclining seats and a smaller steering wheel – no prizes for guessing why – whereupon a friend nicknamed it the 'Chaise Longue'. When he married film actress Zsa Zsa Gabor in 1949, he was most reluctant to give up the apartment he owned because of the large workshop below it, equipped with lathes, presses and tools, so he simply took to going over to the marital home each evening with an overnight bag and fresh clothes on a hanger, then leaving the next morning for the comfort of his workshop. In Mallorca he drove a Ford Consul bought from Amherst's old friend, Whitney Straight.

Amherst and Sanders decided to set up a school of art together in Palma. Unfortunately, another feature that the two men had in common was that the actor was no great businessman. An early attempt at venture capital, investing in a business that made lighter, tougher vinyl records, and another specialising in three-dimensional photography, had failed, and in the mid-1960s a piggery and sausage business of Sanders also went under, in circumstances which bankrupted him and earned him censure from the Board of Trade. The joint venture with Amherst was destined to be another failure, but this had less to do with the lack of acumen of the pair, and more to do with Sanders's increasing depression. When he felt he could no longer play the piano to his usual standards, he dragged it outside and smashed it up. He sold his Mallorca home in the winter of 1971 and immediately regretted it. The following April, Amherst was staying at Glin Castle when the news was announced that Sanders had committed suicide in a hotel room in Castelldefels, near Barcelona. A friend of the Fitz-Geralds, Ursula Leslie, came to dinner that evening and recalls that 'Amherst was heartbroken, he couldn't eat a thing'.[3]

On the last evening of the 1960s, Amherst attended a New Year's Eve party in Palma and, unusually for him at the time, struck up a friendship with a woman his own age. Marguerite Barbrook was born in 1903 and raised in Bristol, in the west of England. Of Anglo-German descent, she travelled widely as a child and became a gifted linguist. Her experience of the Second World War was more peripatetic than most. At the outbreak of hostilities she was a journalist in Johannesburg, but, eager to contribute to the war effort, she first became commandant of an Egyptian internment camp for displaced German and Italian women, and then enjoyed spells as a radio broadcaster in Beirut and Jerusalem. Her first peacetime role was as Cypriot correspondent to Kemsley Newspapers, reporting to its foreign news manager, Ian Fleming.

Upon marriage to Bill Barbrook, a British officer whom she had met while with a news agency in war-riven Italy, they first set up a venture growing bananas in Cyprus, and then bought into a termite-exterminating business in Rhodesia. Living in retirement in Palma, her husband died suddenly and in widowhood Marguerite began a new period of wanderlust, taking a keen interest in mysticism and reincarnation. She frequently spent time in the US, helping to coordinate the search for the legendary island of Atlantis.

Marguerite recorded her first recollections of Amherst as 'a tall, elegant man, of tremendous appeal and impeccable manners'.[4] She was still more impressed when she first shook hands with him, and became aware of the damage done by the broken jack which had dropped the truck on his hand more than 40 years before. Her 'physic counsellor' had recently advised her that a man who had lost a finger would be entering her life.[5]

For Amherst, Marguerite, a short, well-built woman in her late 60s, hardly fitted the brief for the ideal woman he had defined in a letter to Veronica – he was on the lookout for a woman in her mid 40s, neat, trim and charming – but he found he had much in common with Marguerite's febrile mind and itchy feet, and they struck up a close friendship. In particular, Amherst had formed unorthodox but firmly held views on what life might be like in space, and in Marguerite, a woman who viewed certain archaeological remains in the Middle East as the landing sites of prehistoric astronauts, he found a willing listener.

He was working on an early draft of a book to be called *The Giant Leap to Hyperman*, which would encapsulate his theories on the benefits to Mankind of living in an environment of reduced gravity. He was convinced that sex in space would result in a state of increased ecstasy, and that babies thus conceived might be born with astounding intelligence.

This was right up Marguerite's street, and she agreed to collaborate on the book. In a strange echo of the days 45 years earlier, when Amherst had pored over the drawings for the AC's supercharger on the floor of the Grosvenor Hotel, so he lay on Marguerite's living-room floor, dictating while she typed.

Amherst would continue musing for the rest of his days about 'how *wonderful* it would be to conceive a child in space',[6] but he never found an organisation willing to take him there, nor a woman keen to conduct the experiment with him. Marguerite, on the other hand, proceeded to adopt ever more extreme notions, coming to believe, for example, that she was the reincarnation of Queen Victoria. The last paragraph of her autobiography reads, 'When my life mission is fulfilled, I hope to transcend earthly life, never to reincarnate, but to make return visits for service from another dimension of eternity, perhaps the Fifth Dimension.'[7] For the sake of Amherst's reputation, it is perhaps for the best that *The Giant Leap to Hyperman* never saw the light of day, and that Marguerite was neither trim nor 45.

One man was of particular help to Amherst during these difficult times. Three years his junior, John Millar had been educated at Charterhouse, chose business over university and, aged just 17, began his highly successful career as sales manager of an electric radiator company. Though his widow Joanna is uncertain how he and Amherst met, it seems likely that, directly or indirectly, their independent racing activities at Brooklands would have brought them into contact. Millar played an important role in wartime aircraft procurement, acquiring for RAF Coastal Command the Catalina flying boat and the Hudson patrol bomber – in which Amherst flew some six hours during his ATA service. Post-war, Millar built a fortune with his company, Avica Equipment, which specialised in aircraft, rocket and satellite components. By the late 1960s he had settled in Monaco with Joanna. Amherst's trips to stay with them over the Monaco Grand Prix weekend became one of the highlights of his year, and he and Millar remained close for the rest of his life.

Another figure to support Amherst was Edward Douglas-Scott-

Montagu, the third Baron Montagu of Beaulieu. Born in 1926, Lord Montagu was educated at Eton and New College Oxford, and served in Palestine with the Grenadier Guards. He founded his famous motor museum on his beautiful Hampshire estate in 1952, and added to it the world's first motorcycle museum four years later. He looked upon Amherst as 'a British motor racing hero'[8] and invited him for several extended stays at Beaulieu. Palace House became yet another location where Amherst worked on *The Miracle of Santa Clara*.

It was no simple matter for Amherst to lug the canvas around Europe. In order to take the painting back to England from Mallorca, he fashioned an aluminium tube for it, which he could attach to the roof of his car. One trip from the Mediterranean to Beaulieu took Amherst three full days at the wheel of an old Renault 4, its top speed in a strong, cold headwind limited by the huge tube to 60mph (97kmh). Still, he enjoyed his stays at Beaulieu; for all the wonderful automobilia nearby – including the 1964 *Bluebird* in which Donald Campbell, son of his former client Sir Malcolm, had pushed the world land speed record past 400mph (644kmh) – he also enjoyed the local wildlife and was amused that traffic had to give way to the wild horses of the New Forest.

Living at Beaulieu enabled Amherst to keep track of a Rolls-Royce Phantom and Ferrari GT which he had bought and was having restored in Woking, Surrey. Indeed, at one stage he entertained ideas of finding a small village in the south of France where he could set up an artist's studio and vintage car shop.

These plans were to go by the board because of a new project. Over the years Amherst had developed many racing cars and designed an aero engine, an aircraft, space vehicles and missiles, yet, since the *Storm Petrel*, the hydroplane which had 'flown' on the River Cam in 1920, it seems he had stayed away from the water. Suddenly, in February 1972, he took it into his head to buy the *Anchie*, a 40ft German sloop that had come on the market in Barcelona. The boat was fitted with a 50hp diesel engine, and could sleep up to seven passengers and crew, and Amherst considered she would give him a handy return once she had been restored.

In classic Amherst fashion the vessel proved to be anything but a good investment – though it did help to heal his relationship with his son, who today has mixed memories of the *Anchie*:

It was mahogany throughout, and rotten to the core. The only time we sailed it off to some island for the day, the winches came off in our hands! I ended up in a Spanish naval shipyard rebuilding the entire bottom of that boat, complete with copper fasteners, replacing all of the wooden hull; that took three months alone. It even sank once. I returned from LA six months later and floated it, then we sold it, but really it owned us. We had lots of fun though. Mallorca at that time was fabulous in every way. We were the best of friends then.[9]

Four months after buying the boat, Amherst knew he had made an error, but he was aware of the opportunity it had given him with Charles. He told Veronica that while he now realised buying the *Anchie* had been folly, and renovating her a burden, the great benefit of working on the boat with Charles was that it had given him the opportunity to get to know his son, whom he saw as a wise and kind-hearted young man.

It had taken another project to do it, and during the remaining 20 years of Amherst's life there would be further tensions within the family, but at the age of 71, he had at last found a way of connecting with his son.

In the spring of 1973, Amherst was back in Palma, intent on completing *The Miracle of Santa Clara*. There were other benefits to life there. He had begun a relationship with an attractive Irish woman who was a fine cook and a nurse, and caused him to thank God for his good fortune.

A year later, Amherst gave an interview to the well-known New Zealand-born motor racing writer, Eoin Young. The results appeared in the UK in *Car* magazine, and in Australia in *Sports Car World*, and Amherst rather liked them. *Autocar* published an article about him by Michael Scarlett in July 1975, and a piece by Young on the supercharging of Jack

Kruse's Phantom in a special Rolls-Royce 75th anniversary edition four years later. In November 1983 Amherst was in the press on both sides of the Atlantic: in Canada an interview with him appeared in his sister Veronica's local newspaper in Qualicum, *The News Advertiser*, while in the UK, *Classic and Sportscar* published a wide-ranging article about him by Mike McCarthy, notable for recording Amherst's most extensive published comments on his time working on rocketry and missiles in the US. Two years later *Thoroughbred & Classic Cars* published an interview with him conducted by Brian Palmer. He also popped up occasionally in car club journals such as *Bugantics*, the magazine of the Bugatti Owners' Club, and the Rolls-Royce Enthusiasts' Club's *Bulletin*.

Certain common traits shine through in many of the articles. Deep into old age, Amherst clearly remained a charming, delightful and erudite man to be with. Retirement was a dirty word and not to be contemplated. He owed much to his extraordinary education at Oundle, and he was justifiably proud of his years with Raymond Mays. Conversely, Selwyn Edge was 'not a cosy chap at all',[10] Malcolm Campbell left him 'puzzled and hurt',[11] W.O. Bentley was 'a cold fish',[12] Clive Gallop 'a very tiresome man'[13] and Vincent Burnelli a 'blatherskite'.[14] Each 'closed chapter' and 'rug pulled from under his feet' was someone else's fault. The moments of hubris are outweighed by the fatalism – curious, unfortunate bedfellows.

In his interview with Qualicum's *The News Advertiser*, Amherst outlined the philosophy that saw him through his grief at the loss of Nita and beyond into a busy and fulfilling old age:

> *It's a wonderful life when you make something of it, while you bail the water out of your boat as fast as it's coming in. The hurdles go up in front of you and you take them one by one. If you make one, there's the green pasture to graze in until you're confronted with the next one and you take that. If you happen to miss one, of course everybody notices – briefly – and you either pick yourself up and go on or fall back and give up. Of life I am very thankful. I praise the Lord every time I'm able to take a glass of water. If I'm able to take a glass of scotch, I praise a little more.*[15]

Thus, by moving between Kensington, Beaulieu and Mallorca, with the odd extended trip to his sister's estate on Vancouver Island thrown in for good measure, by devoting himself to painting and car and boat restoration, by giving the odd interview to car magazines, and through the company of good friends and lovers, Amherst gradually found peace again. By the end of the 1970s, the wanderlust had left him and he came back to settle in Kensington, where a new pattern of life began to emerge.

Of particular importance to him, both spiritually and socially, was the proximity of Holland Street to St Mary Abbots, the well-known Anglican church at the junction of Kensington High Street and Kensington Church Street, with the tallest spire in London. There had been a spiritual side to Amherst from his early days. His father had, after all, still been an Anglican minister at the time of his birth and, as a Member of Parliament, had argued passionately during the Cowper-Temple debates on religious education that, 'Englishmen . . . are seriously concerned that each child shall be brought up with some knowledge of the relations of the creature to the Creator, and of time to eternity, with its consequent influence over conduct and character.'[16]

That use of the word 'Creator' rather than 'God' was one Amherst would take to in later life, almost as though covering his bases. He had received a strongly orthodox Christian education at Windlesham House under the influence of 'Mrs Charles', he had been expected to attend service daily in the chapel at Gonville & Caius while at university, and he remained first and foremost an Anglican to the end of his days. Yet, over the course of his long life, his enquiring mind meant that he embraced and considered all manner of alternative spiritual thought.

During the 1930s, for example, Amherst dabbled with Vitalism, the doctrine which argues that, beyond the laws of physics and chemistry, some 'vital spark' plays a part in the processes of life, even though mainstream science had largely discounted the principle by this time. Fifty years on, he was so impressed by Pope John Paul II that he considered him a living saint and was inspired to paint his portrait.

Yet at the same time, each Thursday evening Amherst would go to meditate for 90 minutes with followers of the Yogi saint Paramahansa Yogananda, the advocate of 'Kriya Yoga'. In a letter to John Millar, he explained that practising yoga kept him sane, and in love with life and the Creator.

Since 1977 the Revd Ian Robson had been vicar of St Mary Abbots and, quite apart from coming to know the spiritual Amherst, another reason for their close friendship was that before becoming a man of the cloth, he had previously worked for General Motors, and had risen to the position of western regional manager for Vauxhall. Robson recalls:

He was a good friend. I knew him pretty well. There were many sides to him. He was very complex. I remember first seeing him. I couldn't miss him. He was wearing vivid colours, a green jacket and a black beret. His connections with the church were wonderful. He never missed Eucharist. He was there every Sunday. He was intrigued by the person of Jesus, and very sacramentally aware. Towards the end, when he was too ill to come to church, I took communion to him regularly.

He was very friendly, very affectionate and caring, and very good with young people. When new parishioners came to church I knew I could always introduce them to Amherst, because he would make them feel so welcome.[17]

One person to meet Amherst at a St Mary Abbots garden party in the mid-1980s, and who became a good friend, was Antonia Spowers. At the time, she was a self-employed decorative artist, and would not actually begin her career as an award-winning sculptor until some two years after Amherst's death. She was living in Battersea, and had gone over to Kensington to visit her mother:

He was a dashing-looking old boy in a white suit and a kipper tie. He was a man of so many interests. You could never suppose from talking to him he was as old as he was. He was elegant and stylish, and thoroughly mentally engaged. His friends were all younger, he enjoyed being with the young. He was quite Americanised and was less straight-laced than many of his contemporaries, and I think this caused him to veer away from his background. He enjoyed the weekly yoga sessions in the hall; they may have provided a connection to California for him. He was good company at dinner, and liked good food and wine. He enjoyed the Chelsea Arts Club too. He was a polymath, a renaissance man, and his paintings had the Renaissance about them. They weren't innovative, but they were charming, tender, loving records of people as he knew them.[18]

Another woman who met Amherst through St Mary Abbots was American artist Paula McColl:

He was extremely charming and good company. He was quite a dandy, and would wear a flower in his lapel. He was going through life in a creative way, and aged quite gracefully. He had an attractive, red-headed girlfriend late in life. He was devoutly religious, and would toast 'the Creator' before dinner. Meals were fun – there would be extended weekend gatherings with the focus very much on meals. He was a great ghost storyteller too! He was a good friend, I respected him, and honoured his passing.[19]

In between bouts of illness, Amherst's daughter Janie had put her *cordon bleu* cookery lessons to good effect, regularly cooking for 40 people on NBC's *Saturday Night Live* television programme, and going on to work for singer Art Garfunkel and for the Rolling Stones. Then she too began to spend more time in Kensington, and to care for Amherst. He welcomed her presence and tried in turn to help her bear the burden of her eye problems.

Well into his 80s, Amherst kept himself in reasonable shape with daily walks into Kensington Palace Gardens and Hyde Park, and thought nothing of walking the five-mile round trip to his favourite shops on Regent Street. There is no doubt that his creative mind remained as sharp as ever. He was convinced he could design a motorcycle to take on the Japanese, and upset the neighbours when the mound of motorcycle components under a tarpaulin at the front of his house grew ever larger. He even came up with an idea for a bidet lid which he planned to patent.

But, as at the beginning of his career, Amherst's last major projects were automotive, and it is to those we now turn.

Chapter 18

THE FINAL AUTOMOTIVE PROJECTS

In 1968 Graham Hill added a second World Championship to the title he had won with BRM. He was back with Lotus by this time, and his victory helped to pick the team up from the devastating death of their long-time team-leader Jim Clark earlier in the year. Hill's fifth Monaco Grand Prix win in seven years came the following May, but an enormous accident in October's US Grand Prix resulted in two broken legs. Through sheer determination he was on the grid for the South African Grand Prix just five months later. The same grit won him victory in the 1972 Le Mans 24-Hours alongside Henri Pescarolo in a Matra, giving him the final element in a unique 'triple crown' of World Championship, Indy 500 and Le Mans. Even when it became clear to him that no Grand Prix team would give him a drive in 1973, he simply went to tobacco firm Wills and persuaded them to sponsor his own team.

The Embassy Hill team set up base in Feltham, on the other side of Heathrow Airport from Amherst's old workshop in Stanwell Moor, and campaigned a Shadow in 1973 and a pair of Lolas in 1974 without success. That autumn saw Andy Smallman arrive from Shadow. He modified the Lola so extensively that it became known as the Embassy Hill GH1. A brief indication of the potential now within the team came the following April at the Spanish Grand Prix, when German driver Rolf Stommelen took his GH1 into the lead, only for the rear wing to detach itself from the car, which flew over a barrier and killed a marshal and four spectators.

Two weeks later, Monte Carlo, the scene of so much success for

Graham Hill, witnessed what once would have been unthinkable: he failed to qualify for the Monaco Grand Prix. Though he would not formally announce his retirement as a driver until the British Grand Prix, it was his last competitive outing in a Formula One car. By the time of the Belgian Grand Prix at the end of the month he had recruited his successor. Tony Brise, a 23-year-old Birmingham University graduate, was setting that year's Formula Atlantic championship alight, and some saw him as a future World Champion. Brise promptly repaid Hill's faith by recording seventh fastest qualifying time, to earn himself a fourth-row grid slot alongside reigning World Champion Emerson Fittipaldi.

Someone more than three times Brise's age was also doing his bit for the Embassy Hill team. Amherst and Hill had remained in contact over the years. While recuperating from his leg injuries in the winter of 1969, Hill had written his autobiography, *Life at the Limit*, deliberately choosing not to employ a ghostwriter, and sent a dedicated copy to Amherst.

Now, six years on, Amherst proposed to Hill that he may be able to improve the performance of the team's Cosworth engines. This, in spite of the fact that, by the end of the 1974 season, the Cosworth DFV, the most successful Formula One engine ever, had won some 78 World Championship Grands Prix over the previous eight years, and would win almost as many again over the next eight. This, in spite of the fact that Embassy Hill's Cosworths were maintained by Nicholson-McLaren, the company responsible for the engines that had just driven Fittipaldi to his title, and would power James Hunt to his in 1976.

As the 1975 season drew to a close, Amherst commenced regular drives over to Feltham to examine one of the team's DFVs. He concluded that the engine suffered from inconsistent flow through the cylinder head, and that this could be eradicated by fitting a brass one. In the short time left to the Embassy Hill team, it proved impossible to test Amherst's theory in practice, and certainly John Nicholson, of Nicholson-McLaren, was unaware of it when asked: 'What a wonderful story but certainly not one I know about. Just think of the weight and centre of gravity!'[1]

Nevertheless, Hill looked upon Amherst as part of the team and invited him to join them at the Paul Ricard circuit near Marseilles when winter testing began there in early November. Smallman's striking GH2 had been launched the previous month, sporting ultra low-line side-pods, and then taken to Silverstone for Brise to run it for a dozen laps – 'enough to know that it'll be a good car'[2]. That first Paul Ricard test proved disappointing, understeer preventing Brise getting near his French Grand Prix pace in the GH1 four months earlier.

A second visit to the circuit towards the end of the month proved much more successful; a telex sent back to Feltham during the test reads 'GH2 now faster than GH1'.[3] Amherst was not with the team on this occasion. In fact, it was not planned for Hill to be there either, but he flew down to the south of France in his twin-engine Piper Aztec, N6645Y, towards the end of the test to monitor progress for himself.

Thus it was that when he set off on the afternoon of Saturday 29 November for the return trip, flying with him were not only Brise and Smallman, but team manager Ray Brimble and mechanics Terry Richards and Tony Alcock, too. All six men perished at 2129 hours local time when the plane crashed in thick fog on Arkley golf course in Hertfordshire, some three nautical miles short of its intended destination, Elstree aerodrome. The report of the Accidents Investigation Branch of the Department of Trade concluded: 'The reason for the aircraft's descent into the ground could not be established but the possibility cannot be excluded that the pilot was mistaken as to his exact distance from the airfield and believed himself to be closer in than in fact he was.'[4]

Hill's funeral was held the following Friday in the Cathedral and Abbey Church in St Albans. Among the 3,000 mourners was Amherst. He had lost his brother in an air accident 45 years before and knew well the pain the families of the six men were going through, but perhaps a part of him was also thinking that his final front-line motor racing project had died with them.

In retrospect, a fascinating hint of the scale of his Grand Prix ambitions at this time had emerged the summer before the accident. In the closing paragraphs of an article about Amherst published in *Autocar* in July, Michael Scarlett had written:

> *He tends to winter at Palma, but comes here a lot, visiting old friends, proposing new ideas – 'talking to one or two people trying to get some support for a formula 1 engine'. We pricked up our ears. 'If I build it, it would run at 15,000rpm. My whole philosophy is revs – way back to the Bugatti' . . . Might it be a modification of an existing engine? 'No, I would do a complete engine.' Amherst Villiers has ideas on this, but understandably will not publish them.*[5]

So Amherst had been looking beyond the Cosworth at his own engine, and what a design it would have been. It is clear that, just as with his four-wheel-drive ambitions for BRM in 1961, he had read the Formula One rulebook thoroughly. The current formula had been in place since 1966, and permitted a maximum engine capacity of 3 litres. Nine years on, the engine doing most of the winning was the V8 Cosworth DFV, but in addition to BRM, Matra also had a V12, while Ferrari and Alfa Romeo preferred the flat-12 approach. Different though they may have been in configuration, they were all naturally aspirated and they all shared a 3-litre capacity.

Ever since 1966, however, the rulebook had offered the alternative option of an engine half the size, but turbocharged. The first team finally to take this route was Renault, whose 1.5-litre turbo made its debut at the British Grand Prix of 1977 and first won a Grand Prix two years later. That opened the floodgates, and the turbo gradually assumed dominance in Formula One, Ferrari becoming the first winners of the Constructors' Championship with one in 1982, and the normally aspirated Cosworth taking the last of its 155 Grand Prix wins in the back of Michele Alboreto's Tyrrell in Detroit a year later.

Yet eight years earlier Amherst had been planning a 1.5-litre turbo. Moreover, as he explained in old age to Antonia Spowers' son Hugo, it would have been a four-cylinder, two-stroke: 'His reasoning was simple: with a four-stroke you get a bang every second revolution, whereas with a two-stroke, you get a bang every time the piston comes up, so you have more bangs per stroke!'[6]

Towards the end of his life Amherst was interviewed by land speed record historian Steve Holter for a television documentary. Holter was astonished when Amherst suddenly started talking about a very different concept for a Grand Prix engine:

> We talked about it in a break in the interview while the cameraman went to fetch some film. He told me he had designed it 'for a chap who used to drive in Grands Prix but was now building his own cars'. I thought it might be John Surtees, I didn't think of Graham Hill. We were having a chat about the Cosworth DFV, and he said there was a much more effective way to deliver high revs and more power.
>
> It was a horizontally opposed engine, with the pistons coming in rather than out. That required two crankshafts, which seemed over-complicated to me, but he was quite clear. There were fewer moving parts, and a much smaller flywheel in the centre, so much higher revs. 'Much more spin for your power' is how he summed it up. He never actually said it had been built, but it was clear that he had put an incredible amount of thought into it. He had considered issues like poor engine braking and high oil consumption, and he could sketch the basic design straight off and quote dimensions and weights.[7]

Into the winter of 1975 Amherst actually had draughtsmen working on detailed design drawings for this extraordinary engine in an office in Richmond upon Thames, handily placed between his Kensington home and the Hill works in Feltham. One of the many unfortunate aspects of Graham Hill's fatal air accident is that it brought the project to a premature conclusion. Nevertheless, the audacious nature of this astonishing concept, and the idea that a septuagenarian could scrutinise the Formula One rulebook and identify, ahead of state-sponsored Renault, that the 1.5-litre turbo option had been lying there, unregarded and discounted, ever since 1966, are to Amherst's considerable credit.

As his final front-line motor racing chapter closed, so Amherst's attention swung back to the project he had first envisaged two years earlier, and which would eventually consume him. Opinions differ as to how he came to acquire a Rolls-Royce Phantom III; some say he found chassis number 3AZ138, registration DJJ 401, languishing in a field during 1973, but Piers Carlson, who had moved from California to London with Eleanor and their children some years earlier, remembers Amherst buying it from a car dealer in Neasden, in north London: 'It was essentially a funeral car – boxy, not pretty.'[8]

What Amherst had in mind was nothing less than 'the most fabulous Rolls-Royce ever'.[9] He drew up plans for a glamorous, five-seater sedanca body with a stunning colour scheme, the body in ice-blue larkspur, the soft-top in cream. He had an even more ambitious concept for the Phantom's 7.3-litre, V12 engine: 'Mr Supercharger' would fit it with twin-turbochargers! It was the kind of car for touring down to Monte Carlo or Nice, and a fitting project for Amherst to engage upon.

An early step was to have the engine overhauled and overdrive fitted, but at this stage the chassis still lacked a body, and Amherst only committed serious time and capital to the car once he turned 80. He commissioned Stanley Brunt Engineering, based in Silverdale, near Newcastle-under-Lyme in Staffordshire, to undertake the installation of the superchargers and bench-testing of the modified engine, and engaged a coachbuilding firm named Brockham's, in Goring-on-Thames, Oxfordshire, to build and fit the sedanca body.

Thus might DJJ 401 have remained, the project of a sprightly octogenarian with a fertile mind, who also enjoyed his walks in the park, St Mary Abbots on Sunday mornings, yoga on Thursday evenings, and dinner parties in the company of good friends less than half his age – were it not for Rolls-Royce launching its Bentley Mulsanne Turbo at the Geneva Motor Show in March 1982. Implicit in the car's name, and explicit in the company's marketing material, were links to Bentley's glorious past at Le Mans, and Amherst became eager to exploit his own, albeit tenuous, connections with the race.

At the time, his involvement with the Blower Bentley was severely compromised and had lasted only months, while the car itself may have broken the lap record at Le Mans in 1930, and been given credit for 'breaking' Caracciola's Mercedes, but in reality it was the Speed Six Bentleys which harried the German car into retirement and won the race. But ever since, the Blower had been an integral part of the legend of Bentley at Le Mans and, starting with the Californian articles in the 1960s and continuing with British car magazine interviews in the 1970s and 1980s, Amherst had done an effective job of embellishing his own profile, too. That he had actually come to live comfortably within his own legend is demonstrated by the letter he presented to Richard Perry, then Managing Director of Rolls-Royce Motors, and Michael Dunn, the company's Director of Engineering, in March 1983. In it, he described himself as the last surviving link between the Blower Bentley and the turbocharged Mulsanne.

The occasion was a lunch at London's Dorchester Hotel, during which Amherst made two proposals to Perry and Dunn. First, that Rolls-Royce should either pay for the remaining work on the Phantom to be completed, that cost estimated by Amherst to be £15,000, or complete the work themselves, in return for the company being able to use the car for PR purposes. Second, that he should act as a consultant on the design of a new high-performance car.

Amherst concluded by telling the two men that his reputation would lead to great interest in the project, which would be a pleasing and profitable experience for both parties. That final comment would come to ring hollow.

Attached to the letter was an itemised list of the work undertaken on DJJ 401 to date and, crucially, of the outstanding work. Included on this latter list were the rebuilding of the engine with thin-wall big-end shells, thick crown pistons and special exhaust valves, and brake-testing the modified engine and turbo installation.

Perry did not take up Amherst on his offer of consultancy, but he was interested in the idea of completing the outstanding work on the Phantom in return for utilising it for PR activity. On 25 May he wrote to Amherst, proposing that a Rolls-Royce quality engineer named Ian Rimmer should meet with him to examine the car, and explaining that Rolls-Royce was interested in taking the car to its Crewe plant, where it would be completed as a training exercise in its Experimental Department, under the supervision of Rimmer.

In early June Rimmer met with Amherst at Brockham's to examine the car, and his verdict was clearly sufficiently positive for Perry to enter into a contract with Amherst later that month. The agreement comprised a simple text, little more than 200 words long, drawn up on Rolls-Royce Motors Limited paper, and was poorly-drafted. It commenced, 'The following points constitute the principle agreement reached between Rolls-Royce Motors Limited and Mr Amherst Villiers',[10] prompting one to ask what subsidiary agreements might also have been made? Indeed, Amherst would subsequently point to his contract with Brunt's for the engine work, and the quotation Brockham's had given for the coachwork, copies of which he had given Rimmer, with an implicit expectation that Rolls would honour them. The concluding words of the contract with Rolls-Royce were even looser: 'All of the foregoing has been drawn up as a reflection of the agreement reached on the above date.'[11] If this was a 'reflection', where was the agreement itself?

Bizarrely, the work outstanding on the car was barely mentioned, the only reference being, 'Rolls-Royce Motors Limited will complete the restoration of the motor car after completion of the exterior bodywork.'[12] Crucially, from Amherst's perspective, at least he would be able to rely on the title of the contract, 'PHANTOM III TURBO PROJECT'.[13] He was, as we have seen, no great businessman, but for Rolls-Royce to permit itself to be bound by such an imprecise document, open to a wide range of interpretation, was most unfortunate.

Still, most contracts are negotiated and signed, then filed away to never see the light of day again, and there is no doubt whatsoever that both parties entered the project on that basis, expecting it, as Amherst had said, to be a pleasing and profitable experience. To that end, he amicably ended his association with both Brunt's and Brockham's, and sent the car to Crewe in September 1983. During the following January he enjoyed another lunch, this time at L'Escargot restaurant in London's Greek Street, in the company of Rimmer, Ian Adcock, head of Rolls-Royce's PR function, and two journalists to whom Adcock had offered the story of the turbocharged Phantom as a joint exclusive.

In March, Amherst felt it appropriate to send Perry a letter, enclosing a form of supplementary agreement containing seven short clauses. One of these read that Rolls would complete and test the turbocharged car at their own expense in return for defined PR work, without itemising the work to be completed and tested, or stating where the PR work had been defined. Another read that the company would deliver the car to him by 1 October 1985, free from all charges, in concours condition, and in perfect working order. In spite of the imprecise nature of the document, Perry responded the following month to confirm that it formed a *'suitable supplement to the Agreement dated 29th June 1983 and that these documents together record the whole of our understanding. I do hope that the Phantom III project will be a great success and I shall watch it with interest.'*[14]

Two months on, all still seemed well. Rimmer wrote to Amherst, telling him that Adcock hoped that the completed car could be exhibited at the Motor Show in October.

It was only in the summer, when Perry was promoted to another position within Rolls-Royce, and Rimmer allocated other responsibilities, that Amherst first became nervous. This everyday occurrence in corporate life had unnerved him more than once when working in America, and his subsequent meeting with Rolls' director of engineering Michael Dunn did nothing to dispel his concerns, Dunn querying the cost and necessity of engine bench tests.

Worse was to follow. On 28 February 1985 Peter Ward, Perry's successor as managing director of Rolls-Royce Motors, wrote to

Amherst to advise him that the company had decided to carry out no further work on the car. Specifically, Rolls would not fit turbochargers, and could not undertake a bench test until September of the following year. Ward advised Amherst that he could either have the car back in its current form, or that the company would complete the work to his exact requirements, but at a substantial cost to him. One particular sentence also made it clear that the company had dropped any plans to use the car for PR purposes: 'Nor should prospective customers be misled into believing that the conversion has been engineered to our normal standards.'[15]

For Amherst, someone with a very high, almost naive degree of trust in his fellow-man, and someone with a great respect for Rolls-Royce, it was a savage volte-face. He felt entirely confident that Rolls-Royce was contractually bound to deliver the turbocharged car to him in just seven months, free from all charges, in concours condition, and in perfect working order. As such, he felt his only option was to turn to the justice system, in which he had an even higher trust. A letter to his sister Veronica refers to this moment. He explains that the company has reneged on its agreement with him, and that a lawyer has advised him that he has a sound case for breach of contract. In the end, he finally issued a writ against Rolls-Royce in November 1986.

Even then, he refused to let the stress get to him, and sought to busy himself on an even more ambitious project. He came up with plans for a high-performance touring car. Its 4.5-litre, 16-cylinder engine would have a 120-degree V configuration, permitting a particularly low bonnet line. Fitted with four turbochargers, the engine would deliver 1,000bhp. His young friend Hugo Spowers assisted in the creation of a one-fifth scale model of the car to support a presentation of the project to Aston Martin's chief executive, Victor Gauntlett. Aston Martin chose not to proceed with Amherst's proposal, but years later Spowers would look upon the quad-turbo Bugatti EB 110, and wonder what might have been.

In the meantime, Amherst's friend Lord Montagu of Beaulieu tried to bring about an out-of-court settlement with Rolls-Royce, appealing directly to Sir David Plastow, chairman and chief executive of Rolls-Royce Motor's ultimate parent company, Vickers plc. In August 1988 he wrote to Plastow, stating, 'I think in the long run a sensible settlement now would probably save a lot of embarrassment and after all Amherst is getting on now.'[16] Plastow replied a week later, explaining that the amount of work required to complete the car – even without fitting the superchargers and bench-testing the engine – had proved to be much greater than contemplated, such that the company had now spent more than £100,000 on the project. Turbocharging had been ruled out by Rolls's Engineering Department because 'such additional power and torque would be detrimental to the powertrain',[17] but he anticipated that the car would be complete in all other respects and delivered to Amherst by the end of the following month. He concluded by thanking Lord Montagu 'for alerting us to his [Amherst's] concerns and we will, of course, do everything possible to ensure a satisfactory and amicable outcome.'[18]

Montagu reported this back to Amherst, telling him, 'I feel that under the circumstances you should wait until the car is delivered and unless there are serious faults in it, I suggest you should perhaps agree to accept the situation. Legal cases always cost money and it would seem for all concerned an unnecessary exercise.'[19] He was also keen that Amherst, now aged 87, should step back from stressful confrontation with Rolls, and instead think about writing an autobiography. He proposed that a motoring journalist named Jon Pressnell should support him in this endeavour, but Amherst never met him and did not pursue the idea, preferring to focus on righting what he saw as the injustice done to him.

He found it impossible to accept that Rolls-Royce had entered into a contractual obligation to complete the work on the 'Phantom III *Turbo* Project' [author's italics] and return the car to him in perfect working order and concours condition, only after its own quality engineer had examined the car and reviewed the outstanding work, yet now, almost three years after the date by which the car should have been returned to him, it still was not finished, and would never be turbocharged.

The dispiriting dialogue between Amherst and Rolls dragged on into the following year, as did work on the car. Lord Montagu visited Amherst in Kensington and, though still keen to spare his friend the stress of a court action, was impressed by the strength of his case. In April, he wrote again to Plastow:

I in no way wish to interfere with your negotiations with him but having now had a closer look at the evidence which he has marshalled with considerable diligence, I am persuaded that I should write to you to say that if what he says is correct, going into court would reflect very badly on Rolls-Royce. As an old friend of Rolls-Royce, he is very reluctant to do so and I am therefore writing to you once more to ask whether you might take a personal interest in this case, as I believe it would be of benefit to all concerned.[20]

Plastow replied a week later. The engine had dropped a valve on initial test, and had had to be removed and sent to a specialist repairer 'yet again'.[21] However, all being well, the car would be ready for return to Amherst within three or four weeks. As for the legal action, an envoy had been sent to discuss a possible settlement with Amherst. However, since Rolls had now spent in excess of £200,000 on the car, his request for compensation of £100,000, in addition to the car, was thought to be 'grossly excessive'.[22]

The row lumbered on towards the High Court. Even Amherst's vicar, the Revd Ian Robson, tried to intercede. At one point in his career with General Motors he and Plastow had been colleagues, and Robson invited Vickers' chairman to lunch, along with Amherst, in the hope of finding a settlement. Robson recalls, 'It was quite harmonious and charming, but achieved nothing.'[23]

The very day before Amherst's action for breach of contract finally reached the law courts, Robson inadvertently found himself interceding again. Over Sunday lunch, he was explaining that a parishioner of his would be up in court against Rolls-Royce the following day. A guest interrupted and asked him not to say any more; he was Judge John Prosser, and he would be presiding over the case in the morning.

On Monday 1 July 1991 the 90-year-old Amherst got his day in court. He was frail and suffering from cancer of the bladder, but resolutely determined, and resolutely supported by his daughter Janie, who wore a towel around her head to protect her damaged eyes from the bright sunlight. Antonia Spowers had them over to dinner early that week: 'They were hyped up on the adrenaline of it all, but they both knew it was early days and they were up for the long haul.'[24]

During that first day, Amherst's counsel, Peter Brunner QC, introduced his client as 'a legendary figure in the field of car design',[25] and referred to his work on the Blower Bentley, *Bluebird* and the Brescia Bugattis, and to his contribution to the BRM engine that had won Graham Hill his first World Championship. He went on to describe Amherst's plans for the Phantom, thus providing the press with the following morning's headlines. 'Rolls-Royce sued over failure to build "most fabulous car"' wrote *The Times*, [26] while the *Daily Telegraph* weighed in with 'Designer, 90, sues Rolls over "fabulous Phantom"'.[27] Both newspapers published photographs of an elderly, frail Amherst and blind-folded Janie. Lord Montagu's advice from two years earlier – 'going into court would reflect very badly on Rolls-Royce' – seemed prescient.

Into the second day of the action, Amherst began to give evidence, and wasted little time in blaming Michael Dunn for Rolls-Royce's apparent change of heart, giving *The Times* another arresting headline, 'Hatchet man killed car project',[28] but on the third day DJJ 401 itself took centre stage. The car had been brought down to the Royal Courts of Justice from Crewe, and Judge Prosser, a Bentley owner himself, went out to the car park to view it, and then to take a ride in it. A Rolls-Royce expert witness named Richard Barton took the car out on to the road, with Prosser alongside him in the front passenger seat, and Amherst and Brunner in the back. Barton drove them down the Strand, over Waterloo Bridge, back over Lambeth Bridge and along the Embankment. Not very far perhaps, but far enough for Prosser to form a damning assessment of the car.

Back in the court room, Amherst was asked by Brunner for his own opinion of DJJ 401. He replied that it had ended up 'a bastardised thing – a sort of folly',[29] and this, together with photographs of the car at the law courts, dominated the following morning's press reports of the third day of the case. However, by the time these were being read over the breakfast tables and in the railway carriages of Britain, Amherst's fortunes had taken a catastrophic turn for the worse. The previous evening he had fallen heavily at home, breaking his hip, and been rushed to St Mary's Hospital.

The case was adjourned the next morning, but it seems that this was the least of Amherst's concerns. The cancer was an issue, of course, but in terms of his physical injuries, he was stabilised quickly, considered sound enough to undergo a hip replacement operation which was judged a success, and able to go home from hospital within a month of the fall. Nevertheless, something was missing. The indomitable spirit that had supported him through numerous sleepless nights on the Bugattis and on the *Villiers Superchage*, and had fuelled his dogged challenge of Rolls-Royce nearly 70 years later, had been extinguished. Antonia Spowers was one of those who helped Janie nurse Amherst once he came home, and says that the fall 'took all his confidence away; his mental capacity fell away'.[30]

Another friend shaken by the deterioration in his spirits was John Millar. He had phoned St Mary's from Monte Carlo for regular updates on Amherst, and been told he was recovering well. But, in a letter of 22 July, he told Amherst that when he first spoke to him on the phone, 'you sounded so depressed I began to wonder whether they were telling you how marvellously you were recovering from the hip operation'.[31] Tragically, although Amherst was on the mend physically, mentally it was as though a light had gone out.

Nevertheless, Judge Prosser agreed to the unusual step of

reconvening the case at Amherst's home. On 27 August, less than four weeks after he had left hospital, the court came to his Holland Street studio to continue listening to him give evidence. It was soon clear that he was not well enough, and Prosser adjourned the case to a date to be scheduled in the following legal term, beginning in October. Even then, he would require 'the utmost detail'[32] that Amherst was able to continue giving evidence. Sadly that would never prove to be the case, and almost five years would pass before Janie, as executor of her late father's estate, took his breach of contract action against Rolls-Royce back to the High Court – and, after a 15-day hearing, won. Judge Prosser again presided over the case, and awarded Janie damages of £160,000, based upon a value of the car in concours condition of £200,000, less its actual current value, which he thought might be £40,000 – though she was actually able to sell it for considerably more. Prosser also allowed interest for three-and-a-half years, and awarded the bulk of the costs against Rolls-Royce, and those costs incurred since the start of the trial on an indemnity basis. This was an indication of Prosser's disapproval of the way the company had conducted its defence: 'I do not wish to use emotive words, but the case could have been settled at any time. Instead they brazened it out and fought tooth and nail.'[33]

During his judgment, Prosser was as positive in his recollections of Amherst as he was critical of the work Rolls-Royce had put into the Phantom, calling it 'well below standard'.[34] He described Amherst as 'a legend in his own lifetime'[35] who took pleasure in his efforts to 'move the frontiers of mechanical power ever forward'.[36] As for the car, quite apart from the fact that turbochargers had never been fitted, the pram-irons had been put on the wrong way round, rivets could be seen through the chrome and paintwork, and he could recall a 'horrible noise'[37] from the steering box when turning from left to right.

More than a dozen years on from the conclusion of the case, and more than 17 years after Amherst's High Court description of the car as 'a bastardised thing – a sort of folly', what is one to make of this deeply unfortunate affair? Rolls-Royce may well have bastardised the Phantom, but where did the folly lie?

Well into old age, Amherst's searing brain kept coming up with fresh ideas and, as with any creative thinker, they were not all equally brilliant or practicable. British Rail, for example, listened politely to his proposal for a change in the gauge of the national rail network in pursuit of greater passenger comfort, but decided that the vast cost of re-laying every mile of track in the country, rebuilding every bridge, and reboring every tunnel made his idea a non-starter. Similarly, the Vatican did not proceed with his plans for an art school in Rome, and President Reagan chose not to respond to his offer of help on the 'O'-ring problem that had brought catastrophe to the Challenger space shuttle.

The restyling and supercharging of his old Phantom III should have been a wonderful final project for an energetic and creative elderly man, but getting Rolls-Royce involved on a free-of-charge basis in return for using a 50-year-old car for PR purposes was another idea that should perhaps have been turned down. It was Amherst's belief in his own legend, and perception of himself as the sole surviving link between the Blower Bentley and the Bentley Mulsanne, that led him to propose it. If only, like his plans for the UK's rail network, the art school in Rome, or the sealing of the joints on the space shuttle's rocket boosters, the proposal had been vetoed, much distress could have been avoided. The tragedy is that Rolls-Royce not only went along with Amherst's proposal. It contractually agreed to deliver on it, manifestly failed to do so, and then brazenly stuck to its position all the way to the High Court. It was a shameful way to treat an old man.

It is appropriate to ask if Amherst was at fault in setting with Rolls-Royce a budget expectation of only £15,000 for the outstanding work. After all, the company ended up expending more than £200,000, and that was without fitting the turbochargers or testing the engine in this configuration. But Amherst itemised what he understood this work to comprise when he presented his original proposal to Perry and Dunn back in March 1983. He showed quality engineer Ian Rimmer the car, and gave him copies of his contract with Brunt's, the engine restorers, and the quotation from coachbuilders Brockham's. In other words, even if he gravely under-estimated the cost of completing the project to his design, he gave Rolls-Royce every opportunity to establish its own budget.

That leaves the question of Amherst's design. Was it appropriate to turbocharge a pre-war Rolls-Royce? One expert to whom Amherst turned during the affair was Malcolm Barber. Today he is CEO of Bonhams & Butterfields, but at the time he was a member of Sotheby's car team, and had recently brought the gavel down on its sale of the famous ex-Woolf Barnato 'Blue Train Bentley'. Amherst invited Barber to Holland Street twice to discuss the Phantom. In weighing up his options, he wanted to know what the car was worth, whether he decided to sell it, or simply use the valuation as a reference point in his negotiations with Rolls-Royce.

'He was a charming guy,' says Barber. 'I'd love to have known him better. I did admire him, and I could see what he was trying to do. He put me in a difficult position really. Here was a folk-hero of legend, but the car was a one-off, and you'd have had to find a one-off fan – or preferably two – to really determine the value of it. And the car market had peaked, prices were tumbling . . .'[38]

Another authority who rated the design was Lord Montagu. A couple of months before the case reached the High Court, he wrote to Amherst saying, 'There is no question that a Turbocharged Rolls designed by such an expert as you would have made a most interesting and valuable car.'[39]

In conclusion, it seems Amherst's only error was engaging Rolls-Royce in the project. Only Amherst, with his unique blend of engineering talent, creativity, hubris and lack of acumen, could have ended up in such an unfortunate situation. The last word on this wretched case goes to Joanna Millar, the widow of Amherst's great friend, John: 'I am afraid my own opinion was that Amherst was not on top of the transaction as he was not a business man, but an artist in every sense of the word, and maybe some of that drama could have been avoided.'[40]

Back in late August 1991, after the abortive attempt to take Amherst's evidence at his home, Janie had told the press, 'My father is very distressed and is fighting to stay alive so that he will be able to give his testimony.'[41] Regrettably, this proved to be beyond him. His spirit was broken, and the cancer was spreading. For Janie and his closest friends, the task became one of making him comfortable and at peace. The Revd Ian Robson played a part, regularly taking communion to him.

The end came on Thursday 12 December, three days after his 91st birthday. Janie and Antonia were with him, Janie chanting over him, when he slipped away. Antonia: 'It was peaceful and without pain.'[42]

Six days later, Amherst's mortal remains were cremated at Putney Vale Cemetery, the final resting place of pre-war motor racing heroes Richard Seaman and Kenelm Lee Guinness. It was the last service of the day, held at 4 o'clock, and outside it was already dark. The Revd Robson led a brief ceremony for a small group of family and friends. It was Antonia who went down to the town hall to register Amherst's death. Under Occupation she wrote: 'Automotive and Aero/Astronautic Engineer and Portrait Painter (retired).'[43] He would have liked that – except for 'retired'!

Chapter 19

THE RENAISSANCE MAN
WITHOUT A MEDICI

S ome eight weeks after Amherst's death, on 31 January 1992, Sir
Peter Masefield's obituary of him was published in *The Times*. It
was a highly affirmative picture of the man Masefield had known for
more than 50 years. In fact, the published version omitted lines that
would have painted Amherst in still more positive light – 'always good
company, and retaining his enthusiasm in a wide range of interests
right to the end . . .'[1] Nonetheless, the penultimate paragraph made
fascinating reading: 'Villiers was a remarkable man. If he had
accorded the same priorities to his business relationships as he did to
his inanimate achievements there were few heights he might not
have scaled.'[2]

Among the car magazines, the best obituary by far was published
two weeks later, in *Autocar & Motor* (the two titles had merged in
1988). It was written by the motoring journalist who perhaps
understood Amherst best and was most sympathetic to him, Mike
McCarthy. Like his wide-ranging *Classic & Sportscar* article of November
1983, it was well balanced, devoting as much space to his rocketry
and missile work as to his racing cars. The central illustration was a
portrait shot of Amherst as an old man. Surrounding it were images
of Raymond Mays and Peter Berthon sweeping around the Lower Ess
at Shelsley Walsh in an early variant of the *Vauxhall Villiers*, Mays
getting ready for the off in *Cordon Rouge*, Graham Hill posing next to
his portrait, and Amherst at the wheel of his restored Blower Bentley
in the California sun. McCarthy's final two paragraphs are quoted
in full:

For all his genius, Villiers seemed to have flaws: perhaps he rubbed people up the wrong way, had no commercial aptitude, was too much of a dreamer, or couldn't suffer fools gladly. Whatever, he was forever 'having the rug pulled from under him' (his own words) and unfortunately such problems dogged the last months of his life. He had dreamed of creating a twin-turbocharged Rolls-Royce Phantom III, to be built by Rolls-Royce. In the end, unhappy with the results, he sued the company, but died before matters were sorted out.

To those who knew him, he was charm personified, erudite and witty, a fund of knowledge and a fascinating conversationalist. He will be missed.[3]

There, in the closing paragraphs of the obituaries by those writers who knew him best, lies the great conundrum that is Charles Amherst Villiers. He was wonderful company, he possessed immense skill across a bewildering range of endeavour, but he found it easier to walk away, or to call in his lawyer, than he did to engage in reasoned dialogue. How much greater could he have been, what consistent, lasting success could he have achieved, if he had learned a little humility along the way, and if he had ever learned how to get on with his colleagues? If he had not blamed each reverse on a 'rug-puller', if he had considered instead his own role in a failure or a parting of the ways, he may have been able to apply lessons that would have helped him to avoid a situation, or take a different decision, in the future.

Motor racing historian Doug Nye has fascinating insights on this aspect of Amherst:

I met him five or six times in old age, and he did have that confidence about him that only Englishmen of his class and education have. But he did fall into the trap in old age whereby if anyone rejected one of his ideas, they were 'pig-headed' or 'lacking in vision', or 'dull, grey bureaucrats'. He was very much the Renaissance Man, but he really needed a Medici alongside him to achieve consistent success, and I think vanity prevented him from identifying that need. He had a proven track record and when he got his backside in gear he was darned successful, but I've always wondered if he was out of his period. He would have soared in the mid-Victorian period, the Age of the Engineer. He would have been enormously successful, like another Brunel. Or maybe his rightful place was alongside the mavericks who've dominated motor racing recently. But either way, I think he was out of his time.[4]

Amherst's tragedy is that the vanity Nye identified in him in old age had always been there. Consider his reaction, in June 1931, to failing his Ground Engineer's Licence examination. Most people who fail an exam realise that either they did not put sufficient effort into their work and resolve to do better next time, or that they are not well suited to the subject and move on to something else. Either that, or someone close to them gives them a nudge and points out that they ought to reach one of those conclusions.

Amherst's response was to fire off a letter of some 1,000 words to *Flight* magazine. It began:

Permit me to bring to your notice the monstrous manner in which aircraft inspection is operating in this country. Extraordinary powers have been recklessly invested in the Licencing Department of the Air Ministry, which are being used without discretion and to the most extreme detriment of Civil Aviation in its most important aspect – individual enterprise.

It concluded:

We cannot be expected to support indefinitely a system of bureaucracy which stands between our right to build and enjoy a better and higher form of civilisation. Of course, the whole trouble is that the final controlling authorities should be young, practical men who fly, and not a lot of obstructive permanent officials who have been allowed by national apathy to worm their way into positions of vital national importance.[5]

Quite apart from the damage this torrent of pomposity must have done Amherst as he made his first strides in aeronautic engineering, the letter does betray a vanity that should have been pricked years earlier. If he had only had a little humility to sit alongside his undoubted talent, he would have learned from his mistakes and not repeated them. It is fascinating, for example, to consider that, having concluded the Gloster IV seaplane was too fast for any available runway to convert to landplane configuration, Amherst sold it and bought a Gloster VI – a faster seaplane! Consider, too, his departure from the *Bluebird* project: if he had managed to overcome his frustrations with working for Malcolm Campbell sufficiently long to have been part of the team which finally broke the world land speed record, might he not have found the patience to cope better with the challenges of life in corporate America, and enjoyed greater success with his space and missile projects?

Enough of Amherst's liabilities. Let us consider his assets. His most consistent success was achieved in the automotive world. That an undergraduate could develop *Quicksilver* to the point that Raymond Mays – new to motor sport himself – could dominate Inter-Varsity competition and enjoy considerable success at Brooklands, on hill-climbs and in sprints speaks volumes. For Amherst's partnership with Mays on the Brescia Bugatti to deliver such stepped increases in performance that Ettore Bugatti himself should invite them out to Molsheim to examine the car, and then give them a second one, speaks louder still.

Could Amherst have investigated, in advance of that challenging 1925 season, whether the detachable cylinder head of the 1.5-litre AC engine was capable of withstanding the rigours of supercharging in any other way than giving it a go? Perhaps. Should he have given more thought to the weight and cooling implications of fitting the AC with a two-seater body? Unquestionably, but, on the domestic pre-war motor sport scene, just as with Formula One today, consistent success was well nigh impossible, and if Amherst had not suffered the odd reverse along the way, then he probably would not have been trying sufficiently hard to earn all the success Mays went on to enjoy with the car known variously as the *Vauxhall Villiers* and *Villiers Supercharge*, which was still breaking records when it was 12 years old.

Amherst may not have felt able to stay part of Malcolm Campbell's team to witness in person the fruits of his labours – Campbell's snatching of the world land speed record at Pendine in February 1927 – but his real contribution to *Bluebird* was the development potential he designed and (at least partly) built into the car, so that through further design evolutions, largely led by Reid Railton, it was able to break the record another seven times.

Perhaps the world's first supercharged Rolls-Royce, Jack Kruse's Phantom, and the extraordinary, one-off, engine/blower unit Amherst designed for it, were a rich man's flight of fancy, but both *Bluebird* and the Phantom demonstrate that, aged not yet 28, Amherst had effortlessly made the leap from development engineer to design engineer.

It is ironic that the automotive project with which Amherst is most associated, the supercharging of the Blower Bentley, involved him in little more than three months' design work and resulted in, with the exception of the AC, the least successful of his racing cars. But the vehicle has become a landmark in design and one of the most desired classic cars of all. Besides, what red-blooded Englishman – or Anglo-American, to give Amherst a more accurate description – would not want the unique title of the Man Who Supercharged Bond?

Another, more abstract, aspect of Amherst's automotive work deserves mention. He may not have played a central role at BRM, but his presence at Bourne clearly made a difference to a team so used to failure that its owner had delivered the ultimatum, 'Win, and make some money, or I'll close you.' He helped turn them into world champions. Moreover, he was more than 60 years old when he poked around in Formula One's rulebook and came up with his idea for four-wheel-drive, and was in his mid-70s when he designed his unique, 2-stroke, 1.5-litre turbo for Graham Hill. These are the kind of creative pursuits of 'the unfair advantage' that, once in a while, deliver extraordinary results, and Amherst deserves recognition for them.

Finally, there is the overall role he played in the development of British motor sport. With *Quicksilver*, *Cordon Rouge*, *Cordon Bleu* and the *Villiers Supercharge*, Amherst gave Raymond Mays the platforms for consistent success on which he laid the foundations of ERA and BRM. Without BRM, the frustrated Tony Vandervell would never have founded Vanwall. It was Colin Chapman's work on the 'tear drop' body of the Vanwall which brought him a step nearer taking Lotus into Grand Prix racing to overhaul Cooper; and without Cooper, would Jack Brabham have founded the Grand Prix team which Bernie Ecclestone would acquire and use as the basis for his domination of Formula One, or would Bruce McLaren have set up his eponymous team? To claim a direct link between Amherst and Lewis Hamilton would be fanciful in the extreme. Nevertheless, he did play a critical role in the early days of British motor sport, and the Blower Bentley and his work at BRM clinch it; Amherst's star in the firmament of British motor racing may be distant, but it burns brightly.

As for his aeronautic work, it is true that neither of his two most important projects, the Maya engine and the V-1000 double-decker troop transporter and transatlantic passenger plane, made it into production. However, they are further evidence of the assuredness with which he moved from development engineer to designer. That Amherst undertook these designs on opposite sides of the Atlantic from one another, in a field quite different from the automotive world in which he had worked for more than ten years, is again to his considerable credit.

Nor can one be overly critical of his failure to find sustained success during his time as a businessman in the 1930s. He may have over-estimated demand for automotive superchargers, and under-estimated competition against the Maya, but prolonged business success requires not only inspiration and perspiration; it needs an elusive confluence of timing, opportunity and economic circumstance. The enterprises of many men and women with far more commercial acumen than Amherst have failed through the absence of one of those jigsaw pieces. For every entrepreneur who makes a fortune, there are thousands who do not, and the number of businessmen who have been successful in more than one field, as Amherst tried in the 1930s, is small indeed. One can only salute him for his endeavour, and wonder what might have been the outcome if he had been in the right kind of partnership.

Amherst was, by his own admission, a 'projects man'. He needed partners to determine which one had the optimal chance of sporting or business success. Raymond Mays played that role for much of the 1920s, but was so obsessed with achieving motor racing success that he could not possibly have followed his friend into performance road cars, never mind civil aviation, while Thomas Hay may well have provided capital, but not business leadership.

The lead times between design and project execution in space technology may be decades, and it is therefore difficult to judge the significance of most individuals to the US space programme. This is particularly true of Amherst, who not infrequently quit before becoming aware of the fruits of his labour. Just six years after he resigned as technical manager of Boeing's Lunar Systems Group, the company's *Lunar Orbiter 1* began its photography of the moon's surface that would prove key to choosing the right landing locations for the Apollo missions. We cannot know if Amherst's work played a part in this, but thanks to his former colleague at Bendix, Bill Ficken, we do know that the 'Villiers Gyro' led to the company's work on the US Navy's Polaris and Poseidon missiles. We also know that his work on rockets and missiles was highly valued. Why else would Douglas, with a large workforce of its own and numerous American competitors from which to headhunt a project engineer, invite a 62-year-old man from Kensington to join Project EMPIRE?

Art, like beauty, is in the eye of the beholder, and for every admirer of Amherst's portraiture, there is someone else who considers it too realistic and lacking in artistic interpretation. Suffice it to say that if arguably the mid-20th century's most famous portrait painter, Pietro Annigoni, or London's National Portrait Gallery, agreed with Amherst's critics, then he would not have been invited to spend months in Annigoni's Florentine studio, and his work would not have spent years on display in one of the world's most prestigious galleries.

So it can be seen that, over his 91 years, Amherst justly earned the label given to him by his friend Antonia Spowers on his death certificate – Automotive and Aero/Astronautic Engineer and Portrait Painter – and that he possessed great talent in each of those fields. The question remains, did the sheer breadth of his talent prevent him from achieving still more. Had he concentrated on one discipline, had he focused on either cars, or planes, or rockets, and simply enjoyed portraiture as a hobby, would he have been more successful?

The answer to that question is very probably yes, but to ask it at all is to misunderstand Amherst Villiers. In his early 60s there came a period during which he studied under the most famous portrait painter of the day, assisted in the detail design of a World Championship-winning Grand Prix engine, and was brought across the Atlantic to help establish the optimal way to send a man to Mars. Why would he want to focus on one field when, at an age most people retire, he could be 'project man' across a range of subjects most people would find bewildering?

There were times when he found working with colleagues a challenge, when his vanity should have been pricked, and when he struggled with parenthood, but those observations can be made of many of us. The fact is, Charles Amherst Villiers came from a remarkable family, and lived a remarkable life to the full, across a unique range of endeavour, with immense charm, skill, energy and enthusiasm. For that, we should celebrate him.

NOTES AND SOURCES

Chapter 1: Fiel Pero Desdichado

1. Charles Mosley (ed.), *Burke's Peerage, Baronetage & Knightage 106th Edition* (Burke's Peerage, 1999).

2. Royal Decree of Queen Victoria, 8 July 1876.

3. From the marriage certificate of Ernest Villiers and Elaine Guest, 30 April 1898.

4. University of Limerick, Glucksman Library, Glin Papers, 423/3, Elaine Villiers, letter to Veronica Fitz-Gerald (*née* Villiers, later Veronica Milner) (n.d.).

5. 1901 England Census, Administrative County London, Civil Parish Paddington, Ward of Municipal Borough Hyde Park, www.ancestry.com

6. East Sussex Record Office, AMS6273/3, Political Papers of Edwin Ernest Brown, *Brighton Herald* (25 July 1903).

7. 'Hard Blow for Balfour', *New York Times* (6 April 1905).

8. Hansard, HC (series 4), vol. 151, cols 663–4 (8 August 1905).

9. Ibid., vol. 189, col. 769 (25 May 1908).

10. Ibid., vol. 190, col. 58 (3 June 1908).

11. Ibid., vol. 190, cols 65–71 (3 June 1908).

12. Ernest A. Villiers, 'Finance Bills', letter to *The Times* (15 November 1909).

13. Glin Papers, 423/3, Elaine Villiers, letter to Veronica Fitz-Gerald (*née* Villiers, later Veronica Milner) (n.d.).

14. From the death certificate of Ernest Villiers (26 September 1928).

15. Hansard, HC (series 4), vol. 188, col. 1602, 18 May 1908.

Chapter 2: School

1. Raymond Mays, *Split Seconds* (Foulis, 1951).
2. Ibid.
3. John Nolan, *The News Advertiser* (Vancouver Island, 8 November 1983).
4. Obituary of Peter Morgan, *Daily Telegraph* (23 October 2003).

Chapter 3: *Quicksilver*

1. Cambridge University Archives, SOC.98, records of the Cambridge University Automobile Club and its nominated successor, the Cambridge University Motorcycle Club.
2. Mays, *Split Seconds*.
3. *The Light Car and Cyclecar* (1 January 1921).
4. Mays, *Split Seconds*.
5. Chris Mason, *Uphill Racers: The History of British Speed Hill Climbing* (Bookmarque Publishing, 1990).
6. William Boddy, quoted in the DVD *Brooklands: The Birthplace of British Motorsport* (Brooklands Museum Trust/David Weguelin Productions, 2006).
7. Mays, *Split Seconds*.
8. *The Light Car and Cyclecar* (14 May 1921).
9. Ibid.
10. Ibid. (21 May 1921).
11. Ibid. (25 June 1921).
12. Mays, *Split Seconds*.

Chapter 4: *Cordon Rouge* and *Cordon Bleu*

1. Mays, *Split Seconds*.
2. Donald Parker, 'Amhurst [sic] Villiers talking about the Brescia', *Bugantics*, vol. 53, 2 (Summer 1990).
3. Ibid.
4. Mike McCarthy, 'A Man for All Seasons', *Classic and Sportscar* (November 1983).
5. Donald Parker, 'Amhurst [sic] Villiers talking about the Brescia', *Bugantics*, vol. 53, 2. (Summer 1990).

6. Mike McCarthy, 'A Man for All Seasons', *Classic and Sportscar* (November 1983).

7. Donald Parker, 'Amhurst [sic] Villiers talking about the Brescia', *Bugantics*, vol. 53, 2. (Summer 1990).

8. Ibid.

9. Mays, *Split Seconds*.

10. Ibid.

11. Ibid.

12. Ibid.

13. Ibid.

14. Ibid.

15. Raymond Mays, 'Lowering Hill-Climb Records', *The Light Car and Cyclecar* (29 May 1925).

16. Brian Palmer, 'Villiers', *Thoroughbred & Classic Cars* (November 1985).

Chapter 5: First forays into supercharging

1. Mays, *Split Seconds* (Foulis, 1951).

2. *The Light Car and Cyclecar* (27 March 1925).

3. Ibid. (15 May 1925).

4. Ibid. (15 May 1925).

5. Mays, *Split Seconds*.

6. *The Light Car and Cyclecar* (27 March 1925).

7. *The Brooklands Gazette*, vol. 2, 1 (July 1925).

8. Mays, *Split Seconds*.

9. Ibid.

10. Ibid.

11. *The Light Car and Cyclecar* (25 September 1925).

12. Ibid.

13. *Motor Sport*, vol. 2, 4 (October 1925).

14. Mays, *Split Seconds*.

15. Ibid.

16. Ibid.

17. Ibid.

Chapter 6: *Bluebird*

1. Malcolm Campbell, *My Thirty Years of Speed* (Hutchinson, 1935).
2. Ibid.
3. Ibid.
4. Leo Villa, *Life with the Speed King* (Marshall Harris & Baldwin, 1979).
5. Ibid.
6. Brian Palmer, 'Villiers', *Thoroughbred & Classic Cars* (November 1985).
7. Campbell, *My Thirty Years of Speed*.
8. Ibid.
9. William Boddy, *The World's Land Speed Record* (Motor Racing Publications, 1965).
10. 'A 180 m.p.h. Racer: Captain Malcolm Campbell's 450 h.p. Napier-Lion-Engined Car', *The Motor* (30 November 1926).
11. 'The "Napier-Campbell" Racing Car: Details of Capt. Malcolm Campbell's 450 h.p. New Chassis', *Motor Sport* (January 1927).
12. 'A 180 m.p.h. Racer: Captain Malcolm Campbell's 450 h.p. Napier-Lion-Engined Car', *The Motor* (30 November 1926).
13. Eoin Young, 'Meet Mr Supercharge', *Car* (April 1974).
14. Mike McCarthy, 'A Man for All Seasons', *Classic and Sportscar* (November 1983).
15. Lady Dorothy Campbell, *Malcolm Campbell: The Man As l Knew Him* (Hutchinson, 1951).
16. Villa, *Life with the Speed King*.
17. Ibid.
18. Ibid.
19. Amherst Villiers, 'The Origin and Design of Campbell's Car', letter to *The Motor* (28 February 1928).
20. Mike McCarthy, 'A Man for All Seasons', *Classic and Sportscar* (November 1983).
21. Eoin Young, 'Meet Mr Supercharge', *Car* (April 1974).
22. Steve Holter, conversation with author, 26 March 2008.
23. Ibid.
24. Ibid.

25. Ibid.

26. Leo Villa, and Tony Gray, *The Record Breakers: Sir Malcolm and Donald Campbell, Land and Water Speed Kings of the 20th Century* (Hamlyn, 1969).

27. 'Editorial Notes', *Motor Sport* (February 1927).

28. Amherst Villiers, 'Malcolm Campbell's Napier Lion Car', letter to *The Motor* (7 February 1928).

29. Ibid.

30. Brian Palmer, 'Villiers', *Thoroughbred & Classic Cars* (November 1985).

Chapter 7: The first supercharged Rolls-Royce

1. Donald Parker, 'Amherst Villiers: A Happy Reunion with a Former Flight of Fancy', *Rolls-Royce Enthusiasts' Club Bulletin*, vol. 192 (May–June 1992).

2. 'Curiosities at Brooklands: Interesting and Amusing Sights which have Lately Been Seen at the Track', *The Autocar*, 7 October 1927.

3. Charles B. Lowe, 'Supercharging a Rolls-Royce', letter to *The Autocar* (28 October 1927).

4. Tom Clarke, 'Stately Supercar' (part 1), *The Automobile* (June 2002).

5. Brian Palmer, 'Villiers', *Thoroughbred & Classic Cars* (November 1985).

6. Mays, *Split Seconds*.

7. Eoin Young, 'PI Blower: Amherst Villiers and his Amazing Blower Rolls-Royce', *Autocar* (26 May 1979).

8. Ibid.

9. Eoin Young, 'Amherst Villiers – The Man Behind The "Blower" Bentley', *Sports Car World* (April 1974).

10. Donald Parker, 'Amherst Villiers: A Happy Reunion with a Former Flight of Fancy', *Rolls-Royce Enthusiasts' Club Bulletin*, vol. 192 (May–June 1992).

11. Ibid.

Chapter 8: The *Villiers Supercharge*

1. Desmond Fitz-Gerald, 28th Knight of Glin, personal diary, 27 October 1928.
2. Mays, *Split Seconds*.
3. Simon Taylor, *The Shelsley Walsh Story: A Century of Motorsport* (Haynes, 2005).
4. Mays, *Split Seconds*.
5. Ibid.
6. Ibid.
7. Doug Nye, conversation with author, 14 September 2006.

Chapter 9: The enigma of the Blower Bentley

1. Sir Henry ('Tim') Birkin, *Full Throttle* (Foulis, 1937).
2. Ibid.
3. W.O. Bentley, *The Autobiography of W.O. Bentley* (Hutchinson, 1958).
4. Ibid.
5. Mike McCarthy, 'A Man for All Seasons', *Classic and Sportscar* (November 1983).
6. Ibid.
7. Elizabeth Nagle, *The Other Bentley Boys* (Harrap, 1964).
8. Michael Hay, *Blower Bentley: Bentley 4½ Litre Supercharged* (Number One Press, 2001).
9. Eoin Young, 'Meet Mr Supercharge', *Car* (April 1974).
10. *Amherst Villiers Superchargers*, facsimile of 1929 brochure (Motormedia Publications, n.d.).
11. Eoin Young, 'Meet Mr Supercharge', *Car* (April 1974).
12. Ibid.
13. Mike McCarthy, 'A Man for All Seasons', *Classic and Sportscar* (November 1983).
14. Brian Palmer, 'Villiers', *Thoroughbred & Classic Cars* (November 1985).
15. Hay, *Blower Bentley*.
16. Piers Carlson, conversation with author, 4 September 2008.
17. Birkin, *Full Throttle*.

18. Ibid.

19. Hay, *Blower Bentley*.

20. Desmond Fitz-Gerald, 28th Knight of Glin, personal diary, 1 October 1929.

21. Ibid., 7 October 1929.

22. Hay, *Blower Bentley.*

23. Law Report, 22 October, High Court of Justice, Chancery Division, 'Injunction against Bentley Motors, Amherst Villiers *v.* Bentley Motors, Limited', *The Times* (23 October 1929); Law Report, 25 October, High Court of Justice, Chancery Division, 'Superchargers on Bentley Motors: Expiry of Injunction, Amherst Villiers *v.* Bentley Motors, Limited', *The Times* (26 October 1929).

24. Birkin, *Full Throttle*.

25. Nagle, *The Other Bentley Boys*.

26. Birkin, *Full Throttle*.

27. Ibid.

28. Ibid.

29. Bill Lambert, letter to Dorothy Paget, 5 September 1930.

30. Birkin, *Full Throttle*.

31. Ibid.

32. Ibid.

33. Malcolm Barber, conversation with author, 21 February 2008.

34. Lord Montagu of Beaulieu, *The British Motorist: A Celebration in Pictures* (Macdonald, 1987).

35. 'The Le Mans 24-Hour Race', *The Motor* (24 June 1930).

36. Doug Nye, conversation with author, 17 December 2007.

37. Dan Gurney, conversation with author, 3 January 2008.

38. John Bentley, conversation with author, 15 May 2007.

Chapter 10: The businessman

1. *Amherst Villiers Superchargers*, facsimile of 1929 brochure (Motormedia Publications, n.d.).

2. 'Leading Men in the British Motor Industry: Amherst Villiers' (May 1932), reproduction of article together with *Amherst Villiers Superchargers*

(1929), facsimile of brochure (Motormedia Publications, n.d.).

3. Bruce Pounds, conversation with the author, 16 August 2008.

4. Mays, *Split Seconds*.

5. Ibid.

6. Ibid.

7. 'A Combination and a Form Indeed', *The Aeroplane* (14 April 1937).

8. Richard J. Daley Library, Chicago, Special Collections and University Archives, Century of Progress Collection, Series 1, General Correspondence, 1925–37, box 28, Phil Henderson, letter to Amherst Villiers, 9 June 1932.

9. Century of Progress Collection, Series 1, General Correspondence, 1925–37, box 28, E. D. Langworthy, letter to Amherst Villiers, 19 July 1932.

10. Ibid., J. Parker Van Zandt, letter to Amherst Villiers, 29 August 1932.

11. Ibid.

12. Century of Progress Collection, Series 1, General Correspondence, 1925–37, box 28, E.D. Langworthy, letter to Amherst Villiers, 19 July 1932.

13. 'Court and Social', *The Times* (29 May 1933).

14. 'Conquest of Stratosphere, Realm of Speed, Goal of Powers', *Charleston Daily Mail* (14 August 1932).

15. 'New Companies Registered', *Flight* (22 March 1934).

16. 'A Combination and a Form Indeed', *The Aeroplane* (14 April 1937).

17. Hugo Spowers, email to the author, 3 December 2008.

18. 'A Combination and a Form Indeed', *The Aeroplane* (14 April 1937).

19. 'British Commercial Aircraft: The Current Range Reviewed', *Flight* (21 January 1937).

20. 'The Right Engines for Light Aeroplanes', *Flight* (18 March 1937).

21. 'The Industry', *Flight* (7 October 1937).

22. 'Light Aircraft Power Units', *Flight* (23 April 1936).

23. Eoin Young, 'Meet Mr Supercharge', *Car* (April 1974).

Chapter 11: War

1. E. C. Cheesman, *Brief Glory: The Story of A.T.A.* (Harborough, 1946).
2. Wg Cdr Eric Viles, conversation with the author, 6 December 2006.
3. Cheesman, *Brief Glory*.
4. Diana Barnato Walker, *Spreading My Wings* (Patrick Stephens, 1994).
5. Desmond Fitz-Gerald, 28th Knight of Glin, personal diary, 8 November 1942.
6. 'The Greatest Armada', *The Times*, 14 November 1942.
7. 'Offensive On U-Boats', *The Times*, 13 November 1942.
8. 'A High Command communiqué broadcast from Berlin and recorded here by the Associated Press', *New York Times* (12 November 1942).
9. 'Claim Liner Torpedoed: Nazis Now Say it is the Queen Elizabeth, Not a Warship', *New York Times* (13 November 1942).
10. Glin Papers, 422/7, Elaine Villiers, letter to Veronica Fitz-Gerald (later Milner) (20 May 1943).
11. Canadian Car & Foundry Co. Ltd, Technical Development Department, Report No. TR-003, *Long Range Aircraft Projects* (n.d.).
12. Ibid.
13. Mike McCarthy, 'A Man for All Seasons', *Classic and Sportscar* (November 1983).

Chapter 12: Rocketry

1. Mike McCarthy, 'A Man for All Seasons', *Classic and Sportscar* (November 1983).
2. Ibid.
3. Brian P. Macfie and Philip M. Nufrio, *Applied Statistics for Public Policy* (M.E. Sharpe, 2006).
4. Mike McCarthy, 'A Man for All Seasons', *Classic and Sportscar* (November 1983).
5. *Journal of the American Rocket Society*, 75 (September–December 1948).
6. 'Trends in Guided Missiles', *Journal of the American Rocket Society*, 73 (March 1948).
7. 'Navy Plans Rocket Tests', *Journal of the American Rocket Society*, 73 (March 1948).

8. Glin Papers, 424/6, Elaine Villiers, letter to Veronica Milner, 3 August 1956.

9. Desmond Fitz-Gerald, 29th Knight of Glin, conversation with the author, 29 September 2006.

10. Brian Palmer, 'Villiers', *Thoroughbred & Classic Cars* (November 1985).

11. Bill Ficken, emails to the author, 12 and 16 February 2009.

12. Glin Papers, 424/8, Elaine Villiers, letter to Veronica Milner, 2 September 1956.

13. Mike McCarthy, 'A Man for All Seasons', *Classic and Sportscar* (November 1983).

14. Glin Papers, 426/4, Elaine Villiers, letter to Veronica Milner, 20 March 1958.

15. Mike McCarthy, 'A Man for All Seasons', *Classic and Sportscar* (November 1983).

Chapter 13: Painting

1. Brooklands Museum Library, Amherst Villiers, letter to John Millar (n.d.).

2. http://www.metmuseum.org/toah/hd/tita/ho_36.29.htm

3. Churchill Papers, Winston Churchill, letter to Amherst Villiers, 29 October 1958.

4. Glin Papers, 425/9, Elaine Villiers, letter to Veronica Milner, 8 August 1957.

5. Glin Papers, 424/11, Elaine Villiers, letter to Veronica Milner, 6 November 1956.

6. Brooklands Museum Library, Archbishop Bruno B. Heim, open letter, 12 November 1984.

Chapter 14: BRM

1. Doug Nye, *B.R.M. – The Saga of British Racing Motors: Volume 2, Spaceframe Cars 1959–1965* (Motor Racing Publications, 2003).

2. Ibid.

3. Alex Osborn, conversation with the author, 7 December 2008.

4. Raymond Mays and Peter Roberts, *BRM* (Cassell, 1962).

5. Mike McCarthy, 'A Man for All Seasons', *Classic and Sportscar* (November 1983).
6. Alex Osborn, conversation with the author, 7 December 2008.
7. Doug Nye, conversation with the author, 31 January 2009.
8. Ibid.

Chapter 15: 'Bond drove it hard and well'

1. Ian Fleming, *Moonraker* (Jonathan Cape, 1955).
2. Ian Fleming, *Casino Royale* (Jonathan Cape, 1953).
3. 'Playboy Interview: Ian Fleming', *Playboy* (December 1964).
4. Andrew Lycett, *Ian Fleming* (Weidenfeld & Nicolson, 1995).
5. Lucy Fleming, talk at launch of *Devil May Care*, 8 May 2008.
6. Ian Fleming Archive, early manuscript of *Casino Royale*.
7. Brad Frank, conversation with the author, 7 October 2008.
8. Fleming, *Casino Royale*.
9. Ibid.
10. Ibid.
11. Ian Fleming Archive, early manuscript of *Casino Royale*.
12. Fleming, *Casino Royale*.
13. Ibid.
14. Ibid.
15. Fleming, *Moonraker*.
16. Ibid.
17. Ibid.
18. Ibid.
19. Ibid.
20. Ibid.
21. Ian Fleming Archive, Ian Fleming, letter to J. B. Reed of The Bowater Paper Corporation Ltd., 30 June 1954.
22. Charlie Higson, *Double or Die* (Puffin, 2007).
23. Ibid.
24. Lycett, *Ian Fleming*.
25. Ian Fleming, *Chitty-Chitty-Bang-Bang The Magical Car: Adventure Number One* (Jonathan Cape, 1964).

26. William Boddy, letter to the author, 24 September 2006.

27. *Casino Royale* (Danjaq, LLC; United Artists Corporation; Columbia Pictures Industries, Inc., 2006).

28. Robert Wade, email to the author, via Nick Pourgourides, 16 May 2007.

Chapter 16: California

1, 'Veteran – Edwardian – Vintage: A Section Devoted to Old-Car Matters', *Motor Sport* (March 1963).

2. Bruce Pounds, conversation with the author, 16 August 2008.

3. Eleanor Carlson, conversation with the author, 4 September 2008.

4. Ibid.

5. Bruce Pounds, conversation with the author, 16 August 2008.

6. Ibid.

7. Ibid.

8. Ibid.

9. 'James Bond's Personal Sports Car', *Evening Outlook* (13 August 1966).

10. Piers Carlson, conversation with the author (4 September 2008).

11. Wally Wilson, 'Palisades Resident Zooms Around in 1930 Winner of Le Mans Race', *Evening Outlook* (n.d.).

12. Ibid.

13. Ibid.

Chapter 17: After Nita

1. Andrew Gold, email to the author, 23 December 2004.

2. Amanda Severne, conversation with the author, 15 January 2008.

3. Ursula Leslie, conversation with the author, 28 February 2009.

4. Marguerite Barbrook, *Sophie: A Victorian Life in the Twentieth Century* (Wilmott, 1995).

5. Ibid.

6. Paula McColl, conversation with the author, 6 May 2007.

7. Barbrook, *Sophie*.

8. Lord Montagu of Beaulieu, conversation with the author, 29 September 2006.

9. Charles Villiers, email to author, 22 February 2009.

10. Brian Palmer, 'Villiers', *Thoroughbred & Classic Cars* (November 1985).

11. Mike McCarthy, 'A Man for All Seasons', *Classic and Sportscar* (November 1983).

12. Brian Palmer, 'Villiers', *Thoroughbred & Classic Cars* (November 1985).

13. Mike McCarthy, 'A Man for All Seasons', *Classic and Sportscar* (November 1983).

14. Ibid.

15. John Nolan, *The News Advertiser* (8 November 1983).

16. Hansard, HC (series 4) vol. 156, cols 1584–9 (10 May 1906).

17. Revd Ian Robson, conversation with the author, 9 May 2007.

18. Antonia Spowers, conversation with the author, 4 May 2007.

19. Paula McColl, conversation with the author, 6 May 2007.

Chapter 18: The final automotive projects

1. John Nicholson, email to author, 4 October 2006.

2. 'Pit and Paddock', *Autosport* (30 October 1975).

3. David Tremayne, *The Lost Generation: The Brilliant but Tragic Lives of Rising British F1 Stars Roger Williamson, Tony Brise and Tom Pryce* (Haynes, 2006).

4. P. J. Bardon, *Piper PA 23-250 Turbo Aztec 'D' N6645Y: Report on the Accident at Arkley Golf Course, Arkley, Hertfordshire, on 29 November 1975* (Department of Trade Accidents Investigation Branch, 1976).

5. Michael Scarlett, 'Amherst Villiers – Engineer and Artist: The Story of a Motoring Name', *Autocar* (12 July 1975).

6. Hugo Spowers, conversation with the author, 2 October 2006.

7. Steve Holter, conversation with the author, 26 March 2008.

8. Piers Carlson, conversation with the author, 4 September 2008.

9. Robin Young, 'Rolls-Royce sued over failure to build "most fabulous car"', *The Times* (2 July 1991).

10. Brooklands Museum Library, 'Phantom III Turbo Project', contract between Amherst Villiers and Rolls-Royce Motors Limited, 29 June 1983.

11. Ibid.

12. Ibid.

13. Ibid.

14. Brooklands Museum Library, Sir Peter Masefield's papers on Villiers *v.* Rolls-Royce, n.d.

15. Ibid.

16. Lord Montagu of Beaulieu, letter to Sir David Plastow, 12 August 1988.

17. Sir David Plastow, letter to Lord Montagu of Beaulieu, 18 August 1988.

18. Ibid.

19. Lord Montagu of Beaulieu, letter to Amherst Villiers, 22 August 1988.

20. Lord Montagu of Beaulieu, letter to Sir David Plastow, 17 April 1989.

21. Sir David Plastow, letter to Lord Montagu of Beaulieu, 25 April 1989.

22. Ibid.

23. Revd Ian Robson, conversation with the author, 9 May 2007.

24. Antonia Spowers, conversation with the author, 4 May 2007.

25. Alastair McCall, 'Designer, 90, sues Rolls over "fabulous Phantom"', *Daily Telegraph* (2 July 1991).

26. Robin Young, 'Rolls-Royce sued over failure to build "most fabulous car"', *The Times* (2 July 1991).

27. Alastair McCall, 'Designer, 90, sues Rolls over "fabulous Phantom"', *Daily Telegraph* (2 July 1991).

28. Robin Young, 'Hatchet man killed car project', *The Times* (3 July 1991).

29. 'Super-Roller became "a bastardised folly"', *The Guardian* (4 July 1991).

30. Antonia Spowers, conversation with the author, 4 May 2007.

31. John Millar, letter to Amherst Villiers, 22 July 1991.

32. 'Villiers too ill to give car evidence', *The Times* (28 August 1991).

33. Robin Young, 'Villiers daughter wins battle with Rolls-Royce', *The Times* (1 August 1996).

34. Ibid.

35. Ibid.

36. Ibid.

37. Ibid.

38. Malcolm Barber, conversation with the author, 21 February 2008.

39. Lord Montagu of Beaulieu, letter to Amherst Villiers, 28 May 1991.

40. Joanna Millar, letter to the author, 26 October 2007.

41. 'Villiers too ill to give car evidence', *The Times* (28 August 1991).

42. Antonia Spowers, conversation with the author, 4 May 2007.

43. From the death certificate of Amherst Villiers, 14 December 1991.

Chapter 19: The Renaissance Man without a Medici

1. Brooklands Museum Library, Masefield, Sir Peter Masefield's final draft of *The Times* obituary of Amherst Villiers, 28 January 1992.

2. 'Obituaries: Amherst Villiers', *The Times* (31 January 1992).

3. Mike McCarthy, 'Renaissance man', *Autocar & Motor* (12 February 1992).

4. Doug Nye, conversation with the author (31 January 2009).

5. Amherst Villiers, 'Ground Engineers' Examinations', letter to *Flight* (19 June 1931).

BIBLIOGRAPHY

Primary Sources

1901 England Census, Administrative County London, Civil Parish Paddington, Ward of Municipal Borough Hyde Park, www.ancestry.com

Accidents Investigation Branch, Report No. C-165, by permission of the Air Accidents Investigation Branch.

Bardon, P. J. *Piper PA 23-250 Turbo Aztec 'D' N6645Y: Report on the Accident at Arkley Golf Course, Arkley, Hertfordshire, on 29 November 1975* (Department of Trade Accidents Investigation Branch, 1976).

Brooklands Museum Library, Amherst Villiers, letter to Monsignor Mario Oliveri, 24 August 1982.

——, Amherst Villiers, letter to Richard Perry and Michael Dunn, 22 March 1983.

——, Amherst Villiers, letter to President Ronald Reagan, 15 April 1986.

——, Amherst Villiers, letter to John Millar, 12 July 1987.

——, Amherst Villiers, letter to Sir Peter Masefield, 11 August 1990.

——, Amherst Villiers, letter to John Millar (n.d.).

——, Archbishop Bruno B. Heim, open letter, 12 November 1984.

——, 'Further to our Agreement 29 June 1983: Phantom III Turbo Project', supplementary agreement between Amherst Villiers and Rolls-Royce Motors Limited, 20 March 1984.

——, 'Phantom III Turbo Project', contract between Amherst Villiers and Rolls-Royce Motors Limited, 29 June 1983.

——, Sir Peter Masefield's final draft of *The Times* obituary of Amherst Villiers, 28 January 1992.

——, Sir Peter Masefield's papers on Villiers *v.* Rolls-Royce, n.d.

Cambridge University Archives, SOC.98, records of the Cambridge University Automobile Club, and its nominated successor the Cambridge University Motorcycle Club.

Canadian Car & Foundry Co. Ltd, Technical Development Department, Report No. TR-003, *Long Range Aircraft Projects* (n.d.).

Canning Brown, Beatrice, letter to the author, 6 July 2008.

Churchill College, Cambridge, The Churchill Archive Centre, Churchill Papers, CHUR 1/49 112, Amherst Villiers, letter to Winston Churchill, 25 July 1951.

——, CHUR 2/536, Amherst Villiers, letter to Winston Churchill, 28 September 1958.

Cowley, W. L., '1927 Schneider Trophy Contest – Collected Reports on British High Speed Aircraft', *Aeronautical Research Committee Reports and Memoranda 1300* (HMSO, 1931).

Coyle, Nick, email to the author, 28 November 2008.

Dyson, John, letter to author, 5 July 2007.

East Sussex Record Office, AMS6273/3, Political Papers of Edwin Ernest Brown, *Brighton Herald* (25 July 1903).

Ficken, Bill, emails to author, 12 and 16 February 2009.

Fitz-Gerald, Desmond, 28th Knight of Glin, personal diary, 27 October 1928.

——, 1 October 1929.

——, 8–11 June 1930.

——, November 1942.

——, January–February 1949.

Forge, Stephen, letter to author, 4 September 2007.

Gold, Andrew, email to author, 23 December 2004.

Hansard, HC (series 4), vol. 151, cols 663–4 (8 August 1905).

——, vol. 156, cols 1584-9 (10 May 1906).

——, vol. 188, col. 1602 (18 May 1908).

——, vol. 189, col. 769 (25 May 1908).

——, vol. 190, col. 58 (3 June 1908).

——, vol. 190, cols 65–71 (3 June 1908).

Houston, Dr Tom, letter to author, 24 July 2007.

——, letter to author, 26 September 2007.

Ian Fleming Archive, early manuscript of *Casino Royale*.

——, Ian Fleming, letter to J. B. Reed of The Bowater Paper Corporation Ltd., 30 June 1954.

——, J. B. Reed, letter to Ian Fleming, 5 July 1954.

Indiana University, Lilly Library Manuscripts Department, L. Russell manuscripts, Amherst Villiers, letter to researchers of John Pearson's *Life of Ian Fleming*, 7 January 1966.

——, Nita Villiers, letter to researchers of John Pearson's *Life of Ian Fleming*, 7 January 1966.

Lambert, Bill, letter to Dorothy Paget, 5 September 1930.

Millar, Joanna , letter to the author, 26 October 2007.

Millar, John, letter to Amherst Villiers, 22 July 1991.

Montagu of Beaulieu, Lord, letter to Amherst Villiers, 22 August 1988.

——, letter to Amherst Villiers, 28 May 1991.

——, letter to Sir David Plastow, 12 August 1988.

——, letter to Sir David Plastow, 17 April 1989.

Nicholson, John, email to author, 4 October 2006.

Norfolk Record Office, MC 84/20, Estate Papers, Didlington Hall Estate, Villiers, Ernest and Guest, Elaine, copy of marriage settlement, 29 April 1898.

Plastow, Sir David, letter to Lord Montagu of Beaulieu, 18 August 1988.

——, letter to Lord Montagu of Beaulieu, 25 April 1989.

Richard J. Daley Library, Chicago, Special Collections and University Archives, Century of Progress Collection, Series 1, General Correspondence, 1925–37, box 28, Henderson, Phil, letter to Amherst Villiers, 9 June 1932.

——, Langworthy, E. D., letter to Amherst Villiers, 19 July 1932.

——, Parker Van Zandt, J., letter to Amherst Villiers, 29 August 1932.

Riley, Gordon, email to author, 16 November 2008.

Royal Airforce Museum, Department of Research & Information Services, Air Transport Auxiliary Records, Ferry Record for Amherst Villiers.

Spowers, Hugo, email to author, 2 September 2008.

——, email to author, 3 December 2008.

Trost, Maxine emails to author, 17 and 18 December 2007.

University of Limerick, Glucksman Library, Glin Papers, 422/7, Elaine Villiers, letter to Veronica Fitz-Gerald (*née* Villiers, later Veronica Milner), 20 May 1943.

——, 422/15, Elaine Villiers, letter to Veronica Fitz-Gerald, 8 February 1947.

——, 423/3, Elaine Villiers, letter to Veronica Fitz-Gerald (n.d.).

——, 424/6, Elaine Villiers, letter to Veronica Milner, 3 August 1956.

——, 424/8, Elaine Villiers, letter to Veronica Milner, 2 September 1956.

——, 424/11, Elaine Villiers, letter to Veronica Milner, 6 November 1956.

——, 425/9, Elaine Villiers, letter to Veronica Milner, 8 August 1957.

——, 426/4, Elaine Villiers, letter to Veronica Milner, 20 March 1958.

——, 427/1, Amherst Villiers, letter to Veronica Fitz-Gerald, 12 July 1946.

——, 427/2, Amherst Villiers, letter to Veronica Fitz-Gerald, 6 June 1947.

——, 427/3, Amherst Villiers, letter to Veronica Fitz-Gerald, 24 September 1946.

——, 428/1, Amherst Villiers, letter to Veronica and Ray Milner, 2 July 1954.

——, 428/3, Amherst Villiers, letter to Veronica and Ray Milner, 12 August 1955.

——, 428/5, Amherst Villiers, letter to Veronica and Ray Milner, 26 October 1958.

——, 429/2, Amherst Villiers, letter to Veronica and Ray Milner, 1 December 1960.

——, 429/3, Amherst Villiers, letter to Veronica Milner, 12 December 1960.

——, 429/4, Amherst Villiers, letter to Veronica and Ray Milner, 27 December 1960.

——, 429/6, Amherst Villiers, letter to Veronica and Ray Milner, 20 July 1961.

——, 429/19, Amherst Villiers, letter to Veronica Milner, 8 October 1962.

——, 429/22, Amherst Villiers, letter to Veronica and Ray Milner, 16 April 1963.

——, 430/2, Amherst Villiers, letter to Veronica and Ray Milner, 1 September 1965.

——, 430/10, Amherst Villiers, letter to Veronica and Ray Milner, 28 October 1966.

——, 431/1, Amherst Villiers, letter to Veronica Milner, 7 December 1969.

——, 431/10, Amherst Villiers, letter to Veronica Milner, 5 March 1970.

——, 431/15, Amherst Villiers, letter to Veronica and Ray Milner, June 1972.

——, 431/18, Amherst Villiers, letter to Veronica and Ray Milner, 17 March 1973.

——, 431/22, Amherst Villiers, letter to Veronica and Ray Milner, 15 February 1972.

——, 432/2, Amherst Villiers, letter to Veronica and Ray Milner, n.d.

——, 432/8, Amherst Villiers, letter to Veronica Milner, 6 July 1977.

——, 433/1, Amherst Villiers, letter to Veronica Milner, 20 January 1983.

——, 434/3, Amherst Villiers, letter to Veronica and Ray Milner, 7 October 1956.

——, 434/6, Nita Villiers, letter to Veronica Milner, 26 January 1963.

——, 434/8, Nita Villiers, letter to Veronica Milner, 3 May 1963.

——, 434/10, Nita Villiers, letter to Veronica Milner, 4 November 1964.

——, 434/13, Dr. Bagshaw, notes on Nita Villiers' medical record, 4 September 1968.

——, 437/5, Amherst Villiers, letter to Veronica Milner, n.d.

——, 528/2, Amherst Villiers, draft notes on *The Giant Leap to Hyperman* (n.d.).

Villiers, Amherst, Certificate of Marriage to Marietta Strakosch, 30 July 1932.

Villiers, Charles Amherst, Birth Certificate, 9 December 1900.

Villiers, Charles Churchill, email to author, 22 February 2009.

Villiers, Ernest, Death Certificate, 26 September 1928.

Wade, Robert, email to the author, via Nick Pourgourides, 16 May 2007.

Further Reading

'A 180 m.p.h. Racer: Captain Malcolm Campbell's 450 h.p. Napier-Lion-Engined Car', *The Motor* (30 November 1926).

'A Combination and a Form Indeed', *The Aeroplane* (14 April 1937).

Aherne, Brian (assisted by George Sanders and Benita Hume), *A Dreadful Man: A Personal, Intimate Book About George Sanders* (Simon and Schuster, 1979).

'A High Command communiqué broadcast from Berlin and recorded here by the Associated Press', *New York Times* (12 November 1942).

'Air Speed Record Attempt', *Flight* (16 May 1930).

Askew, Mark, 'Rare Jeep Photo Archive: A Flying Willys Jeep – the Rotabuggy', *Jeep World* (August 2004).

Baker, David, *The Rocket: The History and Development of Rocket and Missile Technology* (New Cavendish Books, 1978).

Barbrook, Marguerite, *Sophie: A Victorian Life in the Twentieth Century* (Wilmott, 1995).

Barnato Walker, Diana, *Spreading My Wings* (Patrick Stephens, 1994).

Beaulieu, Lord Montagu of, *The British Motorist: A Celebration in Pictures* (Macdonald, 1987).

'Bendix Aviation Corporation, Eclipse-Pioneer Division, Teterboro, New Jersey', American Institute of Aeronautics and Astronautics, Historic Aerospace Site booklet (n.d.).

Bentley, W.O., *The Autobiography of W.O. Bentley* (Hutchinson, 1958).

Bird, Robin, *Top Secret War Bird of World War Two* (Lord Birdforth, 2004).

Birkin, Sir Henry ('Tim'), *Full Throttle* (Foulis, 1948).

Boddy, William, *The History of Brooklands Motor Course 1906–1940* (Grenville, 1957).

——, 'The Sprint Events of the 1920s', *Motor Sport* (April 1955).

——, *The World's Land Speed Record* (Motor Racing Publications, 1965).

Bradley, W. F., *Ettore Bugatti* (Motor Racing Publications, 1948).

'British Commercial Aircraft: The Current Range Reviewed', *Flight* (21 January 1937).

Brooke, Christopher, *A History of Gonville and Caius College* (Boydell Press, 1985).

Brown, Don Lambert, *Miles Aircraft Since 1925* (Putnam, 1970).

Bryce, Ivar, *You Only Live Once, Memories of Ian Fleming* (Weidenfeld & Nicolson, 1975)

Cadwaladr, Margaret, *In Veronica's Garden* (Madrona, 2002).

Campbell, Captain Malcolm, *My Thirty Years of Speed* (Hutchinson, 1935).

——, 'Some Experiences with the World's Fastest Car', *Motor Sport* (December 1925).

Campbell, Lady Dorothy, *Malcolm Campbell: The Man As I Knew Him* (Hutchinson, 1951).

Canning Brown, Beatrice, *Austin Seven Competition History: The Cars and Those Who Drove Them, 1922–1939* (Twincam, 2006).

Cheesman, E. C., *Brief Glory: The Story of A.T.A.* (Harborough, 1946).

'Claim Liner Torpedoed: Nazis Now Say it is the Queen Elizabeth, Not a Warship', *New York Times* (13 November 1942).

Clarke, Tom, 'A Stately *Super*car: A Supercharged Phantom I, Part I', *Flying Lady* (September–October 2001).

——, 'A Stately *Super*car: A Supercharged Phantom I, Part II', *Flying Lady* (November–December 2001).

——, 'A Stately *Super*car: A Supercharged Phantom I, Part III', *Flying Lady* (January–February 2002).

——, 'Stately Supercar' (part 1), *The Automobile* (June 2002).

——, 'Stately Supercar' (part 2), *The Automobile* (July 2002).

Cooper, Peter J., *Farnborough: 100 Years of British Aviation* (Midland, 2006).

'Court and Social', *The Times* (24 April 1928).

'Court and Social', *The Times* (29 May 1933).

'Curiosities at Brooklands: Interesting and Amusing Sights which have Lately Been Seen at the Track', *The Autocar* (7 October 1927).

Curthoys, M. C, 'Sanderson, Frederick William (1857–1922)', *Oxford Dictionary of National Biography* (Oxford University Press, 2004).

Demaus, A. B., *Motor Sport in the 20s* (Alan Sutton Publishing, 1989).

Eaton, Godfrey, *The Brescia Bugatti* (Profile Publications, 1967).

Edge, S. F., *My Motoring Reminiscences* (Foulis, 1934).

'Editorial Notes', *Motor Sport* (February 1927).

Eves, Edward, 'Vauxhall Villiers', *Autocar* (15 October 1983).

Fleming, Ian, *Casino Royale* (Jonathan Cape, 1953).

——, *Chitty-Chitty-Bang-Bang The Magical Car: Adventure Number One* (Jonathan Cape, 1964).

——, *Chitty-Chitty-Bang-Bang The Magical Car: Adventure Number Two* (Jonathan Cape, 1964).

——, *Chitty-Chitty-Bang-Bang The Magical Car: Adventure Number Three* (Jonathan Cape, 1965).

——, *Live and Let Die* (Jonathan Cape, 1954).

——, *Moonraker* (Jonathan Cape, 1955).

Flight, 1930–7.

Frenz, Horst (ed.), 'Maurice Maeterlinck: The Nobel Prize in Literature 1911', *Nobel Lectures, Literature 1901–1967* (Elsevier Publishing Company, 1969).

Gilbey, Quintin, *Queen of the Turf: The Dorothy Paget Story* (Arthur Barker, 1973).

Guest, Bertie, *The Guest House Volume 1* (self-published, 2006).

——, *The Guest House Volume 2* (self-published, 2006).

Hallums, E., *The Quality of Work and The Quality of Art: A Study on Bugatti* (Mithra Press, 1979).

'Hard Blow for Balfour', *New York Times* (6 April 1905).

Harvey, Chris, *Austin Seven* (Oxford Illustrated Press, 1985)

Hay, Michael, *Blower Bentley: Bentley 4½ Litre Supercharged* (Number One Press, 2001).

Henry, Alan, *The 4-Wheel Drives: Racing's Formula for Failure* (Macmillan, 1975).

Higham, Peter, *The International Motor Racing Guide: The Complete Reference from Formula 1 to NASCAR* (David Bull, 2003).

Higson, Charlie, *Double or Die* (Puffin, 2007).

Holter, Steve, *Leap Into Legend: Donald Campbell and The Complete Story of the World Speed Records* (Sigma Press, 2002).

Hough, Richard, *Tourist Trophy: The History of Britain's Greatest Motor Race* (Hutchinson, 1957).

'James Bond's Personal Sports Car', *Evening Outlook* (13 August 1966).

Jenkinson, Dennis, 'The Racing Cars of Ron Horton', *Motor Sport* (April 1978).

Jenkins, Roy, *Churchill* (Macmillan, 2001).

Journal of the American Rocket Society, 75 (September–December 1948).

Karslake, E. K. H., 'Great Racing Marques: III Bugatti', *Motor Sport* (May 1927).

Kimes, Beverly Rae, and Winston S. Goodfellow, *Speed, Style and Beauty: Cars from the Ralph Lauren Collection* (MFA Publications, 2005).

Koelle, H. H., *Nova and Beyond: A Review of Heavy Launch Vehicle Concepts in the POST-SATURN Class* (Technical University Berlin, 2001).

Konings, Chris, *'Queen Elizabeth' at War* (Patrick Stephens, 1985).

Lang, Mike, *Grand Prix! Race-by-Race Account of Formula 1 World Championship Motor Racing: Volume 1 1950 to 1965* (Haynes, 1981).

——, *Grand Prix! Race-by-Race Account of Formula 1 World Championship Motor Racing: Volume 2 1966 to 1973* (Haynes, 1982).

——, *Grand Prix! Race-by-Race Account of Formula 1 World Championship Motor Racing: Volume 3 1974 to 1980* (Haynes, 1983).

Law Report, 22 October, High Court of Justice, Chancery Division, 'Injunction against Bentley Motors, Amherst Villiers *v.* Bentley Motors, Limited', *The Times* (23 October 1929).

——, 25 October, High Court of Justice, Chancery Division, 'Superchargers on Bentley Motors: Expiry of Injunction, Amherst Villiers *v.* Bentley Motors, Limited', *The Times* (26 October 1929).

'Leading Men in the British Motor Industry: Amherst Villiers' (May 1932), reproduction of article with *Amherst Villiers Superchargers* (1929), facsimile of brochure (Motormedia Publications, n.d.).

'Light Aircraft Power Units', *Flight* (23 April 1936).

Lowe, Charles B., 'Supercharging a Rolls-Royce', letter to *The Autocar* (28 October 1927).

Lycett, Andrew, *Ian Fleming* (Weidenfeld & Nicolson, 1995).

McCarthy, Mike, 'A Man for All Seasons', *Classic and Sportscar* (November 1983).

——, 'Renaissance man', *Autocar & Motor* (12 February 1992).

Macfie, Brian P., and Philip M. Nufrio, *Applied Statistics for Public Policy* (M. E. Sharpe, 2006).

Macintyre, Ben, *For Your Eyes Only: Ian Fleming + James Bond* (Bloomsbury, 2008).

Maroger, Jacques, *The Secret Formulas and Techniques of the Masters* (Studio Publications, 1948).

'Marriages, Sir Hill Child and Miss Villiers', *The Times* (1 December 1925).

Mason, Chris, *Uphill Racers: The History of British Speed Hill Climbing* (Bookmarque Publishing, 1990).

Mays, Raymond, 'Lowering Hill-Climb Records', *The Light Car and Cyclecar* (29 May 1925).

——, *Split Seconds* (Foulis, 1951).

Mays, Raymond, and Peter Roberts, *BRM* (Cassell, 1962).

Mosley, Charles (ed.), *Burke's Peerage, Baronetage & Knightage 106th Edition* (Burke's Peerage, 1999).

'Motoring Sportsmen: Mr. Kenelm Lee Guinness', *Motor Sport* (February 1926).

'Motoring Sportsmen: Mr. Woolf Barnato', *Motor Sport* (November 1925).

Motor Sport, vol. 2, 4 (October 1925).

'Mr. G. E. Villiers's Death: A Witness on "An Error of Judgement"', *The Times* (16 September 1930).

Mundy, Harry, 'Tenacity Rewarded, An Analysis of the 1.5 litre vee-8 B.R.M. Part Two: The Engine', *Autocar* (2 November 1962).

Nagle, Elizabeth, *The Other Bentley Boys* (Harrap, 1964).

'Navy Plans Rocket Tests', *Journal of the American Rocket Society*, 73 (March 1948).

Newcomb, T. P., and R. T. Spurr, *A Technical History of the Motor Car* (A. Hilger, 1989).

'New Companies Registered', *Flight* (22 March 1934).

Nixon, Marni, and Stephen Cole, *I Could Have Sung All Night* (Billboard, 2006).

Nolan, John, *The News Advertiser* (8 November 1983).

Nye, Doug, *B.R.M. – The Saga of British Racing Motors: Volume 1, Front Engined Cars 1945–1960* (Motor Racing Publications, 1994).

——, *B.R.M. – The Saga of British Racing Motors: Volume 2, Spaceframe Cars 1959–1965* (Motor Racing Publications, 2003).

——, *The United States Grand Prix and Grand Prize Races 1908–1977* (Batsford, 1978).

Obituary: Amherst Villiers, *The Times* (31 January 1992).

Obituary: Peter Morgan, *Daily Telegraph* (23 October 2003).

'Offensive On U-Boats', *The Times*, 13 November 1942.

Osborn, Alec, 'The Fascination of Engines: Formula 1 to Farm Machinery', Institution of Mechanical Engineers Presidential Address, 2006.

Palmer, Brian, 'Villiers', *Thoroughbred & Classic Cars* (November 1985).

Parker, Donald, 'Amherst Villiers: A Happy Reunion with a Former Flight of Fancy', *Rolls-Royce Enthusiasts' Club Bulletin*, vol. 192 (May–June 1992).

Parker, Donald, 'Amhurst [sic] Villiers Talking About the Brescia', *Bugantics*, vol. 53, 2 (Summer 1990).

Paul, Ned, 'Bridge in Crime Fiction', *Mr Bridge* (n.d.).

Pearson, John, *The Life of Ian Fleming* (Jonathan Cape, 1966).

——, *James Bond: The Authorised Biography* (Century, 2006).

Phillips, Ian, 'Tony Brise', *Autosport* (4 December 1975).

'Pietro Annigoni, 78, Dies in Italy; Noted for Portrait of Elizabeth II', *New York Times*, 30 October 1988.

'Pit and Paddock', *Autosport* (30 October 1975).

'Playboy Interview: Ian Fleming', *Playboy* (December 1964).

Portree, David S. F., *Humans to Mars: Fifty Years of Mission Planning* (NASA Monographs in Aerospace History Series, Number 21 (2001).

Posthumus, Cyril, *The Roaring Twenties: An Album of Early Motor Racing* (Blandford, 1980).

Pudney, John, *A Pride of Unicorns: Richard and David Atcherley of the RAF* (Oldbourne, 1960).

'Pupils Zoom to Record', *Kettering Evening Telegraph* (29 June 1991).

'Record Speeds in French Grand Prix', *The Motor* (23 September 1930).

Scarlett, Michael, 'Amherst Villiers – Engineer and Artist: The Story of a Motoring Name', *Autocar* (12 July 1975).

Sewell, J. D. W., 'A Meeting with Amherst Villiers', *Bugantics*, vol. 37, 2 (Summer 1974).

'Sir Henry Birkin's Racing Launch – The "Ida"', *Sir Henry Birkin Memorial Rally* (1993).

Taylor, Simon, *The Shelsley Walsh Story: A Century of Motorsport* (Haynes, 2005)

The Brooklands Gazette, vol. 2, 1 (July 1925).

'The Greatest Armada', *The Times*, 14 November 1942.

'The Industry', *Flight* (7 October 1937).

'The Le Mans 24-Hour Race', *The Motor* (24 June 1930).

The Light Car and Cyclecar (1 January 1921).

——, (14 May 1921).

——, (21 May 1921).

——, (25 June 1921).

——, (27 March 1925).

——, (25 September 1925).

'The "Napier-Campbell" Racing Car: Details of Capt. Malcolm Campbell's 450 h.p. New Chassis', *Motor Sport* (January 1927).

'The Napier-Campbell Transmission System: Construction of the Epicyclic Gear-box Designed by Mr Maina', *Motor Sport* (March 1928).

'The Right Engines for Light Aeroplanes', *Flight* (18 March 1937).

Tipler, John, *Graham Hill: Master of Motor Sport* (Breedon, 2002).

Trayes, F. E. A. (ed.), *Biographical History of Gonville and Caius Colleague, vol. v* (Cambridge University Press, 1948).

'Trends in Guided Missiles', *Journal of the American Rocket Society*, 73 (March 1948).

'Veteran – Edwardian – Vintage: A Section Devoted to Old-Car Matters', *Motor Sport* (March 1963).

Venables, David, *Brooklands, The Official Centenary History* (Haynes, 2007).

Villa, Leo, *Life with the Speed King* (Marshall Harris & Baldwin, 1979).

Villa, Leo, and Tony Gray, *The Record Breakers: Sir Malcolm and Donald Campbell, Land and Water Speed Kings of the 20th Century* (Hamlyn, 1969).

Villiers, Amherst, 'Ground Engineers' Examinations', letter to *Flight* (19 June 1931).

——, 'Malcolm Campbell's Napier Lion Car', letter to *The Motor* (7 February 1928).

——, 'The Origin and Design of Campbell's Car', letter to *The Motor* (28 February 1928).

Villiers, Charles A. H., *The Villiers in Africa*, MA diss. (University of Edinburgh, 1986).

Villiers, Ernest, 'Finance Bills', letter to *The Times* (15 November 1909).

——, 'Stirring up the Pool', letter to *The Times* (27 January 1914).

Watkins, David, Antony Ratcliff, Nicholas Thomson and John Mills, *A Home in Town: 22 Arlington Street, Its Owners and Builders* (Batsford, 1984).

Whittall, W., 'The Design of "Blue Bird"', letter to *The Motor* (14 February 1928).

Wilson, Wally, 'Palisades Resident Zooms Around in 1930 Winner of Le Mans Race', *Evening Outlook* (n.d.).

Witty, Chris, obituaries of Tony Alcock, Ray Brimble, Terry Richards and Andrew Smallman, *Autosport* (4 December 1975).

Wray, Vamplew, 'Paget, Dorothy Wyndham (1905–1960)', *Oxford Dictionary of National Biography* (Oxford University Press, 2004).

Wyatt, R. J., *The Austin Seven* (Macdonald, 1968).

Young, Eoin, 'Amherst Villiers – The Man Behind The "Blower" Bentley', *Sports Car World* (April 1974).

——, 'Meet Mr Supercharge', *Car* (April 1974).

——, 'PI Blower: Amherst Villiers and his Amazing Blower Rolls-Royce', *Autocar* (26 May 1979).

Young, Robin, 'Rolls-Royce sued over failure to build "most fabulous car"', *The Times* (2 July 1991).

——, 'Villiers daughter wins battle with Rolls-Royce', *The Times* (1 August 1996).

Films and DVDs

Brooklands: The Birthplace of British Motorsport (Brooklands Museum Trust/David Weguelin Productions, 2006).

Casino Royale (Danjaq, LLC; United Artists Corporation; Columbia Pictures Industries, Inc., 2006).

Websites

McMillan, Paul, post to *The Aviation Forum*, http://forum.keypublishing.co.uk (13 November 2008).

The Metropolitan Museum of Art, http://www.metmuseum.org/toah/hd/tita/ho_36.29.htm

INDEX